Becoming an Effective Psychotherapist

Becoming an Effective Psychotherapist

Adopting a Theory of Psychotherapy That's Right for You and Your Client

Derek Truscott

American Psychological Association • Washington, DC

Published by
American Psychological Association
750 First Street, NE
Washington, DC 20002
www.apa.org

To order
APA Order Department
P.O. Box 92984
Washington, DC 20090-2984
Tel: (800) 374-2721; Direct: (202) 336-5510
Fax: (202) 336-5502; TDD/TTY: (202) 336-6123
Online: www.apa.org/books/
E-mail: order@apa.org

In the U.K., Europe, Africa, and the Middle East, copies may be ordered from
American Psychological Association
3 Henrietta Street
Covent Garden, London
WC2E 8LU England

Typeset in Meredien by Stephen McDougal, Mechanicsville, MD

Printer: Edwards Brothers, Inc., Ann Arbor, MI
Cover Designer: Naylor Design, Washington, DC
Technical/Production Editor: Devon Bourexis

The opinions and statements published are the responsibility of the authors, and such opinions and statements do not necessarily represent the policies of the American Psychological Association.

Library of Congress Cataloging-in-Publication Data

Truscott, Derek, 1959-
    Becoming an effective psychotherapist : adopting a theory of psychotherapy that's right for you and your client / Derek Truscott. — 1st ed.
        p. ; cm.
    Includes bibliographical references and index.
    ISBN-13: 978-1-4338-0473-1(hc); ISBN-10: 1-4338-0473-5(hc)
    ISBN-13: 978-1-4338-0993-4(pb); ISBN-10: 1-4338-0993-1(pb)
    1. Psychotherapy—Philosophy. 2. Psychotherapy—Practice. I. American Psychological Association. II. Title.
    [DNLM: 1. Psychotherapy—methods. 2. Psychological Theory. WM 420 T873b 2010]

    RC437.5.T78 2010
    616.89'14—dc22   2009001830

British Library Cataloguing-in-Publication Data
A CIP record is available from the British Library.

Printed in the United States of America
First Edition

In loving memory of Ken,
who showed me how to live life deliberately

Contents

Foreword

Experience is the name everyone gives to their mistakes.
—Oscar Wilde, *Lady Windermere's Fan*

t the ripe old age of 29, psychologist Saul Rosenzweig (1936/2002) published an article titled "Some Implicit Common Factors in Diverse Methods of Psychotherapy." Swimming against the current of "mine-is-best-schoolism" coming to dominate the field of psychotherapy, the newly minted Harvard PhD argued that factors shared by all approaches were responsible for successful care. Seventy plus years of research have since confirmed what Rosenzweig surmised: The similarities between competing models of therapy (e.g., the therapist, the relationship, the goodness of fit, the creation of hope and expectancy, the presence of a healing ritual or structure) are far more important than the differences (cf. Duncan, Miller, & Sparks, 2004; Hubble, Duncan, & Miller, 1999).

As a graduate student, I was familiar with both Rosenzweig and the common factors literature. Portions of Jerome D. Frank's (1961) *Persuasion and Healing* had been assigned in one of my classes. I had also volunteered as a research assistant for Michael Lambert, an outcome researcher whose own work and review of the literature figured prominently in the common factors arena (Lambert, 1979, 1986). None of my professors, as far as I could tell, was a zealous supporter of any particular brand of therapy. Indeed, *The Skilled Helper* by Gerard Egan (1979) and *Principles of Psychotherapy* by Irving B. Weiner (1975) were the two primary texts assigned in my first class on counseling—hardly partisans in the battle between warring psychotherapy factions. And then, I met my first client.

Watching the grainy black-and-white videotape of that session is painful despite the passage of more than 2 decades. I still grimace when I watch it, alternately peering between the fingers covering my face and then, when it's too much to bear, looking away. Two fuzzy images occupy the frame. Each would be indistinguishable from the other were it not for the wide-open, almost luminescent eyes of the one seated on the left. Me—the deer in the headlights.

At no other time in my life, neither before nor since, have I felt so woefully unprepared. The person sitting opposite me was suffering, tremendously. And believe me, any knowledge I had in regard to the role of common factors in psychotherapy seemed inadequate to the task at hand. After reflecting feelings for 10 minutes—the one thing I knew how to do—the conversation sputtered out. "What was I supposed to do now?" I wondered. Listen? Did that. Form a therapeutic relationship? Did that, too. Ensure goodness of fit? Yep, in fact, I must have said at least a dozen times already, "So what I hear you saying is . . . ?" That left two possibilities: (a) applying a healing therapeutic ritual or structure and (b) creating hope or positive expectation.

At that time in my training, I knew a little about a lot of different treatment approaches. In my 1st-year "Survey of Psychotherapies" course, I'd studied the 13 models described in the pages of Raymond Corsini's (1979) *Current Psychotherapies*, carefully reading and rereading, underlining and outlining each. Learning how to do therapy from such a work, however, was about as likely as becoming a master chef by eating at a smorgasbord. Moreover, I realized that even if I could competently and expertly apply all 13 approaches outlined in Corsini's volume, I still had no idea which one to use with this person. For these reasons, I decided to wait with the ritual and focus instead on creating hope.

"It's always darkest before the dawn," I said in my most compassionate voice, to which my client quietly responded, "Yes," and then began crying, sobbing actually.

More headlights.

That session, more than any other single event in graduate school, shaped the arc of my professional career. Soon thereafter, I left the common factors behind, considering them too vague to be of value in day-to-day clinical work. I became a man on a mission, determined to figure out how to do therapy the right, most effective way (S. D. Miller, 2004). I went to workshops, sought out consultation with noted experts, and attended various supervision groups. For a number of years I worked with a team of researchers, developing a specific model of psychotherapy. Ultimately, though, our own research would direct me back to the common factors.

The evidence is clear and overwhelming: No differences in efficacy exist between bona fide psychotherapy approaches (Duncan, Miller, Wampold, & Hubble, in press). Although the passion with which the developers of models present their findings and the worldwide trend toward "specific treatments for specific diagnoses" may make this finding hard to believe, meta-analytic studies leave no doubt (Ahn & Wampold, 2001; Baskin, Tierney, Minami, & Wampold, 2000; Imel, Wampold, Miller, & Fleming, 2008; S. D. Miller, Wampold, & Varhely, 2008; Shadish & Baldwin, 2002). The conclusion is inescapable. As Rosenzweig (1936/2002) stated,

> If . . . theoretically conflicting procedures . . . can lead to success, often even in similar cases, then therapeutic result is not a reliable guide to the validity of theory . . . It takes but little reflection to arrive at the . . . conclusion [that] . . . factors that are operating in several different therapists may . . . have much more in common than have the factors alleged to be operating. (pp. 5–6)

Research establishing the general equivalence of disparate treatment models and the existence of a core group of common factors is often and mistakenly interpreted to mean that "anything goes." Nothing could be further from the truth. As I discovered the day I met with my first client, it means that therapists and clients must each find an approach that works for them. How I wish I would have had the book you have in your hands right now.

Becoming an Effective Psychotherapist: Adopting a Theory of Psychotherapy That's Right for You and Your Client is a remarkable work. Based on more than 70 years of collective wisdom and research on the common factors, it does what no volume on the subject has done to date. Specifically, it uses the science of the common factors to help readers sort through the myriad therapeutic alternatives and find an approach that works best for them and their clients. Consider yourself fortunate.

Scott D. Miller, PhD
Center for Clinical Excellence
Chicago, Illinois

Preface

Most therapists-in-training feel anxious about doing psychotherapy. To attempt to help another human being overcome difficulties in living is a tremendous responsibility. Therefore, it is not surprising that therapists-in-training want to learn how to do psychotherapy properly. When presented with a variety of apparently quite dissimilar approaches to psychotherapy, however, many become rather bewildered. "Why not just tell me which one is the right one?" is a common refrain. Of course, many books on theories of psychotherapy exist, and it is not my goal to merely add another to their number. What makes this book unique is that it is based on the premise that there is no "right" system in the absolute sense. There is an approach that is right for each therapist and each client, however. My intention is to help you adopt a theory that is right for you by virtue of its being based on an understanding of the world that is compatible with your own. Additionally, I hope to show how you can be an effective therapist by honoring the worldview of those who seek your help and collaborating within a shared rationale for change.

The purpose of this book is to help you do the following:

1. Appreciate the value of the varied approaches to psychotherapy.
2. Be knowledgeable of the leading theories of psychotherapy and their rationale.
3. Be knowledgeable of interventions associated with the theories covered and their appropriate application.
4. Adopt a theory for practice that you believe in so that you might maximize your satisfaction and effectiveness as a therapist.

What this book does not do is compare and contrast the various theories and systems of psychotherapy. Not only has this been done at great length elsewhere, but also it does not aid therapists in adopting a theory that is right for them. Each psychotherapy's strengths and weaknesses are not essential features that make it what it is. Aspects that one commentator might consider a weakness could be considered a strength by another. Our preference for one theory of therapy over another is in large part based on a fit between that theory's assumptions about the human condition and our own. This probably explains why debates about the superiority of one theory over another can become so heated—it feels like our basic approach to life is being attacked. I have chosen to avoid critiquing anyone's fundamental beliefs about the nature of being human and instead have focused on how each has an internal consistency and usefulness.

This book is written primarily for use in senior undergraduate or graduate courses intended to train practitioners in psychotherapy and counseling. Such courses are often called "Systems of Counseling and Psychotherapy" or "Theories of Psychotherapy." This book is also appropriate for practicing therapists who desire to gain a deeper understanding of theories of psychotherapy and refine their personal approach. I have endeavored to write it so that counselors, social workers, psychologists, psychiatrists, and all who practice the "talking cure" will find this book helpful.

Of course, no survey of theories of psychotherapy could ever be complete without being impracticably voluminous—there are at least 250 extant theories and many more theorists. I have found from reading other books, however, that trying to cover too many theories requires a curtness that does justice to none. I have therefore used rather drastic principles of selection. I have tried to give a sympathetic account of those theories that (a) are representative of the foundational worldviews underlying the psychotherapeutic enterprise, (b) have significantly shaped the practice of psychotherapy, and (c) continue to be relevant to current practice. A consequence of this is that I cannot give some theories the coverage they deserve on the basis of their merits. For this I apologize.

There are also approaches currently in vogue that are not covered in this book. For this I do not apologize, because "truth is the daughter of time," and their contribution remains to be determined. Like all who are students of history, I have a strong aversion to what is fashionable. It is my furtive goal that readers might come to be as wary of therapeutic fads as I am.

I also feel compelled to note that it is obviously impossible to know as much about every theory as those who specialize in them know. I have no doubt that each one I have covered is better known to many others than to me. If, however, this were sufficient reason to not undertake the task, then books such as this would surely never be written. I am in awe of the intellect and perceptiveness of all of the progenitors of the theories presented in this book. To explicate a system for relieving human suffering is one of the most worthwhile endeavors anyone could undertake. I have tried to present each theory in such a way that the reader might share some of the respect and admiration that I feel.

I have taught a course on systems of psychotherapy for the better part of a decade. On the basis of my experience, I encourage you to embrace two complementary attitudes as you strive to learn the material in this book:

1. Dare to be mistaken.
   - develop an informed opinion, even if unsure of your ideas, and
   - refine your opinion by finding truth in what you oppose and fault in what you espouse.
2. Keep an open mind.
   - accept no fact or opinion uncritically—it might be misleading, and
   - reject no fact or opinion impetuously—it might be useful.

It is my intention that *Becoming an Effective Psychotherapist: Adopting a Theory of Psychotherapy That's Right for You and Your Client* be useful to you in becoming a confident and effective therapist. I would therefore appreciate any comments or feedback you might want to share with me about this book. I promise to consider them thoughtfully and to incorporate those that I can if I should have the opportunity to write another edition. You can contact me via e-mail at derek.truscott@ualberta.ca.

Acknowledgments

had the incredible good fortune to meet a delightful person and remarkable psychologist in graduate school by the name of Diane Zanier. She gave generously of her time, insight, and intelligence in helping me to write this book. You, the reader, should thank her as much as I do for making it much better than it would have been without her input. To the extent that it fails to be as good as it could, you can thank me.

To Steve Knish and Jim Evans, I remain forever grateful. They have helped me to continue to believe in the value of psychotherapy when seemingly everyone around us did not. The countless, precious hours that the three of us have spent talking about how to be good therapists are those from which this book was conceived. Perhaps even more significantly, Jim and Steve have taught me what it means to be a true friend and to believe in myself. I could not have written this book without them.

Working with the editors of the American Psychological Association's Books department was an absolute delight, from the encouragement of Linda McCarter, through the generous guidance of Emily Leonard, to the meticulous feedback of Devon Bourexis.

I am indebted to my mother for her passion and courage, my father for his gentleness and curiosity, and my brother for his loyalty and integrity. They will always be with me, and I would not have it any other way.

My wife and sons are my life. The love that I feel for and from them is a part of this book in a manner beyond words.

Becoming an Effective Psychotherapist

Adopting a Theory

1

People have known and experienced the healing power of talking and relating to other human beings since the earliest recorded times (J. D. Frank & Frank, 1991; Wampold, 2001a). In ancient societies, reparative talk occurred most frequently within religious practices, which was then the dominant system of thought for making sense of our place in the world. It was in the late 1800s that Sigmund Freud introduced his "talking cure"—the modern Western concept of *psychotherapy*. By doing so, Freud wrested therapeutic conversations from the domain of religion and into secular medical practice. Soon thereafter, physicians, social workers, psychologists, counselors, and others undertook therapeutic conversations with adults, children, families, and couples in an effort to cure any number of individual, social, and community ills. In most Western cultures, psychotherapy is now generally accepted and valued as a helping modality that can reduce human suffering and improve our quality of life.

In the time following Freud, psychotherapy has come to be understood as a unique craft that requires specialized skills to achieve remedial results (Freedheim, 1992). Also during this time, however, a plethora of approaches to psychotherapy with apparently incompatible ways of conceptualizing therapeutic practice have emerged. These include psychodynamic, behavioral, existential, person-centered, gestalt, cognitive, systemic, feminist, and constructivist approaches, among others. Indeed, theories of psychotherapy have proliferated—conservative estimates are that there are some 250 distinct approaches (Goldfried & Wolfe, 1996)—to the point that not one of them can claim dominance.

The task confronting the modern practitioner of healing conversation, therefore, is how to choose one form of therapy over another. The answer lies in understanding how psychotherapy works.

How Does Psychotherapy Work?

Evidence based on over 40 years of research, involving hundreds of studies and thousands of clients, provides consistent support for the conclusion that psychotherapy in its many diverse forms is highly effective (Lambert & Ogles, 2004). The *effect size* (i.e., the statistically standardized difference between the averages of two groups) of psychotherapy on personal distress for those receiving it compared with those who do not is 0.80 (Wampold, 2001b). This is a large effect (Cohen, 1988), and in practical terms it means that the average person who receives psychotherapy is better off than 79% of those who do not and that psychotherapy accounts for 14% of the variance in mental health outcomes (Wampold, 2001b).

Given that psychotherapy is effective and given the number of different theories with their often very different conceptual principles, prescribed interventions, and procedural proscriptions, a reasonable question to ask is, Which one of them is correct? Which theory explains how psychotherapy works and therefore is the one that should guide practice? The studies that support the efficacy of psychotherapy also overwhelmingly support another very important conclusion: There are no significant differences in the effectiveness of any system of psychotherapy over another (Ahn & Wampold, 2001; Chambless & Ollendick, 2001; Lambert & Ogles, 2004; Wampold et al., 1997). Although there are some well-conducted studies that have shown some differences between therapies (e.g., Dimidjian et al., 2006), the number of studies that show significant differences is what one would expect by chance given the total number of studies that have been conducted (Wampold et al., 1997). Therapists' belief in one theory over another, adherence to a particular therapeutic system, or application of a specific treatment technique has no consistent impact on whether they are more or less successful in relieving psychological distress or promoting mental health (Wampold, 2007). Additionally, the benefits of psychotherapy are minimally, if at all, related to any specific treatment techniques, such as making transference interpretations, prescribing homework to dispute irrational beliefs, or role playing conflicted aspects of oneself (Ahn & Wampold, 2001). These conclusions hold for both psychotherapy in general and treatments developed for particular disorders, such as depression (Elkin, 1994) and anxiety disorders (J. J. Sherman, 1998; Tarrier et al., 1999).

Some practitioners—and a good number of those who would tell therapists how they ought to practice—have difficulty accepting the absence of theoretical superiority or treatment specificity. Others find these results entirely consistent with their practical experience. Therefore, there is considerable debate within the literature about whether specific psychotherapies have specific effects (e.g., Castonguay & Holtforth, 2005; Craighead, Sheets, Bjornsson, & Arnarson, 2005; DeRubeis, Brotman, & Gibbons, 2005; Kazdin, 2005; Wampold, 2005).

Of course, these findings typically exacerbate psychotherapists' anxiety: If one therapy is not better than another one is, then how does a psychotherapist decide how to practice? Without evidence-based guidance, are we not vulnerable as a profession to passing fads, where self-defined therapists can offer whatever they fancy—tickle therapy, sensory deprivation, or aura transmogrification—as viable treatments for serious mental health problems? Perhaps we need to ask a different question. Perhaps we ought to ask, How does psychotherapy work? In fact, the answer to this question can guide how we should practice.

Jerome D. Frank (1910–2005; see Figure 1.1), in his seminal work *Persuasion and Healing: A Comparative Study of Psychotherapy,* explained that psychotherapy works by establishing a circumstance that is characterized by three aspects (J. D. Frank, 1961; J. D. Frank & Frank, 1991). First, the treatment must involve activities consistent with a therapeutic rationale that is believable to the therapist and the client. Second, a client must seek help from a practitioner who the client believes to be helpful. Third, the client must experience a collaborative relationship with the therapist. In support of this model, meta-analytic studies (Wampold, 2001b) revealed that the most powerful effect sizes in relation to outcome are 0.60 for the therapist's belief in the treatment, 0.55 for therapist helpfulness, 0.45 for the degree of client–therapist collaboration, and 0.40 for the client's belief in the treatment.

This understanding of how therapy works has a number of implications for practice. First, clients must seek the help of the therapist. It is no coincidence that the only form of psychotherapy to be tested and found ineffective is *critical-incident stress debriefing,* an approach in which individuals exposed to disastrous events are educated about the possible effects of exposure and encouraged to share their feelings and perceptions about the event (Mitchell & Everly, 1996). The circumstances under which it has been found to be ineffective were in hospital units where uninvited therapists debriefed patients who had medical treatment for early miscarriage and burns (van Emmerik, Kamphuis, Hulsbosch, & Emmelkamp, 2002).

FIGURE 1.1

Jerome D. Frank. Printed with permission of the Alan Mason Chesney Medical Archives.

Second, to be helpful, therapists should strive to collaborate with clients by establishing a common understanding of the nature of the client's problem and an agreed-on means by which to bring about its remediation (Wampold, 2001a, 2007). Duncan, Miller, and Sparks (2004) called this finding the client's *theory of change*. By finding a theory of change that is acceptable and believable for the therapist and the client, we can work collaboratively toward shared goals through agreed-on tasks (Horvath & Greenberg, 1994). Sometimes the client will have an explicit model: "I want to learn to express my emotions." Often it is implicit: "If I could just figure out what is wrong with me, I would know what I need to do with my life." In either case, it is not the ultimate truth of the model that is predictive of change; it is the shared belief in it. The relative worth of any form of psychotherapy over another is not assumed. If the therapist has a philosophical, logical approach to practice, for example, and the client has a pragmatic, action-oriented approach to life, then therapy is highly unlikely to be successful. It would be just as likely to be unsuccessful if the therapist was behaviorally oriented and the client was predisposed toward self-reflection and seeking personal insight. Although it may be possible to convince clients that their understanding of their problems and the solutions are incorrect and they should adopt the therapist's understanding, considerable time and effort will have to be devoted to the task in proportion to the degree of dissimilarity, and there is no guarantee of results. Indeed, it is much more likely that clients will not return, and the therapists as well as the clients will experience the other as "difficult" or "nonresponsive."

Third, note that techniques are not entirely irrelevant to outcome. Rather, techniques are integral to effective practice if they constitute an activity consistent with the treatment rationale and are a plausible means by which to achieve desired results (Wampold, 2001a, 2007). Stated quite plainly, you need to do something during therapy, and what you do ought to make sense to the client.

Why Should I Adopt a Theory?

If no theory is more effective than another, why adopt a theory at all? A theory of practice is an organized set of assumptions that provides a framework for (a) generating hypotheses about what change processes will further therapeutic goals, (b) formulating specific tasks to facilitate desired change processes, and (c) evaluating progress toward the goals of therapy. Theory serves as a heuristic that aids practitioners in selectively attending to and organizing the vast amounts of information available in therapy. Stated more simply, theory helps therapists know how to proceed. Having a theory of practice is like having a map of the psychotherapeutic territory.

Practicing from a consistent theoretical base also helps therapists to be more consistent in their practices and thereby better able to identify whether trying something new is helpful. More than one writer has likened the relationship between theory and practice in psychotherapy to that in music (Schacht, 1991). Just as a musician must be fully grounded in musical theory to be able to improvise well, so too must a psychotherapist be grounded in—without being bound by—theory.

Note that adopting a theory based on a particular system of psychotherapy is not synonymous with preferring a particular intervention strategy. Behavior modification need not be the exclusive domain of behaviorists or transference interpretation of psychoanalysts. Theoretical preference does influence how practitioners behave in practice—behaviorists are more likely to give instruction and psychoanalysts are more likely to make interpretations—although not as much as most theoreticians would have us believe (Wogan & Norcross, 1985). Believing in a theory does lead to a preference for interventions consistent with our assumptions about how to facilitate desired change processes—such as increased frequency of new behavior or verbalizing new insights—as we would hope. The challenge is to allow ourselves to remain open to alternative conceptualizations, as will be discussed in chapter 11 of this volume. Again, the idea is to be guided by theory, not blinded by it.

The most common approach to psychotherapy among practitioners is *eclecticism* (Norcross, Prochaska, & Farber, 1993), an atheoretical approach in which interventions are selected from any system of psychotherapy. The therapist selects procedures that address the particular problem presented by a particular client, rather than drawing only from the therapist's preferred theoretical system. From a pragmatic point of view, the merits of eclecticism are obvious: Do what works. After all, theory is for therapists, not clients.

What seems to draw therapists to eclecticism is the desire to be flexible in their approach to helping clients, that is, to be responsive to the uniqueness of client problems, characteristics, and circumstances. Seen in this light, we can appreciate the virtue of such an approach. Indeed, therapists with an integrative–eclectic approach are more likely to feel skillful and efficacious and to experience professional growth than those who are allied with a single approach (Orlinsky & Rønnestad, 2005). There is also some evidence that rigid adherence to the interventions of any one theoretical approach results in diminished treatment effectiveness (Castonguay, Goldfried, Wiser, Raue, & Hayes, 1996; W. P. Henry, Schacht, Strupp, Butler, & Binder, 1993; W. P. Henry, Strupp, Butler, Schacht, & Binder, 1993). Conversely, therapists who have no salient theoretical allegiance are more likely to feel ineffective, dissatisfied, and stagnant (Orlinsky & Rønnestad, 2005).

What makes eclecticism especially difficult to adopt as an approach to practice, however, is that therapists still need some theory to guide their decision as to what technique to use with what problem for each client. In fact, most therapists who profess to be eclectic are practicing a form of *syncretism* in that they are applying interventions they are familiar and comfortable with in an essentially random manner (McBride & Martin, 1990). There are hundreds of theories of psychotherapy, each with its own interventions. How could one practitioner know how to apply the right intervention for the right client under the right circumstances to address all problems? Moreover, remember that interventions devoid of a shared, plausible rationale are not the active ingredient of psychotherapy.

For our purposes, eclecticism is problematic because it does not provide a framework for practice, placing practitioners at risk of losing their way in therapy and thereby failing to be helpful or actually causing harm to clients. In addition, without a plausible rationale we do not have common grounds from which to form a collaborative theory of change with our clients, further decreasing the likelihood of a positive outcome. Therefore, we need a map—that is, a theory—to serve as our guide. However, not just any theory will do; remember that our belief in the theory we use is highly predictive of our success. What we need is a theory in which we can believe (Vasco, Garcia-Marques, & Dryden, 1993).

What Theory Should I Adopt?

The facts and methods of any scholarly undertaking, including psychotherapy, are based on *assumptive worldviews*—assumptions about the nature of reality (Howard, 1985; Lyddon, 1989a; Maher, 2000). An assumptive worldview essentially serves as a filter by which humans selectively attend to the vast amount of potential data available as they try to understand the world around them (Koltko-Rivera, 2004), just as a psychotherapeutic theory helps psychotherapists to make sense of the potential data in therapy (Hansen & Freimuth, 1997; Poznanski & McLennan, 1995). At an individual level, one's worldview is one's personal theory of how best to live his or her life (Prilleltensky, 1989; Unger, Draper, & Pendergrass, 1986). Preference for one theory of therapy over another is in large part dependent on the fit between that theory's basic premises and one's personal assumptions about how the world works (J. A. Johnson, Germer, Efran, & Overton, 1988; Poznanski & McLennan, 2003; Schacht & Black, 1985). Thus, understanding your own assumptive worldview is the starting point for adopting a theory of psychotherapy that is the best fit for you (Drapela, 1990).

On the basis of a review of the many different ways that psychotherapists' theoretical orientations have been measured, Poznanski and McLennan (1995) concluded that a two-dimensional model best captures their underlying beliefs: analytic versus experiential and objective versus subjective. By incorporating these two dimensions into a four-celled conceptual model, each of the major systems of psychotherapy can be reliably mapped onto one of the quadrants (Poznanski & McLennan, 1995, 1999; Sandell et al., 2004), as depicted in Figure 1.2.

By organizing theories in this way, we can generate a conceptual profile of similarities and differences among them—a "periodic table of the psychotherapies," if you will. As we do so, we can see more clearly what R. B. Miller (1992) described as models of the nature of psychological reality—or assumptive worldviews—on which each of them is based. In fact, we can see how the different systems of psychotherapy reflect the most important attempts in Western philosophy to understand the nature of reality. Is it any wonder, then, that there is such debate about which system of psychotherapy is the right one? Philosophers have been

FIGURE 1.2

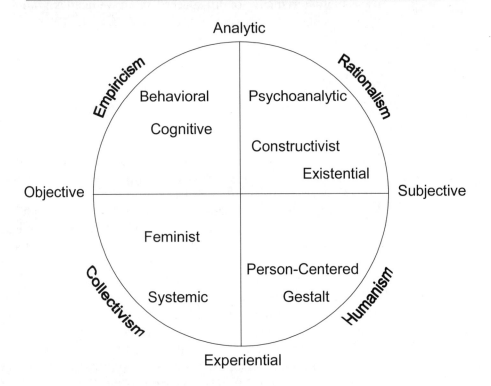

Taxonomy of the systems of psychotherapy.

debating for centuries how reality can be truly known, and they have not reached a consensus about which worldview is the correct one. Each of these philosophical worldviews is valid up to a point, and each has its limitations (Bevan, 1991; Rychlak, 2000). The strengths of each address the weaknesses of the others, without quite managing to completely explain the human condition. It may just be that our merely mortal minds are incapable of grasping the cosmos—"A hand cannot grasp itself," as the Buddhists say. However, take heart: Remember that to the best of our knowledge with respect to effective psychotherapy, it doesn't matter that no system is the "correct" one. It matters that we adopt a theory of practice in which we believe, and the well-honed worldviews of history's greatest philosophies serve as terrific starting points in our quest. The worldviews are empiricism, rationalism, humanism, and collectivism.

Empiricism values rational thought applied to objective experience and is the worldview underlying what is traditionally referred to as *science*. The empirical worldview assumes that people are reactive and separate from—yet determined by—their environments. Human behavior is the result of learning and the product of situation-specific forces. Although life is seen as having many obstacles and struggles, there is always a light at the end of the tunnel; problems can be solved through direct action. People are seen as having conflicts with difficult situations in which they find themselves. Problems in life are the result of current external situations or learned habits that can be mastered through the appropriate application of technique or technology. Emotional responses to irrational thoughts are eliminated or at least controlled by substituting rational thoughts. Psychotherapies based on empiricism use carefully selected strategies deliberately applied to specific problems to achieve concrete, measurable outcomes. Each client is approached as a case study or an experiment of $N = 1$, where hypotheses are tested and new ones are generated in light of the results. Prediction and control are valued. The results of other like-minded therapists and researchers are valued and applied, if appropriate, to one's own situation. Adopting strategies and undertaking activities that have been proven effective are encouraged. The therapist's role is one of technical consultation and instruction. The therapist approaches problems with a sense of optimism and a "can do" spirit. Therapeutic instruction in the form of rational thinking or adaptive behaviors is designed to modify clients' cognitions and actions to bring them more in line with the demands of reality. Pragmatism is the order of the day, with improved role functioning (e.g., parent, spouse, breadwinner) and coping skills as goals.

Rationalism values rational thought applied to subjective experience. The rationalistic worldview assumes that only by first understanding ourselves can people truly understand the world around us. Participation in the intellectual and emotional process of self-reflection is the means by which one achieves greater self-understanding. Patterns of our deepest levels of subjective and emotional processes and influences of the past on the present can be discovered and understood. As our understanding of ourselves changes, we are better able to make rational decisions. Personal imperfections are accepted as inevitable expressions of one's humanness and as a basis for self-improvement. In the rationalist worldview, human possibility is limited. Indeed, a certain degree of resignation is considered healthy. Honest self-perception and freedom from illusion are the goals—to reconcile the ideal with what is possible. In Freud's famous words, the best that one can hope for is to exchange "irrational misery for common unhappiness" (Breuer & Freud, 1895/1955, p. 305). The limitations of life are accepted; not all is possible, not all is redeemable, not all potentialities are realizable. Nothing can be done to undo the tragic or traumatic facts of one's life. The clock cannot be turned back, death cannot be avoided, and human nature cannot be perfected. The client and the therapist engage in a search for patterns and processes in the understanding of old meanings and then create ones that are more logical. An introspective, subjective, skeptical stance on the part of the client and therapist is called for, with the therapist encouraging a thoroughgoing internal focus. The therapist aids the client in the expression of feelings and thoughts around key influential understandings, encouraging a detailed description of events and reflecting empathically on what is said. The therapist identifies with the client's problems and personal failings through the human ability to resonate with similar tragedies in our own lives.

Humanism values growth-promoting subjective experience. The humanistic worldview assumes that people are intrinsically motivated toward development, growth, and socially constructive behavior. Problems arise when this intrinsic motivation is thwarted or usurped. Problems are understood as developmental challenges that are typically accompanied by emotional disequilibrium. Rather than being viewed as deficits to be remedied, problems are seen as being powerful opportunities for the emergence of a more evolved self. People are understood to be fundamentally active, complex, purposive, autonomous, and creative individuals. Life is seen as having fulfilling and adventurous possibilities and is to be lived in the present moment. Individuality is idealized and natural. Everyone has a creative spark that can be nurtured through the promotion of free, uninhibited, and authentic self-expression. Risk taking, the pursuit of a unique lifestyle, and the continuous search for self-actualization are the goals of humanism. Empathic contact between the therapist and the client fosters self-acceptance, self-understanding, and growth toward a fully functioning self. A therapeutic relationship of unwavering acceptance, rather than action or explanation, is the focus of therapy. It allows clients to fully integrate all aspects of their true selves. Emotional experience has a functional role in facilitating change and is thus encouraged. Feelings are seen as safe, even when painful, and they warrant being fully experienced to bring rich meanings to life. With personal growth comes increased capacity for achieving creative solutions and new forms of knowledge. People can become vibrant, socially engaged, and artistically expressive. A satisfying life is gained by finding an overarching purpose and direction that includes values centered on being more attuned, sensitive, and responsive to others. Strengths and talents are assets and gifts to be appreciated and used in the service of others.

Collectivism values growth-promoting objective experiences with others and is the dominant worldview of most non-Western cultures. The metaphor of complex, integrated, organic processes that "grow" toward healthy functioning is central to collectivism. The collectivistic worldview assumes that social context is what gives life meaning and purpose and that people and groups are active, purposeful, autonomous, creative, and integrated into a social matrix and inherently strive toward healthy functioning. Individuals cannot be understood independent of interpersonal influences, and personal problems are best solved if we involve others in the solution. Individuals and systems have reciprocal influences on each other such that changes to social systems bring about changes to individuals and vice versa. Change in one component of the system—whether within the individual or within the larger social system—will produce a change elsewhere in the system. Problems in living are seen as by-products of systemic malfunction and are thus considered indicators that something needs to be addressed in the way the system is functioning. Although outcomes are not completely predictable, systems have a propensity for self-regulation such that liberation of any aspect of the system will tend to produce an increased capacity for generating creative solutions. Change is thus not a cumulative event, but it is a transformative process. Changes to structures bring about changes to individuals by way of changing their relationship to others within the system. Therapists working from a collectivist perspective take an active role in directing changes to systems, and clients are expected to be actively involved. A good fit between individual and system is sought in order to achieve strong interpersonal ties and multisided, nurturing relationships. Unhealthy social roles, such as sexist and racist stereotypes, are challenged and replaced with egalitarian ones. *Communion*—contact, openness, and noncontractual cooperation between persons—is seen as the ideal state.

Adopting a Theory for Practice

Once a preferred assumptive worldview has been identified, it is possible to proceed to narrowing down choices to a psychotherapeutic system, then to theory, and in some cases, to a particular theorist (Hansen & Freimuth, 1997). A *system of therapy*, also sometimes referred to as a *school* or *paradigm* (Cottone, 1992), represents the application of a given assumptive worldview to psychotherapeutic practice. Because it is so closely linked to assumptive worldview, the system level cannot be validated—or invalidated—by evidence. This is because the nature of what constitutes evidence is defined by the epistemological assumptions underlying each system (Bohart, O'Hara, & Leitner, 1998; Messer, 1985; R. B. Miller, 1992). Someone who believes that knowledge is subjective, for example, will not be convinced by empirical data that knowledge is objective. Similarly, qualitative data cannot prove—or disprove—that knowledge is best gained through objective means. Thus, a particular theory of psychotherapy will feel right if it captures the essence of your way of making sense of the human experience (Freimuth, 1992; Guy,

1987; Vasco et al., 1993). Although some will find your preferred theory similarly compelling, others will not, because their worldview is different from yours.

Systems of therapy should be categorized on the basis of commonalities and differences among their underlying assumptions. The number of different schools that various authors have identified depends on the specificity of beliefs used to discriminate among them (Hansen & Freimuth, 1997). Using the taxonomy of assumptive worldviews presented in Figure 1.2, four major systems of psychotherapy are identified:

1. Empiricism → Cognitive–Behavioral
2. Rationalism → Psychodynamic
3. Humanism → Humanistic
4. Collectivism → Systemic

This level of analysis allows for a bridging from assumptive worldview to theory.

Theory gives content and a sharper focus to the assumptive worldview of a system (Hansen & Freimuth, 1997). Each system is represented by a number of theories that share assumptions about the nature of knowledge and what counts as evidence, while disagreeing on the relative importance or usefulness of key facts. Different theories also prescribe different actions to take in pursuit of goals consistent with their assumptions (Blocher, 1987). Thus, for example, there are psychodynamic theories that emphasize the primacy of the self, or instinctual drives, or internalized relationships (Pine, 1990). Similarly, there are different theories within each of the other systems.

Finally, within each theory there are usually a variety of theorists who differ in their emphasis or presentation of a theory's governing principles. They also often differ in their personal and writing style such that most practitioners find one or another theorist within a theoretical orientation more to their liking, perhaps even a theoretical "kindred spirit" (Hansen & Freimuth, 1997).

Putting Theory Into Practice

Once you have found a theory that is a good fit with your assumptive worldview—and is thus one you can believe—it is time to put it into practice, that is, to begin to understand how to help people who seek your services. Taking our model of psychotherapy presented earlier in this chapter, readers can think of psychotherapy as the therapist proposing therapeutic *tasks* designed to facilitate *change processes* in order to

TABLE 1.1

Theory Into Practice

Theory	Task	Change process	Goal
Psychoanalytic	Free association	Consciousness raising	Self-understanding
Behavioral	Exposure to feared stimulus	Counter-conditioning	Decrease anxiety
Person-centered	Express negative feelings in a nonjudgmental context	Tolerance for negative feelings	Self-acceptance
Systemic	Reframe anxiety as excitement	New interpersonal patterns	Anxiety no longer a problem

achieve *goals*. To maximize the likelihood of success, the tasks, change processes, and goals should be believable to the client and the therapist. The therapist's job is then to develop a theoretically derived conceptualization of the client's goals and propose tasks consistent with that conceptualization. All theories have such working hypotheses as a way of translating theory into practice (Goldfried, 1980). An example of the application of psychoanalytic, behavioral, person-centered, and systemic theories, respectively, to the treatment of anxiety is presented in Table 1.1.

The following chapters cover nine different theories of psychotherapy: psychodynamic, behavioral, existential, person-centered, gestalt, cognitive, systemic, feminist, and constructivist. I encourage readers to strive to appreciate the value of each of these theories and the assumptive worldview on which each rests. Even if a particular theory does not sit well with you—and some likely will not—remember that many of the clients who seek your services will have worldviews different from yours (Lyddon, 1989a; Lyddon & Adamson, 1992). The ability to understand and value different worldviews and their concomitant psychotherapeutic goals, change processes, and tasks will help you to be more effective with more people more often.

The Novice Psychotherapist

Amanda discovered her interest in psychotherapy during her undergraduate psychology classes. She found that whenever she learned something new about psychology she wanted to know how to apply it to helping people. While she was volunteering at a residential treatment center, she noticed that those who were able to articulate why they were in treatment seemed to gain more from it. Therefore, for a class project, she researched how people make meaning of their circumstances. She discovered Victor Frankl's (1946/1963) *Man's Search for Meaning: An Introduction to Logotherapy*, and "everything fell into place" for her. She found reading Frankl a profoundly moving experience that gave her "the chills" and further deepened her interest in psychotherapy.

A defining moment occurred while Amanda was assisting a patient who was multiply handicapped, severely disfigured, and unable to communicate verbally. Using a keypad, the patient tapped out—letter by painful letter—"Look at me. I am a freak." Amanda looked at her. She looked into her eyes, felt a powerful human connection, and they wept silently together. Amanda experienced an intense helplessness and wished to know what to say or do to help. She decided to pursue graduate studies in professional psychology to learn.

When Amanda got to graduate school, she was very eager to learn how to be an effective therapist. She kept a journal of her experience with the intention of documenting her progress. After 2 years, however, her journal contained only disjointed—albeit helpful— snippets of clinical wisdom gleaned from instructors, supervisors, and classmates. In therapy, she felt anxious, self-conscious, and unsure of herself. Something was missing for her.

Then her mother called one evening concerned about her brother's "extreme" reaction to the death of his pet. She asked Amanda why he was behaving so "illogically." Without stopping to think, Amanda ventured that his reaction may have been an effort to make meaning of the meaninglessness of death. With this, she realized that she made sense of the world through existentialism, and she threw herself into the writings of the existential therapists with a renewed enthusiasm. She found Irvin Yalom's (2002) approach and writings to be particularly amenable, and she even waited for hours at a conference to have him sign a copy of *The Gift of Therapy: An Open Letter to a New Generation of Therapists and Their Patients*. She eloquently described her approach as she entered doctoral school as "joining clients in their experience and being a supportive witness to their confrontation with issues of death, freedom, and isolation so that they can create meaning in a way that best fits their personal experience."

Learning Task

Now that you have been introduced to how understanding worldviews is fundamental to becoming an effective psychotherapist, it is time to identify your personal worldview by completing the task in Exhibit 1.1. Once you have done so, transfer your ratings from the categories in Exhibit 1.1 to the corresponding axes of Figure 1.3. The intersection of the two axes represents 0, and the intersection of the axis with the outer circle represents 4. Connect the four points, making a roughly circular shape. The theories within the area of these four points represent those that are most compatible with your personal worldview.

If you find that you have rated all of the worldviews equally, you could try using a forced-choice rating in which you choose one over the other in each possible pairing: objective versus analytic, objective versus

EXHIBIT 1.1

Identifying Your Personal Worldview

Take your time while you carefully read each of the following four descriptions and rate the degree to which it describes your beliefs:

Ob The world can best be understood by identifying the characteristics of phenomena that represent a stable underlying essence. The best approach to understanding the world is by gathering measurements that are publicly confirmable. A complete explanation is one in which the common features that account for the functioning of a phenomenon have been classified.

Not at all   0   1   2   3   4   *Completely*

An The world can best be understood by discovering the action of phenomena on one another. The best approach to understanding the world is through logical analysis that enables us to achieve greater degrees of appreciation of the laws of nature. An explanation is complete when the causes of a phenomenon have been identified.

Not at all   0   1   2   3   4   *Completely*

Su The world can best be understood by the person trying to understand it. The best approach to understanding the world is through introspection that culminates in a highly personal result. A complete explanation is a rich, comprehensible description of an experience.

Not at all   0   1   2   3   4   *Completely*

Ex The world is best understood as being driven by developmental processes toward healthy functioning. The best approach to understanding the world is to participate without preconceived notions so that these processes can be appreciated. An explanation is complete when the processes and ultimate function of a phenomenon have been described.

Not at all   0   1   2   3   4   *Completely*

Now transfer your ratings to the following categories:

___ Ob = Objective
___ An = Analytic
___ Su = Subjective
___ Ex = Experiential

---

subjective, objective versus experiential, analytic versus subjective, analytic versus experiential, and subjective versus experiential. Once you have done so, add the number of times you chose each one. Transfer these numbers to the corresponding axes of Figure 1.3.

If you still find that you are having difficulty, you could try rereading the more detailed description of each worldview on pages 10–13, pausing to reflect on each, and then letting your intuition guide you. One

FIGURE 1.3

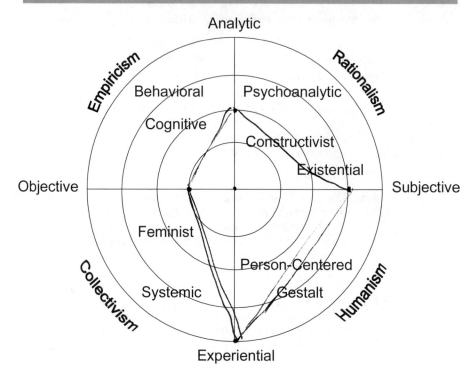

Plotting your psychotherapeutic worldview.

way to do this might be to flip a coin and, before you look at the result, notice whether you are hoping for a particular result. (You may have noticed that your preference for a particular type of evidence is also a clue as to your personal worldview.)

It is not vitally important that you identify the one theory that is right for you. In fact, many therapists find a number of theories amenable. It is most important that you avoid practicing from a theory based on a worldview incompatible with your own. As long as you begin with a compatible theory, you will put yourself on track for a long, satisfying, and effective career during which you will very likely explore many different theories as you develop your personal approach to psychotherapy (as discussed in chap. 11).

Your Reflective Journal

At the end of each chapter you will be invited to add to your own personal reflective journal. The intent is to challenge you to think about your individual perspective on the strengths and weaknesses of each approach. Consolidating what might work best for you is a crucial aspect of your development as a psychotherapist. To choose a particular therapeutic orientation requires thorough and deep processing of the information presented in this volume. Writing is a particularly good way to accomplish this processing. Some may find writing to be rather difficult or unappealing, however, and may prefer to create an audio or video journal, for example. Whatever you choose, I encourage you to find a way that works for you. You might also want to keep a pen and paper or other recording device available while you are reading each chapter so that you can record your thoughts and impressions while they are fresh. Immediate reactions can be a good source of information about yourself, and therefore you may want to record them before they are lost. You will later be asked to reflect on what you found appealing about each approach, what you identified with, what you found difficult to accept, and any unanswered questions you may have.

For this first chapter, begin your journal by recording an autobiographical sketch of how you came to pursue psychotherapy as your career. Think about the turning points in your career as a psychotherapist to date, even if you see yourself as "just a student." What have been the pivotal events that occurred in your life as you became a therapist? What important choices have you made? For example, when did you decide that you wanted to become a therapist? What ideas did you have about what a therapist is and does? How did you come to form these ideas? You might want to consider some of the influences on your choice. Were they familial, personal, or something else? You may also choose to consider some of your formative experiences as a therapist. What is most salient about these experiences for you? Were they your own experiences, someone else's experiences, a persuasive argument, compelling data? Do the content and nature of these influences and experiences inform you about your personal worldview? Take some time to write down your responses to these and any other questions that occur to you.

Summary

For psychotherapy to be effective, a client must seek help from a therapist who he or she believes to be competent, the client must experience a collaborative relationship with the therapist, the treatment must have a plausible therapeutic rationale that is believable to the therapist and client, and it must involve activities and goals consistent with the rationale. On the basis of the available, overwhelming research evidence, no theory of psychotherapy has been found to be superior to another. Rather, what is important is that the practitioner and the client believe in the therapy. A theory provides a framework for (a) generating hypotheses about what change processes will further client goals, (b) formulating tasks to facilitate desired change processes, and (c) evaluating progress toward those goals. Finding a theory in which you can believe involves identifying your assumptive worldview about the nature of the world from among four alternatives: empiricism, rationalism, humanism, and collectivism. Once your personal assumptive worldview has been identified, it is possible to proceed to narrowing down your choices to psychotherapeutic system, theory, and theorist through in-depth study of existing, well-developed theories.

Further Resources

Freedheim, D. K. (Ed.). (1992). *History of psychotherapy: A century of change.* Washington, DC: American Psychological Association.

Hubble, M. A., Duncan, B. L., & Miller, S. D. (Eds.). (1999). *The heart and soul of change: What works in therapy.* Washington, DC: American Psychological Association.

Lambert, M. J. (Ed.). (2004). *Bergin and Garfield's handbook of psychotherapy and behavior change* (5th ed.). New York: Wiley.

Snyder, C. R., & Ingram, R. E. (Eds.). (2000). *Handbook of psychological change: Psychotherapy processes and practices for the 21st century.* New York: Wiley.

Wampold, B. E. (2001). *The great psychotherapy debate: Models, methods, and findings.* Mahwah, NJ: Erlbaum.

Psychodynamic 2

Every therapist, like it or not, is indebted to Sigmund Freud (1856–1939; see Figure 2.1) because he is inarguably the father of psychotherapy. Freud, a physician who wanted to be a scientist, developed his method of psychoanalysis late in the 19th century.[1] Two circumstances make it difficult to summarize his approach to psychotherapy: (a) His writings spanned 45 years, and he continually revised his theories up until his death, and (b) he was not primarily interested in therapy as much as he was in understanding the human mind. Also, his theories about the nature of the mind and particularly the nature and role of child development were and continue to be controversial. Fortunately, one does not need to accept all of Freud's theories or participate in the controversies surrounding them to practice psychotherapy from a psychodynamic perspective.

Prior to Freud's time, emotional difficulties were thought to be the product of demons, weakness of character, or physical causes such as brain lesions. It is probably not overstating the case to say that Freud's greatest contribution was to introduce the nonreligious, nonphysical concept of the *psyche* or mind as a legitimate object of study and target of intervention, thereby ushering in the psychological paradigm of treatment—namely, psychotherapy.

---

[1]The term *psychoanalysis* tends to be used to refer only to the approach to therapy first described by Freud and based on his theory of the nature of the mind, whereas the term *psychodynamic* refers to therapies whose rationale involves unconscious processes first articulated by Freud, without necessarily incorporating all of Freud's theories.

FIGURE 2.1

Sigmund Freud. Printed with permission of the Freud Museum.

Freud came to psychoanalysis by way of neurology. He enrolled at the University of Vienna in 1873 and earned his degree in medicine in 1881. His studies were delayed because he had originally wanted to pursue a career as a biological research scientist, but he found this career path blocked because, as a Jew, he was discouraged from holding a university appointment. Upon graduation, he accepted a position at the Vienna General Hospital. Freud actually wrote the definitive book of the time on childhood aphasias, and it remained in use for decades (Gay, 1988). He eventually established a private practice in medicine in 1886, however, and it was there that he developed and published his ideas on psychotherapy.

Freud traveled to Paris to study with Jean-Martin Charcot, who was using hypnosis to treat physical symptoms that had no apparent physical basis. When he returned to Vienna, Freud tried hypnotic suggestion as a therapeutic tool, with limited success, and he continued searching for an effective means of treating what we now call *psychological disorders*. One of Freud's greatest influences was an account of treatment provided by Josef Breuer, who was a prominent, established Viennese physician. Freud and Breuer became close professionally and personally, and Freud was intrigued by Breuer's descriptions of his clinical cases of *hysteria*—vague physical symptoms inconsistent with what was known about the functioning of the body. He was especially impressed with Breuer's patient, the now-famous "Anna O" (Breuer & Freud, 1895/1955)—who was actually Bertha Pappenheim and who went on to become a prolific author, feminist, social activist, and pioneering social worker (Kimball, 2000). She was helped by what she called the "talking cure" in which she would tell Breuer about her symptoms and gradually uncover the traumatic causes of them. An avoidance of drinking on her part that had no physiological cause, for example, arose out of an incident in which she witnessed a dog drinking from her sick father's water glass and did not warn her father before he drank from the same glass (Breuer & Freud, 1895/1955).

Freud's fascination with Breuer's approach prompted him to refine his technique. He eventually developed the method of *free association*, whereby the client is instructed to report their spontaneous thoughts (see the Psychodynamic Change Tasks section later in this chapter). Using free association, Freud was able to observe how the client was motivated to keep an idea out of awareness and how this disavowal resulted in psychopathology because of impairment in the integrated functioning of the mind.

During Freud's life, unprecedented developments were occurring in the physical and biological sciences. Darwin's theory of evolution, in particular, was very influential across most domains of study. While he attended the University of Vienna, Freud was immersed in important advances in the areas of neurophysiology and neuropathology. Empiricism ruled the day, and particularly influential for Freud was a group of biologists who were attempting to explain biological phenomena solely in terms of physics and chemistry (Bernfeld, 1944). In his early writings, Freud expressed the hope that psychoanalysis would one day be explained entirely in terms of biological processes once science and diagnostic procedures advanced sufficiently.

In response to the medically inexplicable symptomatology that he observed in his practice, however, Freud gradually moved away from an empirical explanation and began to understand mental phenomena as subjectively—as opposed to objectively—determined. In this he was profoundly influenced by the rational approach to knowledge of the classical Greek philosophers, whom he had studied extensively in school. Socrates's famous statement, literally in defense of his own life, that "the life unexamined is not worth living" could well be the rallying call of the psychodynamic therapist. Freud eventually came to make sense of the human condition through a logical analysis of subjective experience. Indeed, he applied his method to his own psyche and underwent an intensive self-analysis that was seminal to his theory of therapy, culminating in his magnum opus, *The Interpretation of Dreams* (S. Freud, 1900/1953). Freud's debt to Socrates even extended to his three-part model of the mind (*ego, id,* and *superego*), which directly parallels the tripartation of the soul in Plato's (1892) *Republic*. Freud was certainly very curious about the human condition beyond merely the mechanics of the mind—he was interested in and wrote freely about the *soul* broadly defined (i.e., not in the strictly religious sense), social mores, and cultural strivings.

This brings us to something that must be said about Freud—English-language readers have been done a disservice (Bettelheim, 1983). Much of what we read is littered with Latin-derived terms such as *ego, id,* and *superego*. The true equivalents of Freud's *Ich, Es,* and *Uber-Ich* are *I, it,* and *over-I* (or *upper-I*). It is sad that the English-language translator—James Strachey—had a political agenda to restrict the practice of psychoanalysis in North America to a medical activity.[2] Freud voiced strong opposition to these efforts (S. Freud, 1926/1959b), but to no avail. Strachey used unnecessarily technical language that obscured the subjective, subtly nuanced, and emotionally imbued connotations of Freud's language. The result is an abstracted, depersonalized, objective version that lost much of Freud's original freshness. For example, in translating *Mutterleib* (literally "womb") as "uterus," Strachey dissociated the term from motherhood (Bettelheim, 1983). In Freud's original German his writings were considered remarkable in their clarity and broad appeal, a claim no one would make about Strachey's English language translations. Indeed, one of the first major awards he received, and of which he claimed to be very proud, was the Goethe prize for literature (Goethe being the German-language equivalent of Shakespeare). In the last decade, a number of translations have appeared that restore the subjective quality of Freud's prose—in particular, Joyce Crick's *The Interpretation of Dreams* (S. Freud, 1900/1999) and *The Joke and Its Relation to the Unconscious* (S. Freud, 1905/ 2003)—and are well worth reading.

Psychodynamic Rationale

Psychodynamic therapy is based on the premise that a satisfying and useful life comes from being honest with oneself (McWilliams, 2004). Such honesty is not easy, however. It is very difficult for us to acknowledge what is painful or unflattering about ourselves. Vanity, sloth, lust, greed, gluttony, envy, and anger—among many other undesirable attributes and impure motives—lurk in our hearts. Thus, we tend to dis-

---

[2]In fairness to Strachey, psychoanalysis was introduced to North America when medicine was trying desperately to counter accusations in the Flexner Report of faddish, unscientific practice. American physicians interested in psychoanalysis needed to be able to describe it in "scientific" language if they had any hope of having it accepted into medical practice (Wallerstein, 1998).

avow them, and they remain unconscious except in modified form or when our conscious mind is otherwise weakened (e.g., when we are asleep or under the influence of certain drugs).

In Freud's classical psychoanalytic formulation, our unconscious, primitive, alogical impulses can only be expressed in a highly modified form if we are to live as social beings. When these impulses build to the point of threatening unmodified release, we feel anxious and try to satisfy the impulse in a way that is compatible with society's dictates and our sense of who we are. To the extent that we are able to effectively manage this compromise, we are relatively happy and symptom free. The extent to which we fail to find a healthy compromise determines the extent of psychological problems we manifest. If the compromise is overly repressive of our impulses, the pressure to seek expression continuously builds to levels that demand attention, leading to anxiety and their eventual expression in a symptomatic form. If unconscious material is expressed in unmodified form, then our behavior is so antisocial that we cannot live harmoniously with others.

Contemporary psychodynamic therapists tend to refer less to primitive impulses and more to unconscious representations of relationships with people who were influential in our young lives—usually our parents. Punishments, prohibitions, praise, and various interpersonal rules are internalized into our developing sense of self. As we grow older, these rules continue to unconsciously influence how we behave—particularly in relation to important people in our present lives—even though they are often no longer relevant or adaptive.

Psychodynamic Goals

Overall, psychodynamic therapy aims at strengthening our sense of self (S. Freud, 1923/1961)—our conscious mind—through logical, rational self-understanding so that our everyday functioning is more flexible and less rigid (McGlashan & Miller, 1982). Thus, we achieve a broadening of our organization of experience so that we can make more realistic life choices and lead satisfying and socially responsible lives. Anxiety is at tolerable levels, ambivalence and uncertainty are reasonably accepted, and instead of irrational misery, we experience normal unhappiness in response to real events. Knowing ourselves deeply and becoming aware of disavowed aspects of ourselves also frees up the energy it takes to keep them unconscious, making more energy available for living consciously. Ultimately, we come to be able to give and receive love and to feel that our lives are meaningfully productive (S. Freud, 1917/1957).

Goals that are more specific than this cannot be established ahead of time because clients will ideally experience openness to new experiences and therefore to new goals that had not occurred to them or that they considered unacceptable or impossible prior to therapy. Thus, when beginning therapy the client agrees to undertake a process of self-understanding.

Psychodynamic Change Processes

The primary and fundamental change process in psychodynamic therapy is to make what is unconscious, conscious—commonly referred to as *insight*—or as Sigmund Freud (1933/1964) said, "Where *It* was, there *I* shall be [italics added]"(p. 80). The change process has the effect of reducing the press of unconscious impulses and the intrapsychic conflict between them and the restrictions of society, while also strengthening one's sense of self so that the demands of reality can be more readily met.

Insight is achieved through making connections between seemingly unconnected aspects of one's experiences. For example, premature ejaculation might be related to impulsiveness in other areas of life, or retarded ejaculation might be related to procrastination. In addition, new meanings can be made of old experiences, such as recognizing that low self-esteem internalized from an unkind parent results in preemptively rejecting others. New experiences of the self and of others are noticed and claimed or reclaimed. These experiences are then incorporated into a more robust sense of self, thereby resulting in expansion of awareness, openness to new experiences, new meanings of experiences, and new self-organizing processes.

Traditionally, insight into unconscious processes was held to be primarily, if not exclusively, responsible for change (Burchard, 1958). Current thinking places greater emphasis on the therapeutic aspects of a corrective relationship with the therapist (see the Evolution and Variations section later in this chapter). A compromise may have been achieved by accepting that the relative contribution of insight and the relationship depend on the particular circumstances of the client's difficulties. Thus, those who suffer from difficulties arising out of early childhood deprivations or abuses may benefit more from relationship factors, whereas those who struggle with developmentally recent issues may benefit more from insight (Wolitzky & Eagle, 1997).

Psychodynamic Change Tasks

The psychodynamic therapist uses a number of tasks toward making the unconscious conscious and facilitating a corrective relationship.

Free association involves having the client say, without censoring, whatever comes freely or unprompted to mind—no matter how seemingly trivial, random, or irrelevant—in a neutral, relaxed circumstance. It is the basis for all psychodynamic change tasks. Freud referred to free association as the "fundamental rule" of psychoanalysis. While the client is free associating, the therapist listens with an unbiased, evenly hovering attention, thus allowing the therapist to comprehend the deeper sense and meaning within the client's unconscious mind.

Free association is, to some extent, an impossible task—we constantly monitor and distort our primitive, socially unacceptable thoughts because they are threatening. The act of trying to say whatever comes to mind permits the client and therapist to observe how the client engages in distortions of unconscious material to avoid anxiety. Insights are thus gained into the nature of the client's conflicts and the anxieties associated with them.

Interpretation is the therapist's verbalization of their understanding of the client's unconscious material to the client. Through interpretation, the therapist strives to communicate an accurate, empathically based, tactful, and well-timed understanding of connections between past and present events that are emotionally meaningful to the client.

Ideally, an interpretation will contain what the client is currently thinking, feeling, and doing in the therapy session; how these parallel the client's life outside of therapy; and how they are related to important events in his or her past. The degree to which the therapist's interpretation meets this standard is judged by the degree to which the client responds positively with more information and a deepening of experience.

Dream analysis involves treating dreams much like the symptoms the client is experiencing. The obvious, *manifest* dream content represents the conscious mind's effort to disguise the hidden, *latent*—but true—content comprising unconscious impulses and their proscriptions. However, because consciousness is weakened during sleep, the therapist can discover the nature of the unconscious conflicts. For this reason, dreams are often referred to as the "royal road to the unconscious" (S. Freud, 1900/1953). The client is encouraged to report any dreams to the therapist, who can then interpret them in much the same way as free associations. In dream analysis the client reports the dream and then free associates on each element of the dream (see the Learning Task section later in this chapter). The therapist offers interpretations in regard to the latent content and its relationship to the client's unresolved unconscious conflicts. With experience, clients can begin to interpret their own dreams.

Analysis of transference involves interpreting the client's thoughts and feelings toward the therapist to facilitate the client in achieving insight into unconscious interpersonal motives and conflicts. *Transference* refers to unconscious, preexisting expectations of others—most important for therapy, the therapist—by which the meanings of interpersonal events are understood. These expectations arise out of our early significant relationships (most often parental) and are usually an important source of present misery if they are based on rigid proclivities to interpret interpersonal events in a certain way.

Transference can be broadly understood as being positive or negative. The therapist must deal with *negative transference* promptly so that the client does not terminate therapy because of an unfavorable perception of the therapist. *Positive transference*, in contrast, is what keeps the client cooperating and collaborating with therapy, and therefore it is dealt with last unless sexual feelings toward the therapist become so strong or frightening to the client as to interfere with therapy.

Therapeutic Relationship

In some ways the psychodynamic therapy circumstance can be thought of as analogous to viewing a sample in a sterile petri dish through a microscope: Concentrated, sustained, unbiased listening permits a glimpse into the human psyche (Schwartz, 2003). The subject matter that is dealt with, unlike the natural sciences, is the subjective experience of the client, however, not the objective material world.

Analytic neutrality is considered an essential ingredient of psychodynamic therapy so that the client's experience is not "contaminated" by the therapist's. It is sometimes referred to as *anonymity* or a *blank screen*. Neutrality is not the same as being indifferent, cold, or detached, however. It is, rather, a stance the therapist takes in relation to the client's conflicts whereby the therapist attempts to behave in a benevolent manner—kind and benign without unduly intruding on the client's subjective experience. The therapist strives to respect the client's uniqueness and individuality without judging from any preexisting set of values. Consistency—of fees, regularity of sessions, therapist interpersonal presentation, and so forth—is an important aspect of neutrality and also provides a safe haven for the client by rendering the therapeutic circumstance predictable and trustworthy.

Countertransference is the therapist's (undesirable) transference toward the client. It interferes with therapy to the extent that the therapist's own needs and expectations are imposed on the client and the therapeutic circumstance. Exploiting the client for personal gain is an obvious example of countertransference, whereas not so obvious perhaps are such things as trying to rescue the client from their unhappiness, seeking the client's approval, adopting an all-knowing "guru" stance, or feeling impatient with the client's therapeutic progress. The absence of counter-transference allows the therapist to maintain neutrality while allowing the client to feel truly understood and thereby safe to explore their inner psyche. It is generally accepted that psychodynamic therapists must undergo psychotherapy to resolve their own transference issues.

Evolution and Variations

Psychodynamic thought continues to be a force in psychotherapy, albeit much less so than among previous generations of therapists. It is interesting to note, however, that the number of psychoanalytic societies and training institutes continues to increase (Kahn, 2002), and there is a substantial body of cognitive, social, developmental, and neurological research that supports the central propositions of contemporary psychodynamic theory (Westen, 1998; Westen & Gabbard, 2002). Although much of Freud's theorizing has not stood the test of time, his postulate that much of conscious mental life is influenced by unconscious mental process certainly has and remains the predominant lay-psychological explanation of why people do what they do in their lives (Epstein, 1994; Westen, 1998).

Given that Freud began his pioneering efforts to uncover the essence of the human condition over 100 years ago, psychodynamic practice has evolved through attempts to incorporate the assumptive worldviews underlying the nonrationalist systems of psychotherapy (see chap.1). Because these are still psychodynamically oriented approaches, they all retain the central role of unconscious motivations. The differences between most of them center on whether our motivations are (a) primarily based in fantasy versus reality (i.e., empiricism), (b) sexual and aggressive versus affiliative (i.e., collectivism), or (c) reductionistic versus holistic (i.e., humanism). Still other variations represent efforts to shorten the length of traditional psychoanalysis, integrate psychodynamic and behavioral theories, and incorporate family systems practice.

Ego psychology follows most directly from Freud's work, and it was in fact developed by his daughter, Anna Freud (1895–1982), Heinz Hartman (1939), and Margaret Mahler (1968) and later honed to a fine edge by Charles Brenner (1982). By studying children, rather than the childhood recollections of adults as Sigmund Freud did, the ego psychologists arrived at a different understanding of the role of childhood development. In ego psychology humans' continuous efforts to adapt to the demands of reality are understood as playing a greater role in their functioning than Sigmund Freud's original emphasis on defense against unconscious impulses (A. Freud, 1936). In this way some of the objective assumptions of empiricism were introduced into psychoanalysis. Erik Erikson's famous psychosocial stages of development (Erikson, 1950), for example, are an ego psychology recasting of Sigmund Freud's theories to take into account the objective (in this case, social) nature of the infant's developmental challenges. Ego psychology therapists follow traditional psychodynamic technique most closely of all of the current variations, maintaining a neutral therapeutic relationship and focusing on interpretation of unconscious conflictual material to bring the unconscious into consciousness. Greater emphasis is placed on the demands in the client's life that prompt defense against unconscious impulses, however, than on fear of their unmodified expression.

Object relations therapy was developed by Melanie Klein (1882–1960), and it draws on the work of Sandor Ferenczi (1938/1980), Freida Fromm-Reichmann (1950), Harry Stack Sullivan (1953), Ronald Fairbairn (1954), and Otto Kernberg (1980). The therapeutic application of object relations has been nicely articulated by Sheldon Cashdan (1988), Jay R. Greenberg and Stephen Mitchell (1983), and Hans Strupp and Jeffery Binder (1984). Like Anna Freud, Klein observed the behavior of babies and infants. Unlike the ego psychologists, Klein (1948) concluded that the real relationship between mother and child in the earliest months of life becomes unconsciously represented in the psyche. The term *object relations* was originally used because the infant is able to relate to other people only as parts—or objects—such as the mother's breast. These relations serve as templates by which all other relationships are understood. The object relations therapists thereby introduced a consideration of collectivism into a still fundamentally rationalist approach. As D. W. Winnicott (1964) wrote, "a baby cannot exist alone, but is essentially part of a relationship" (p. 88). Fairbairn (1958) even wrote of the inner relational world of people in psychological distress as "closed systems" in a manner not unlike a systemic therapist (see chap. 8, this volume). Object relations therapists make particular use of interpretations of transference and countertransference in therapy to facilitate insight into problematic relationship patterns in the client's life.

Self-psychology was developed by Heinz Kohut (1913–1981) and also focuses on the importance of how real relationships influence development. What sets self-psychology apart from other psychodynamic variants, however, is Kohut's (1977) introduction of a more humanistic understanding of the self. To the self-psychology therapist, humans are all seen as striving to become a coherent, functional individual able to achieve his or her full potential. Less-than-perfect parenting—particularly failures in empathy—are experienced as a sense of "optimal frustration" and provide opportunities for the development of a healthy sense of self (Kohut, 1971). The relationship between therapist and client is therefore used to bring about therapeutic change, rather than strictly interpreting transference as in traditional psychoanalysis. In essence, the therapist becomes a parent substitute. Self-psychology therapists try to provide growth-promoting empathic experiences that inevitably fail at times. If experienced in the context of feeling accepted and safe, the client's innate drive toward integration will prompt the incorporation of disavowed unconscious material, ultimately resulting in a more robust and resilient sense of self.

Brief psychodynamic psychotherapy had its beginnings in the years of greater openness to other ways of practicing psychoanalytically following Sigmund Freud's death in 1939. In particular, Franz Alexander (1891–1964) and Thomas French's (1892–1974) description of their experimentation with a range of variations of psychoanalytic technique in their 1946 book, *Psychoanalytic Therapy: Principles and Applications*, was especially influential. They argued for a more flexible approach to treatment and that treatment might be shortened in some instances without sacrificing outcomes. There are now almost as many variations of brief psychodynamic psychotherapy as there are variations of psychodynamic therapy, although most tend toward being relational in their focus. These brief approaches have focused on aspects of psychodynamic theory considered to be well established, often subjecting them to empirical research, which has resulted in a more active approach. Rather than waiting for material to emerge from the client's free associations over months or even years, brief psychodynamic therapists seek unconscious material likely to be central to the client's distress—especially maladaptive and conflictual interpersonal expectations (i.e., transference). Some of the more well-articulated approaches are those by David Malan (1979), Habib Davanloo (1980), Lester Luborsky (1984), and James Gustafson (1986).

Cyclical psychodynamics represents one of the first attempts at integrating psychotherapies. Although originally an effort to reinterpret psychoanalysis in learning theory terms, it evolved into a true integration (Wachtel, 1977, 1997). Paul Wachtel (1940–)sought to take the core concepts of each approach and synthesize them into a broader and more inclusive approach. He posited that early childhood relationships predispose individuals to interact with others in such a way as to maintain old interpersonal patterns—for better or for worse. Our rationalist inner world and our empiricist external reality are seen as continually defining and redefining each other in a recursive fashion. The cyclical psychodynamic therapist uses active, objective change tasks of behavioral therapy (see chap. 3, this volume) to bring about change in the problematic patterns of the client's objective reality. These changes promote new insights into the client's subjective experience which, in turn, generate increased motivation to try new behaviors. Although cyclical psychodynamics is recognized as being an integrative tour de force, it has never been as influential on therapeutic practice as most scholars feel it should be. Perhaps this is because so few therapists are able to reconcile the rational and empirical worldviews underlying it.

Psychodynamic family therapy was pioneered by Murray Bowen (1913–1990)—and to a lesser extent Nathan Ackerman (1908–1971)—and made very influential contributions to family therapy through the application of psychodynamic principles. Bowen (1990) translated psychoanalytic concepts such as resistance and transference into interpersonal terms that could be addressed in the here-and-now experience of the client's (and therapist's) life and the therapy session. Bowen argued that individual problems arise and are maintained in relationship with significant people in our lives, typically our family members. The degree to which our sense of self is individualized and independent from our family system determines our ability to resist being drawn into the emotional reactivity of our families. The more undifferentiated or fused we are, the more dysfunctional our relationships, and thus our lives, are. The Bowenian therapist strives to actively relate to family members without taking sides in the family's interpersonal conflicts (i.e., remaining neutral). By doing so, the recursive cycling of symptoms between marital partners and key family members automatically resolve. It is not surprising that neither Bowen nor his followers ever managed to completely reconcile the rationalist epistemology of psychoanalysis with that of collectivism to produce a true systemic approach to psychotherapy (see chap. 8, this volume).

A Life Worth Living

Brian, a 42-year-old high school teacher, entered therapy because he felt that his life was a disappointment. He said that his wife in particular was complaining that he was increasingly distant and unresponsive. Their sexual activity had diminished from once or twice a month to once or twice a year. Brian found that he usually felt no interest in initiating sex and that if he didn't, his wife rarely made the first move. He felt there was something wrong with him and wanted to get to the root of his problems.

Brian said he remembers embarking on his teaching career "feeling like the world was my oyster." Great career success never materialized, however, and he became increasingly disappointed with his average life. He became preoccupied with fantasies of receiving glorious acclaim and rewards that included—he reluctantly admitted—the amorous attention of beautiful women. As his despondence deepened, his interest in his wife lessened.

Brian found his therapist's demeanor a little off-putting at first, and then he came to appreciate her quiet, comforting manner. He felt relieved when she told him not to make any changes in his life while he was undergoing therapy, and he enjoyed the experience of trying to say whatever came into his mind. He became quite fascinated and curious about what would come forward during each session. He noticed himself thinking about things that he had not thought about for years.

Gradually, as Brian basked in his therapist's supportive, empathic acceptance, he became aware of intense feelings of shame and loneliness stemming from his childhood. He was surprised with himself that even with her unwaveringly uncritical acceptance of everything he had told her, he was reluctant to share these feelings. Eventually he did muster the courage to tell her that he felt fundamentally unlovable and that he could not remember feeling any other way. When she asked whether he felt that he did not deserve her time and attention, he broke down and wept uncontrollably. As he cried deeply and fully, he felt wonderfully, terribly unburdened. After waiting for an appropriate moment, his therapist asked whether what he was feeling had any connection to his relationship with his wife.

The question felt more like an answer. He realized that he had been keeping his emotional distance from his wife because he did not feel worthy of her love and assumed that even though she told him she loved him, she really did not. He felt ashamed as he realized that he unconsciously blamed her for holding back his career by failing to be more supportive.

Brian applied this newfound insight to his marriage with gusto. Although his wife found his enthusiasm a bit overwhelming initially, she gradually accepted that he had made important and lasting changes, their relationship deepened in a profound way, and their marriage thrived. Brian also began to apply himself more conscientiously to his job and experienced a pleasant sense of satisfaction when he earned a long-overdue promotion.

Learning Task

Just as Sigmund Freud (1900/1953) famously undertook the analysis of his own dreams, psychodynamic therapists use dream analysis to gain insight into their own unconscious conflicts. After undertaking the task provided in Exhibit 2.1, take a few moments to write down your reactions and consider how useful you found each of the change tasks (i.e., free association, interpretation, dream analysis, and analysis of transference). Can you imagine proposing any of them to a client? If not, why not? If so, under what circumstances?

Your Reflective Journal

Having now read about the first and therefore oldest theoretical approach to psychotherapy, take some time to record your impressions in your

---

EXHIBIT 2.1

Dream Analysis

Record a dream and prepare the following account as soon after you awake as possible:

1. Allow yourself to focus on each aspect of the dream (time, place, people, mood, etc.).
2. As you focus on each aspect, try free associating either aloud into an audio recorder or through journaling, and take note of the thoughts, images, and feelings of which you become aware.
3. Allow your mind to drift to an earlier time in your life (the earlier the better) that is associated with these thoughts, images, and feelings.
4. As you allow yourself to experience these old thoughts, images, and feelings, ask yourself how they connect with your current concerns, particularly your important interpersonal relationships.
5. Ask yourself how these thoughts, images, and feelings might be connected to your therapeutic practice and your comfort working with particular clients or client problems.

---

reflective journal. In particular, what did you find appealing about the approach, what did you identify with, and what did you find difficult to accept? Could you imagine yourself practicing or undergoing psychodynamic psychotherapy? Why or why not? Do any of the current variations of psychodynamic therapy hold a greater or lesser appeal for you? Do you have any unanswered questions about this approach? If so, what would be the best way for you to answer those questions?

Summary

Psychoanalysis was originally developed by Sigmund Freud at the beginning of the 20th century as a method to understand the human mind, while simultaneously being a treatment for what was then known as hysteria. Psychoanalysis went on to become the progenitor of most psychotherapies practiced today. Although it has evolved and changed over the ensuing 100 years, much has remained constant. Unconscious conflicts are considered to be at the root of mental suffering, and bringing them into consciousness is the means by which that suffering can be reduced. Free association, interpretation, dream analysis, and analysis of transference are the tasks most often used to bring about therapeutic change. The therapist is expected to maintain a neutral, though empathic, attitude toward the client and the client's conflicts. A number of schools of psychodynamic therapy have been developed, with the most commonly practiced forms being variants of brief psychodynamic psychotherapy that focus on the primacy of interpersonal relationships.

Further Resources

CASE READINGS

Freud, S. (1955). Two case histories ('Little Hans' and the 'Rat Man'). In J. Strachey (Ed. & Trans.), *The standard edition of the complete psychological works of Sigmund Freud* (Vol. 10, pp. 1–250). London: Hogarth Press. (Original work published 1909)

Mann, J., & Goldman, R. (1982). *A casebook in time-limited psychotherapy.* New York: McGraw-Hill.

Sholevar, G. P. (Ed.). (1991). *Psychoanalytic case studies.* Madison, CT: International Universities Press.

Winnicott, D. W. (1972). Fragment of an analysis. In P. L. Giovacchini (Ed.), *Tactics and techniques in psychoanalytic therapy* (pp. 455–493). New York: Science House.

RECOMMENDED READING

Auld, F., Hyman, M., & Rudzinski, D. (2005). *Resolution of inner conflict: An introduction to psychoanalytic therapy* (2nd ed.). Washington, DC: American Psychological Association.

Freud, S. (1958). Observations on transference-love (Further recommendations on the technique of Psycho-Analysis III). In J. Strachey (Ed. & Trans.), *The standard edition of the complete psychological works of Sigmund Freud* (Vol. 12, pp. 157–171). London: Hogarth Press. (Original work published 1915)

Freud, S. (1958). On beginning the treatment (Further recommendations on the technique of Psycho-Analysis I). In J. Strachey (Ed. & Trans.), *The standard edition of the complete psychological works of Sigmund Freud* (Vol. 12, pp. 121–144). London: Hogarth Press. (Original work published 1913)

Freud, S. (1958). Remembering, repeating and working-through (Further recommendations on the technique of Psycho-Analysis II). In J. Strachey (Ed. & Trans.), *The standard edition of the complete psychological works of Sigmund Freud* (Vol. 12, pp. 145–156). London: Hogarth Press. (Original work published 1914)

McWilliams, N. (2004). *Psychoanalytic psychotherapy: A practitioner's guide*. New York: Guilford Press.

RECOMMENDED VIEWING

Allyn & Bacon (Producer). (2000). *Object relations therapy with Jill Savege Scharff, MD* [Motion picture]. (Available from Psychotherapy.net, 4625 California Street, San Francisco, CA 94118-1224)

American Psychological Association (Producer). (2004). *Brief dynamic therapy with Stanley B. Messer, PhD* [Motion picture]. (Available from the American Psychological Association, 750 First Street, NE, Washington, DC 20002-4242)

American Psychological Association (Producer). (2008). *Psychoanalytic therapy with Nancy McWilliams, PhD* [Motion picture]. (Available from the American Psychological Association, 750 First Street, NE, Washington, DC 20002-4242)

American Psychological Association (Producer). (2008). *Time-limited dynamic psychotherapy with Hanna Levenson, PhD* [Motion picture]. (Available from the American Psychological Association, 750 First Street, NE, Washington, DC 20002-4242)

Psychological & Educational Films (Producer). (1986). *Three approaches to Psychotherapy III: Part 1. Hans H. Strupp (psychodynamic therapy)* [Motion picture]. (Available from Insight Media, Inc., 2162 Broadway, New York, NY 10024-0621)

Behavioral | 3

Behaviorism has its historical roots in the 17th- and 18th-century European Age of Enlightenment, during which rationality and objectivity were championed over opinion and divine authority. It was John Broadus Watson (1878–1958; see Figure 3.1), however, who set the stage for behavior therapy to come of age. In his now-famous 1913 article, "Psychology as the Behaviorist Views It," Watson stated, "Psychology as the behaviorist views it is a purely objective branch of natural science. Its theoretical goal is the prediction and control of behavior" (p. 158). Emotions, for example, rather than being thought of as transcendental experiences, are understood as visceral bodily reactions; language is not a window to the soul but a laryngeal habit, and so on. Thus, we can see that Watson put his behaviorist psychology squarely in the empiricism quadrant of epistemologies (see Figure 1.2, chap. 1, this volume).

The intellectual climate of the young Watson prized a functional analysis of the role the mind plays in the adaptation of the organism to its environment. James Angell (1867–1949), one of Watson's graduate professors at the University of Chicago, had even predicted in 1910 that the term *consciousness* would disappear from psychology just as had the term *soul*. Angell suggested that a more objective description of human and animal behavior would ultimately prove to be a more profitable way to study psychology. Indeed, Ivan Pavlov's (1849–1936) research on conditioned responses in animals had demonstrated the value of objective measures and terminology in studying higher mental processes.

FIGURE 3.1

John Broadus Watson. Printed with permission of the Archives of the History of American Psychology.

Watson set to work demonstrating the value of his approach for clinical problems. He and Rosalie Rayner[1] conditioned a *fear response* (i.e., phobia) in an 11-month-old child, "Albert B." They repeatedly paired a loud frightening noise—a hammer struck against a steel bar—with the presentation of a white rat that initially elicited no response (Watson & Rayner, 1920). After seven pairings of rat and sound (in two sessions, 1 week apart), little Albert displayed a strong fear response when presented with the rat, and with a rabbit, a dog, and a fur coat, and a negative response to a bearded Santa Claus mask and Watson's hair. His fear did not transfer to his wooden blocks or the hair of Watson's assistants. Watson stated that his intent was to further demonstrate that such a conditioned emotional response could be deconditioned (Watson, 1924), but Albert's mother removed her son from the hospital where the experiment was being conducted (Harris, 1979).

A college friend of Rayner's, Mary Cover Jones, persuaded Watson to help her design an intervention program for children in the institution managed by Jones and her husband. She demonstrated how a child's

[1]Rayner was a 21-year-old graduate student with whom Watson had an affair, resulting in Watson's scandalous divorce from his socially prominent wife, Mary Ickes, and forcing him from academic psychology and into advertising (Benjamin, Whitaker, Ramsey, & Zeve, 2007).

fear could be deconditioned by pairing a desired food with an object that elicited a fear response. The child, in a state of "craving for food" (Jones, 1924a, p. 388), was fed while the feared object was brought within a distance from him that did not prompt a response that interfered with his eating behavior. Over subsequent meals, the object was gradually brought nearer to him until he no longer displayed any fear reaction to the object (Jones, 1924a, 1924b).

Thus, Pavlov's (1927) classical conditioning principles came to be applied to therapeutic ends. It is a curiosity that almost no one followed the applied trail that Watson, Rayner, and Jones established. For quite some years, little interest outside of academic circles was aroused (Samelson, 1981). A decade later—in 1935—Hobart and Willie Mowrer initiated a treatment program for childhood bedwetting (Mowrer & Mowrer, 1938). They put a special pad under the child's bedsheet that would ring a bell when the child urinated. The bell awakened the child, who would eventually wake up in response to a full bladder. This technique proved so successful that it is still in use today.

However, it was not until the 1950s that behavioral principles began to be widely applied to treating human suffering. In particular, B. F. Skinner's (1904–1990) landmark book, *Science and Human Behavior* (1953), established the importance and usefulness of *operant conditioning*—changing the likelihood of a behavior recurring based on its consequences. Although Skinner was more interested in general psychology, he and his student Ogden Lindsey did apply operant conditioning to people with psychotic disorders at the Metropolitan State Hospital in Waltham, Massachusetts (Lindsey, 1956; Skinner, 1954). Their research lead directly to the use of token economy treatment programs in psychiatric hospitals (see the Behavioral Change Tasks section later in this chapter) and classroom management programs in regular and special education classrooms (e.g., O'Leary & O'Leary, 1977).

In England, Hans Eysenck (1916–1997) published his scathing critique of the state of (predominantly psychoanalytic) psychotherapy (Eysenck, 1952) and proposed a more "scientific" (i.e., empirical) approach (Eysenck, 1960). Although Eysenck's conclusion that insight therapies are no more effective than spontaneous recovery was soon shown to be exaggerated (Cartwright, 1955; Luborsky, 1954), he did stimulate considerable interest in behavior-based therapy. Eysenck and his colleagues (e.g., Cyril Franks, Stanley Rachman, M. B. Shapiro) at the University of London's Institute of Psychiatry played a major role in the early development of behavior therapy. Most notably, they developed clinical procedures through the intensive behavioral study of individual cases (e.g., Shapiro, 1961).

In South Africa, Joseph Wolpe (1915–1997) was dissatisfied with psychodynamic therapy and set out instead to apply classical conditioning to the treatment of anxiety disorders. He found considerable success treating anxiety by provoking a bodily response that is incompatible with anxiety while in the presence of anxiety-evoking stimuli. Wolpe called this process *reciprocal inhibition* (Wolpe, 1958) and used muscle relaxation (Jacobson, 1929), social assertion (Salter, 1949), and sexual arousal, among others, as anxiety antagonists to great effect. Although reciprocal inhibition is no longer considered to be a valid explanation of the change process (Rescorla, 1988), Wolpe's work continues to have a major influence on present-day behavior therapy practice.

Because behavior therapy is not the product of one person, there is no completely noncontroversial consensus on what constitutes the behavioral approach to psychotherapy. There is some agreement, however, that it (a) focuses on current—as opposed to historical—determinants of behavior; (b) emphasizes specific, overt behavior as the target of treatment; (c) specifies treatment in objective terms to enable replication and evaluation; and (d) relies on empirical research as the source of treatment hypotheses, techniques, and evaluation (Kazdin, 1978). In sum, behavior therapy represents the application of the science of human behavior (i.e., an analytic, objective, empirical approach) to therapeutic ends.

Behavioral Rationale

Problems in our lives are best dealt with in a precise, methodical, and practical manner. Just as we use scientific methods to find solutions to problems in the natural world—such as the effect of carbon emissions on global warming—we can also seek solutions to personal problems such as depression and managing stress. Although thoughts, feelings, and beliefs are certainly important aspects of the human condition, they are very difficult to measure reliably and therefore are best avoided in our efforts to solve personal problems. What we can do is observe and measure our personal behaviors and evaluate the effect that they are having on producing or maintaining our problems. In fact, empirical research demonstrates that if we change our behavior, then our thoughts, feelings, and beliefs will soon follow suit. Similarly, because events that occurred in the past cannot be altered, we are better off focusing our efforts at changing what we can in the present.

Behavior therapists have found that solutions are more forthcoming if we understand that problematic behaviors are developed, maintained, and changed primarily through learning. If we accept that these behaviors are learned, then they can be unlearned or new behaviors can be learned that will compensate for—or help us to adapt to—problematic ones. Research actually shows that the same principles of learning govern normal and abnormal behavior. Even behavior that stems from biological disturbances can be favorably influenced through interventions based on learning principles.

Given that the focus of the behavior therapist's treatment efforts is behavior, the behavior therapist asks the client to do something about his or her difficulties. Talk is really only useful for gaining information about the nature of a problem, helping to identify what behaviors are the rightful target of change, and communicating instructions for implementing change tasks. Talk is not enough to bring about change. Clients in behavior therapy are asked to actively undertake tasks in their day-to-day lives. The logic is straightforward: The problem occurs in one's life, so this is where changes should occur.

Behavioral Goals

Behavior therapy has as its overarching goal the elimination of unwanted or problematic behaviors and the introduction or strengthening of desired or adaptive behaviors. The therapist approaches each client's circumstances from the perspective of the scientific method. After precisely assessing the nature and extent of the client's problem, individualized behavioral goals are developed that are specific, measurable, and achievable. By being precise about the nature of the problem, the behavior therapist can decide whether a proven existing treatment protocol is applicable. If not, a unique plan is developed on the basis of established learning principles. Equally as important, precision and specificity allow progress toward and attainment of goals to be quantitatively monitored. As a good scientist, the behavior therapist treats each change task as a hypothesis. If the task results in the desired change in the target behavior, then therapy is considered successful. If not, another task is proposed, and the results are assessed until the goals are achieved.

Behavioral Change Processes

Behavior therapy brings about change through two learning processes: stimulus control (i.e., classical conditioning) and reinforcement (i.e., operant conditioning).

Stimulus control involves changing the cues or conditions that occur before behaviors occur. *Prompts* are the cues to perform a behavior, such as a red light at a traffic intersection or a parent asking a child to go to bed. *Setting events* are environmental conditions that elicit behaviors, such as how when riding in an elevator one faces the doors rather than the back wall. Altering the stimuli in our environment can be very influential in changing behavior: for example, avoiding the snack aisle when grocery shopping to reduce consumption of unhealthy food. Sometimes, new associations can be learned in response to stimuli that had previously elicited maladaptive or otherwise undesired behavior, such as phobias. Exposure-based interventions are an example of this approach.

Reinforcement means to strengthen behavior in the sense of increasing the frequency of its occurrence. It occurs when the consequences of a behavior increase the likelihood of its being repeated. If a behavior increases when a reinforcer follows it, this is known as *positive reinforcement*. If a behavior increases when a reinforcer is taken away, this is *negative reinforcement*. For example, eating food is reinforced by the taste of food (positive reinforcement) and the elimination of hunger (negative reinforcement).

To the extent that behavior is maintained by consequences in one's environment, changing environmental reinforcers will produce changes in behavior. This can be facilitated in a number of ways. The most obvious way is to change an individual's environment. Parent training for childhood problems is an example.

Often environments cannot be changed, however, and the focus of intervention can be the individual's behavior. Behaviors can be increased or decreased so that different consequences are elicited in one's environment. Social skills training is an example of this approach.

Behavioral Change Tasks

The behavior therapist draws from a wide range of empirically based interventions. Some of the more commonly used tasks are described in this section.

Exposure-based interventions are the earliest, most studied behavioral interventions and are considered the treatment of choice for fear-based problems such as anxiety and phobias (Barlow, 2002). Exposure-based interventions involve exposure to feared stimuli. They can be delivered in a number of different ways, with in vivo (i.e., in life) being preferred. For example, an individual who is afraid of heights is gradually exposed to heights, a shy person is gradually exposed to social situations, someone afraid to leave their house gradually leaves their house, and so on.

The other method is through imaginal exposure whereby the individual imagines the feared stimuli. Although generally less preferred than in vivo, it is useful when the client is afraid of something that cannot be experienced, such as thoughts or memories, or when the client cannot or will not undertake in vivo exposure.

A relatively new method of exposure is through computer-mediated virtual reality, using a three-dimensional graphical representation of the feared stimuli (Emmelkamp et al., 2002).

The therapist works with the client to develop a hierarchy of feared stimuli to assist the client in becoming unafraid of relatively minor fears, gradually progressing through increasingly fearful stimuli. Therefore, a client might begin with standing on a 6-inch platform before standing in the stairwell of a tall building and, eventually, peering over the balcony railing of a 10th-floor apartment.

To maximize the likelihood that exposure will be effective, presentation of the feared stimuli should be under the client's *control*, of sufficient *intensity* to elicit a fear response, of sufficient *duration* for the client's fear to decrease, of sufficient *frequency* (ideally multiple exposures daily), and be practiced across a *variety of circumstances* (Antony & Swinson, 2000).

Relaxation-based interventions are sometimes implemented in isolation of other tasks for addressing muscle tension, heart rate, blood pressure, and hyperventilation. They are most often used in conjunction with exposure-based interventions. The most commonly used approach is progressive muscle relaxation, whereby clients are instructed to clench and then release each set of muscles: arms, face, neck, shoulders, chest, abdomen, and legs. Often, a recorded set of instructions is provided so that clients can practice at home. With practice, clients can voluntarily induce relaxation without tensing their muscles (Goldfried & Davison, 1994).

Response prevention is a variant of exposure-based intervention, and it involves preventing obsessive–compulsive rituals until the tendency to perform the behavior diminishes. Such rituals typically arise in response to fears because they are usually successful in temporarily reducing the anxiety evoked by stimuli. Preventing such rituals therefore leads to an increase in anxiety. Clients are helped to find some way to do whatever they can that is incompatible or antagonistic with performing their ritual in order to delay it for progressively longer periods. The urge to perform the ritual will gradually decrease and may be eliminated entirely in some cases. If response prevention and exposure are maintained for 2 hours per day for several weeks, then habituation and greater comfort typically ensue (Foa, Franklin, & Kozak, 1998). Response prevention has also been shown to be effective in reducing body dysmorphic disorder, bulimia nervosa, alcohol use, and hypochondrias.

Operant strategies—also known as *contingency management procedures*— cover a variety of interventions that address the environmental stimuli that are maintaining undesired behavior, often with persons who have diminished capacity such as those with autism (e.g., Lovaas, 1977) or severe, chronic mental illness (e.g., Ayllon & Azrin, 1968). *Successive approximation* (or *shaping*) involves reinforcing behaviors that are more like the desired behaviors than the undesired ones along a continuum of small steps. *Token economies* establish an institutional system whereby tokens are given for desired behavior that can be exchanged for items of direct reinforcement, such as food (Ayllon & Azrin, 1968). *Time-out* is a fixed period spent in a less reinforcing environment, contingent on behavior (Brantner & Doherty, 1983).

Social skills training involves the client learning new behaviors that elicit desired behaviors from others. Many difficulties that prompt people to seek therapy are the result of their being unable to interact with others in a manner that satisfies their instrumental and affiliative needs (e.g., Becker, Heimberg, & Bellack, 1987). Social skills training proceeds through a series of steps: (a) identifying problematic interpersonal situations; (b) establishing specific behavioral goals; (c) receiving instruction on and modeling of adaptive behaviors; and (d) rehearsing the new skills and receiving feedback.

Modeling involves having someone demonstrate desired behaviors that the client has never done, and the client then imitates the model. Models can be the therapist, some other person from the client's life, actors in film or television, or video self-modeling (Meharg & Woltersdorf, 1990). Modeling is used extensively in social skills training. A related use is having someone model a behavior that the client has been avoiding because of anticipated negative consequences. The client observes the model performing the behavior without the feared negative consequence, increasing the likelihood that the client will exhibit the behavior.

Therapeutic Relationship

For behavior therapists, a therapeutic alliance is a useful but not necessary and certainly not a sufficient condition for bringing about therapeutic change (Keijsers, Schaap, Hoogduin, & Lammers, 1995; Williams & Chambless, 1990). After all, self-administered treatments and self-help books—in which the therapist is absent or minimally present—have been shown empirically to be highly effective (Hecker, Losee, Fritzer, & Fink, 1996; Swinson, Fergus, Cox, & Wickwire, 1995). There is also the overwhelming body of evidence that a positive therapeutic alliance is highly predictive of positive outcomes independent of type of therapy (Keijsers, Schaap, & Hoogduin, 2000). In behavior therapy, the relationship is understood as an opportunity for modeling desired adaptive interpersonal behavior and as a source of social reinforcement.

The behavior therapist assumes a directive stance throughout treatment because it is the therapist's responsibility to plan and structure the sessions. The target goals, however, are established collaboratively with the client, and there is a periodic, ongoing review of progress toward goals and setting new ones. If progress is not being made, the therapist accepts responsibility for adjusting the therapy. The client is not blamed or labeled "resistant." Rather, failure or lack of progress is understood as information that is incorporated into the revised treatment plan.

The therapist's activity does not mean that clients are expected to be passive. Quite the contrary: Clients are expected to be active, and homework is regularly assigned to practice, strengthen, and generalize to the client's life what has been learned in session. The therapist is responsible for clearly articulating these expectations to the client. As the client becomes more adept at formulating plans and goals, the therapist can become less directive, until therapy can be faded out toward termination of services.

Evolution and Variations

Consistent with its grounding in empirical inquiry, behavior therapy continues to evolve in response to new research findings. Most significant has been the incorporation of cognitive processes (see chap. 7, this volume) into behavioral theory and therapy (e.g., Caballo, 1998; Dobson, 2001). In fact, there are currently few associations devoted exclusively to behavior therapy. The Association for the Advancement of Behavior Therapy, for example, was established in 1966 and recently changed its name to the Association for Behavioral and Cognitive Therapies after many years of debate. Similarly, the European Association of Behavior Therapy, established in 1976, changed its name in 1992 to the European Association of Behavioral and Cognitive Therapy.

No evidence has been put forth that has necessitated a change to the essential rationale and therapeutic relationship of behavior therapy, however. Changing observable behavior through active involvement on the part of the therapist and client has been found to be a remarkably effective approach. Behavior therapy has evolved along the lines of developing and testing applications to particular disorders. Evidence has been accumulated for the efficacy of the behavioral treatment of obsessive–compulsive disorder (Eddy, Dutra, Bradley, & Westen, 2004), panic disorder (van Balkom et al., 1997), bulimia (Lewandowski, Gebing, Anthony, & O'Brien, 1997), and anger disorders (DiGiuseppe & Tafrate, 2003; Sukhodolsky, Kassinove, & Gorman, 2004), among others. Currently, a number of behavior therapists are testing ways of treating the complex disorders typically seen in clinical practice, such as posttraumatic stress disorder in adult women who were sexually abused as children (Cloitre, Koenen, Cohen, & Han, 2002).

Behavioral medicine involves the application of behavioral principles to physical health and illness (Pomerleau & Brady, 1979). Behavioral methods have been effectively applied to (a) the treatment of medical issues such as hypertension (Appel, Saab, & Holroyd, 1985) and chronic pain (Morely, Eccleston, & Williams, 1999); (b) adherence to medical treatments (McComas, Wacker, & Cooper, 1998; Wong, Seroka, & Ogisi, 2000); (c) coping with medical treatments (Redd & Androwski, 1982); (d) the prevention of HIV infection (Kalichman, Carey, & Johnson, 1996); and (e) the prevention of medical disorders such as heart disease, stroke, and some cancers (N. Adler & Matthews, 1994; Metzler, Biglan, Noel, Ary, & Ochs, 2000). In fact, behavior is increasingly becoming recognized as a crucial factor in developing major health problems, with over 50% of health care costs being attributable to the consequences of behaviors such as smoking, alcohol abuse, inactivity, and overeating (Prochaska, 1996). These same behaviors influence the development of conditions such as diabetes, high blood pressure, and obesity, which increases the risk of morbidity and premature mortality. Other behaviors, conversely, can lower the risk of life-threatening illness, such as participating in medical screening for treatable diseases. In light of these findings, behavioral medicine is well positioned to supplement biologically based medical treatment.

Multimodal therapy was developed by Arnold Lazarus (1932–), a student of Joseph Wolpe, with the goal of broadening behavior therapy to include aspects of clients' lives that have been empirically demonstrated to be worthwhile targets of intervention. Clients' troubles are assumed to be the result of a multitude of specific problems, which can be addressed by using a wide range of specific techniques. A systematic technically eclectic approach, multimodal therapy attends to each area of a client's significant *b*ehaviors, *a*ffective responses, *s*ensations, *i*magery, *c*ognitions, *i*nterpersonal relationships, and the need for *d*rugs and other biological factors (*BASIC ID*; Lazarus, 1989). Appropriate techniques—with empirical support whenever possible—are then selected in collaboration with the client to address each difficulty within these modalities. If an impasse should arise during treatment, a second-order BASIC ID is developed, whereby the unresponsive problem is targeted multimodally. If the client presents with a more generalized complaint, such as anxiety or depression, the multimodal therapist works with the client to develop a more specific modality-based understanding of each distressing aspect of the larger problem. The therapeutic relationship is understood in similarly practical terms: The therapist strives to tailor the relationship to that which the client prefers provided therapy remains task oriented (Lazarus, 1993).

Functional analytic psychotherapy (FAP) was initially developed by Robert Kohlenberg (1937–) and Mavis Tsai (1954–) to treat a variety of interpersonal difficulties, including personality disorders, that did not respond to established behavioral (or any other) treatments (Tsai et al., 2008). Not unlike Wachtel's cyclical psychodynamics (see chap. 2, this volume), Kohlenberg and Tsai (1991) recognized that the relationship themes so central to the psychodynamic concept of transference were clinically important, while scientifically inadequate. FAP focuses on the in vivo relationship between the therapist and client as an objective sample of representative behavior from relationships in the client's life. A client who is overly critical or dismissive of the therapist, for example, likely has difficulty forming close relationships with others. The therapist works to establish a genuine, caring, and meaningful therapeutic relationship with the client so that the client will come to find the relationship a source of reinforcement. The therapist's reactions to the client are then used as information to assess and elicit relevant interpersonal behavior about the client and as natural reinforcers. Desired behavior is reinforced in session through honest interpersonal responding about the effect that the client's behavior is having on the therapist. This natural—rather than arbitrary—reinforcer has been found to better sustain generalization of desired interpersonal behavior in the client's life outside of therapy.

A Difficult Child

Falik was referred for therapy by his Grade 2 teacher in response to disruptive disobedience at school. He was described as often talking back, whining, refusing to comply with requests, and occasionally hitting classmates. His parents were very concerned that their son not become known as "a difficult child" and expressed reservations about him being treated by a behavior therapist for fear that it might be seen as further proof of his difficult nature.

The therapist explained that there was nothing "wrong" or "bad" about their son. Rather, he had simply learned to behave in ways that were causing him and others problems. He could learn new behaviors that would help him be happier and get along better with others. Falik's parents were obviously relieved by this explanation and admitted that they had been struggling with similar problems at home. They expressed enthusiasm for treatment.

After further explaining what to expect from treatment and what would be expected of them, the therapist gave them recording sheets and instructed them to record the behaviors that were causing problems, the events that preceded them, and those that followed. After the therapist showed them how to fill out the sheets and answered their questions, the session was concluded.

In the second session, the records were reviewed, and a pattern was noted whereby Falik's problem behaviors were preceded by a request by either parent and followed by a compromise or capitulation. On the basis of this assessment data, a treatment plan was developed that involved Falik's parents being taught how to (a) provide positive attention for their son's desired, prosocial behavior; (b) ignore his noncompliant, inappropriate behavior; and (c) use time-out to control his disruptive behavior. Time-outs were to be implemented by having him sit in a quiet spot for 3 minutes. If he misbehaved during that time, 1 minute would be added to his time-out. Information and instructions were also provided for his teacher to reward appropriate behavior in school with stickers that would be exchanged for treats to be given out by his parents.

In the third and fourth sessions the therapist reviewed the week's recording sheets, noting any changes in the target behaviors and problem solving any difficulties in implementing the treatment program. In response to some inconsistency in administering the program, the therapist observed Falik and his parents in session and then coached them on consistently attending to and rewarding desired behaviors. The therapist also noted in session that they tended to make overly complicated requests of Falik and instructed them how to make simple, direct requests without drawn-out explanations. Once they demonstrated mastery, the therapist concluded the session.

By the eighth session, Falik was behaving more appropriately at school and home. His disruptive behavior had diminished to the point where his teacher did not think it was a concern, and he hadn't struck a classmate for 2 weeks. His parents were delighted with his behavior at home and noted that things were "so much more relaxed" between them. They and the therapist mutually agreed to discontinue therapy.

Learning Task

In order to gain a sense of just how practical behavior therapy can be, complete the task provided in Exhibit 3.1. Be sure to go through the steps thoroughly and apply them methodically. Once you have completed the task, ask yourself how successful you were in achieving the goals you established. If unsuccessful or partially successful, what hypothesis might you postulate to explain your lack of success? How might this hypothesis inform a new behavioral plan? If you had difficulty completing the task, you might even try targeting your difficulty as a behavioral goal.

Your Reflective Journal

Behavioral therapy is the second-oldest theoretical approach to psychotherapy; it is very different from the psychodynamic approach. Take some time to record your thoughts in your journal. In addition to what you may have found convincing about the behavior therapy approach, what you identified with, and what you found difficult to accept, how do you

EXHIBIT 3.1

Applied Behavioral Analysis

Think about a recurring circumstance in your life that troubles you. It might be arguing too often with someone you like or love, overeating junk food, or avoiding something you should do. Now proceed through the following steps:

1. *Operationalize the issue.* Describe the circumstance as specifically and concretely as possible. For example, describe an actual argument: Where did it occur, who was present, and what words were said?
2. *Identify antecedent events.* Describe the behavioral events that occurred prior to the circumstance. For example, what were you doing, feeling, or thinking prior to a junk food binge?
3. *Identify behavior.* Describe in specific detail the behaviors that occurred during the circumstance on which you are focusing. For example, what were you doing while you were procrastinating? Were you watching television, visiting with friends, or worrying?
4. *Identify consequences.* Describe what happened after the circumstance. What specifically was the result of the antecedent event and behavior? For example, did you avoid social contact with your friend for a week following the argument, feel guilty after overeating, or spend all night working after procrastinating?
5. *Establish goals.* Once you have a clear, specific description of the problematic circumstance, see if you can describe a goal you would like to accomplish. Try to incorporate the specific aspects you identified in the preceding four steps to establish an achievable behavioral goal. For example, you might listen to your friend's complete statement prior to responding when you argue, go to the library when an assignment is due rather working in your room, or visit a friend rather than go to the ice cream store when you feel sad.

think about behavior therapy in contrast to psychodynamic therapy? If you had to choose between just those two types of therapies, which would you prefer to apply as a therapist? Which might you prefer to undergo as a client? Are there aspects of one or the other that you might like to incorporate into how you practice without having to accept the approach completely? What does this tell you about your personal approach to therapy? What unanswered questions do you have about this approach, if any? If you do have unanswered questions, how might you answer them?

Summary

Behavior therapy is best conceptualized as a general category of approaches, or a set of related approaches, that have evolved from the theoretical writings, clinical experiments, and empirical studies of behaviorally oriented psychotherapists. There is thus no single definition of behavior therapy. The various therapies are tied together by a scientific approach to solving people's problems. Behavior is understood as changing through either stimulus control (i.e., antecedents that elicit behavior) or reinforcement (i.e., consequences that accelerate behavior). Behavioral goals are based on changes in behavior, observed with methodological rigor. Behavioral change tasks use a variety of strategies to target behavioral problems. Behavior therapies provide great flexibility in treatment targets and interventions, with many different behavioral change tasks that have empirically demonstrated effectiveness. Behavioral therapies have largely been incorporated into cognitive–behavioral therapy, which continues to grow as it is developed and tested for effectiveness for a variety of psychological problems.

Further Resources

CASE READINGS

Barlow, D. H. (Ed.). (1993). *Clinical handbook of psychological disorders* (2nd ed.). New York: Guilford Press.

Cautela, J. R., Kearney, A. J., Ascher, L., Kearney, A., & Kleinman, M. (Eds.). (1993). *Covert conditioning casebook*. Pacific Grove, CA: Thomson.

Eysenck, H. J. (Ed.). (1976). *Case studies in behavior therapy*. London: Routledge.

RECOMMENDED READING

Goldfried, M. R., & Davison, G. C. (1994). *Clinical behavior therapy*. New York: Wiley.

Kanfer, F. H., & Goldstein, A. P. (Eds.). (1991). *Helping people change: A textbook of methods* (4th ed.). Needham Heights, MA: Allyn & Bacon.

O'Donohue, W., & Krasner, L. (1997). *Theories of behavior therapy: Exploring behavior change*. Washington, DC: American Psychological Association.

Spiegler, M. D., & Guevremont, D. C. (2003). *Contemporary behavior therapy* (4th ed.). Pacific Grove, CA: Brooks/Cole.

Wolpe, J. (1991). *The practice of behavior therapy* (4th ed.). New York: Pergamon Press.

RECOMMENDED VIEWING

American Psychological Association (Producer). (1994). *Multimodal therapy with Arnold A. Lazarus, PhD* [Motion picture]. (Available from the American Psychological Association, 750 First Street, NE, Washington, DC 20002-4242)

American Psychological Association (Producer). (1997). *Behavior therapy for obsessive–compulsive disorder with Samuel M. Turner, PhD* [Motion picture]. (Available from the American Psychological Association, 750 First Street, NE, Washington, DC 20002-4242)

Eastern Pennsylvania Psychiatric Institute (Producer). (1969). *Behavioral therapy demonstration* with *Dr. Joseph Wolpe* [Motion picture]. (Available from Penn State Media Sales, 237 Outreach Building, University Park, PA 16802-3899)

Foxx, R., & Gregorich, D. M. (Producers). (1980). *Harry: Behavioral treatment of self-abuse* [Motion picture]. (Available from Research Press, Department 29W, P.O. Box 9177, Champaign, IL 61826-9177)

Milton H. Erickson Foundation (Producer). (1985). *Joseph Wolpe, MD: A case of social anxiety* [Motion Picture]. (Available from the Milton H. Erickson Foundation, 3606 N. 24th Street, Phoenix, AZ 85016-6500)

Existential 4

Existential psychotherapy is fundamentally a philosophical approach that guides the therapist's rationale for therapy. The term *existential* is derived from the Latin root *exsistere*, meaning to "stand forth," "become," or "exist." That is, existentialism assumes existence precedes essence in that an individual cannot be reduced to some essential component or components. *Who* we are is understood as an epiphenomenon arising out of *how* we live our lives. Thus, existential philosophers are concerned with the question of what it means to be fully alive.

Søren Kierkegaard (1813–1855) is generally credited with being the pioneering thinker of what came to be known as existential philosophy. He postulated that people are imprisoned by acquiescence to ideologies about the nature of the world, particularly religious doctrine and scientific detachment. Kierkegaard argued that we should move from trying to live an objectified life and instead acknowledge how our subjective experience of struggling to find truth is central to human existence. It is through this struggle, he urged, that we can expand, deepen, and achieve our full potential as human beings. When we direct our energies toward making our lives easier, we expunge the very challenges that give life meaning and purpose. This is because those subjective states that human beings covet above all others—such as love and happiness—cannot be sought directly. These uniquely valued human experiences can only occur as byproducts of some other activity that has meaning for us. If we were actually able to rid life of unhappiness, therefore, we would also—paradoxically—rid it of joy. And so, like Socrates—that other great rationalist before him—Kierkegaard set out to live a virtuous life consistent with his beliefs by questioning assumptions, ridiculing hypocrisy, doubting the obvious, and rejecting convention.

Friedrich Nietzsche (1844–1900), writing during approximately the same period as Kierkegaard, similarly argued that the scientific, objective approach to living was dominating the intuitive, subjective approach, resulting in a devitalization of the human condition. Like Kierkegaard, Nietzsche argued that truth is subjective and that abstractions such as language can never fully grasp nor communicate the reality of individual existence.

For both Kierkegaard and Nietzsche, life is not about adjustment or normality. Rather, truly healthy persons are those who have *transcended* themselves through disputing the lies of socially defined character, accepting that the universe is meaningless and absurd with no rational direction or scheme, and freeing their human spirit of its conditioned prison. Life is a continual emerging, a becoming of one's true self. As such, we have complete freedom, cannot help but make choices (even not deciding is a choice), and our actions are unpredictable. Only through such an honest appreciation of the worst that life truly is can we create a better life.

Given that existentialists eschew reducing the human condition to an essence and accept that language is inadequate, is it any wonder that they have not produced a simple definition of existentialism? In keeping with its central assumption ("existence precedes essence"), rather than defining what existential philosophy is, it is defined by what existential philosophers do. Therefore, we say that the existentialist is concerned with human predicaments such as alienation, anxiety, inauthenticity, responsibility, dread, anticipation of death, sense of nothingness, and making meaning in a meaningless universe (Angeles, 1992).

Existential psychotherapy arose in Europe in the 1940s and 1950s in the wake of World War II and with awareness of the atrocities committed during that horrific conflict fresh in people's minds. The two leading proponents of existentialism, Ludwig Binswanger (1881–1966) and Medard Boss (1903–1990), expressed dissatisfaction with the prevailing approaches in psychiatry of Freudian drives and behavioral conditioning. They argued that therapists were not seeing patients for who they really were and instead were seeing a projection of their theories about them. Therapists were urged instead to strive to enter the patient's experiential world without presuppositions that preclude true understanding—a "disciplined naivete." Binswanger (1958, 1963), drawing on the work of Martin Heidegger (1889–1976), spoke of how human experience is multiple and complex and takes place on a number of different levels: the *Umwelt* (world around—the environmental and biological), *Mitwelt* (world with others—the social), and *Eigenwelt* (one's own world—the personal). Only by considering all of these aspects of an individual's experience can we begin to "know" them.

Rollo May (1909–1994) is generally considered to be the father of North American existential psychotherapy. With the publication of the book *Existence* (May, Angel, & Ellenberger, 1958), May introduced the work of the European existential thinkers—such as Binswanger and Boss—to an American audience. May came to existentialism after suffering what he called a "nervous breakdown" as a young English teacher. After confronting his own existential issues, he decided to learn psychotherapy from Alfred Adler in Vienna (May, 1985, p. 8). On returning to the United States, where he planned to study psychology, he was unimpressed with the emphasis on behaviorism in academia and instead entered a seminary college. There he met the philosopher–theologian Paul Tillich (1886–1965). Tillich's wide knowledge of religion, philosophy, and art was a tremendous influence on May's approach. In particular, May applied what he learned from Tillich when he contracted tuberculosis, which necessitated his confinement to a sanatorium for 2 years. He was working toward his doctorate at the time, and as he grappled with his mortality (and his dissertation), he found meaning in his suffering. He went on to author such influential works as *Love and Will* (1969), *Freedom and Destiny* (1981), and *The Cry for Myth* (1991).

Irvin Yalom (1931–; see Figure 4.1) is probably the greatest popularizer of existential psychotherapy in North America. Indeed, his book *Love's Executioner and Other Tales of Psychotherapy* (1989) was even a bestseller in the mainstream market, spawning a host of other similar books by therapists hoping to emulate his success. Yalom was influenced by May and has done much to formalize existential psychotherapeutic theory. In his 1980 book, *Existential Psychotherapy*, Yalom organized the breadth of existential theory into four main themes: (a) death, (b) freedom and responsibility, (c) isolation, and (d) meaninglessness. According to Yalom, these existential realities are at the root of our psychological problems and have no ultimate answers. Although some existential therapists may be more optimistic about the ability of people to find solutions to these concerns, it is generally agreed that they are central to the human experience. Yalom characterized existential psychotherapy as a dynamic approach, focusing on conflicts that arise out of the individual's confrontation with the givens of existence. The client's confrontation with death, freedom, isolation, and meaninglessness offers the therapist explicit interpretive content. By consciously considering their personal values and beliefs, clients are provided the opportunity to live more deliberately, authentically, and purposefully, while accepting the inevitable limitations and contradictions of human existence.

FIGURE 4.1

Irvin Yalom. Printed with permission of Irvin Yalom. Photograph by Reid Yalom.

Existential Rationale

Every human struggles to a greater or lesser extent with four concerns of existence. First, there is our involvement in the physical world, in which we struggle with survival versus death. Second, there is a personal dimension, in which we grapple with the tension between freedom and responsibility. Third, there is our activity in the social world with other people, in which we struggle with our need to belong and the possibility of our isolation. Finally, there is a spiritual dimension, in which we seek to find meaning against the threat of meaninglessness. To have a full and satisfying life, people must live with the tension between these opposites and embrace the paradox that we cannot have life without death, freedom without responsibility, love without hate, nor wisdom without doubt.

To approach life from an existential perspective is to see that conflicts are constantly generated by the tensions of human existence. Paradoxes are inevitable, and life flows out of contradictory forces working against and with each other. Our primary task as humans is to recognize the particular tensions that are most salient in our lives. This exploration can lead to a deeper appreciation of what it means to be human, affording us the opportunity to face life's inevitable challenges and adversities. It is up to each of us to create an essence out of his or her own existence. This does not necessarily lead to a nihilistic view devoid of meaning—although it certainly can—but rather to one in which meaning is built out of meaninglessness, order arises out of chaos. Thus, we have an individual and very personal responsibility to live our own lives with awareness and intention.

Difficulties in living arise out of lying to ourselves. We can lie about our relationship to the physical world and deny our frailty (e.g., avoid taking care of our bodies) or excessively tend to our bodies (e.g., through hypochondria). We can lie to others and pretend to be what we think others want us to be or avoid social fulfillment by denying our desire to connect with others. We can lie to ourselves about our own personal agency—"surviving" from one life crisis to the next rather than choosing to create an authentic identity—or be so focused on controlling all aspects of our lives that we feel trapped. Finally, we can lie about our relationship to the unknown and deny meaninglessness by clinging unquestioningly to blind faith or rejecting all belief and living a life without purpose.

Existential Goals

Why am I here? What will happen when I die? How can I find love? What is my purpose in life? What does life mean? From an existential perspective, these questions are at the root of the problems that trouble humans, and each of us must find our own answers to them to live a full, meaningful, and authentic life. No "cures" are offered.

The goal of existential therapy is to embrace the fundamental nature of human existence. It is through awareness of how the concerns of existence are manifest in our own lives that we might find satisfaction and meaning in our lives, with a full recognition of the paradoxes that are an inevitable aspect of the process of living. The therapeutic search is about claiming personal freedom and being open to the world in all of its complexity—authentic living with courage and humility (Tillich, 1952) and in accordance with one's true values, beliefs, and experiences (Buber, 1947, 1970).

Existential Change Processes

In existential therapy, change is understood as occurring through a series of processes. However, *authenticity*—the honest appreciation of the human condition—is the central component in all of the various aspects of personal change.

The first step in changing through existential therapy is *self-awareness*. As existential therapists understand it, self-awareness is awareness of the concerns of existence as they are manifested in our own lives. Greater awareness allows for greater possibilities for freedom. Awareness involves appreciating that we are finite and time is limited, that we have the choice to act and choose our destiny or not, that meaning is not automatic—we must seek it—and that anxiety is essential to living.

Once we become aware of the reality of our lives, we can take responsibility for our choices. Taking responsibility means appreciating that we are free to choose how we live and that we are not the product of victimization, impulses, patterns of reinforcement, or poor parenting. Failure to accept responsibility is to live *inauthentically*. *Existential guilt* arises out of realizing we are not living authentically and is a necessary experience for motivating us to move toward authenticity.

Why am I alone? What do I want from life? Does my life have any purpose? To find the answers to these questions for ourselves and live authentically, we must discard our inauthentic values. This results in experiencing meaninglessness, which is destabilizing. The therapist assists the client to create *authentically informed meaning* to replace old. Searching for meaning involves a struggle to find significance in life. Finding meaning in life is a byproduct of a commitment to creating, loving, and working—*engagement*. Life is not meaningful in itself; people must create and thereby discover meaning.

Existential Change Tasks

Existential therapists are famous for being highly circumspect regarding the use of techniques, cautioning that manipulation begets manipulation. Instead, the process of therapy primarily involves a dialogue between the client and therapist: a conversation. And yet this is not a conversation like those that we typically have with others in our day-to-day lives, the vast majority of which deal with mundane, trivial concerns like the weather, celebrity gossip, sporting events, and the like. The conversation that occurs in existential therapy deals with the fundamental aspects of being human: life, death, purpose, responsibility, and loneliness. To raise and deal with such profound topics, the existential therapist acknowledges the importance of being relationship focused so that the client can experience sufficient trust in the therapist to risk entering into such a potentially terrifying conversation.

This "nontechnique" technique requires a process of careful attention to and focus on the client's experience and unique stance in the world. Abstract or hypothetical constructs are therefore avoided as much as possible. To understand the client's approach to the world is to grapple with the way he or she makes meaning and the particular circumstances and wider context of the client's life. The existential therapist then elicits, clarifies, and helps to put into perspective the client's current problematic issues and contradictions.

The existential therapist will use change tasks inasmuch as they arise out of a deep understanding of the client's experience. In an effort to help a client who is struggling with issues of responsibility, for example, the therapist may interrupt the client at an opportune moment with the comment, "When you say *can't* do something, aren't you really saying you *won't* do it." (May & Yalom, 2005). The general principle is to prompt a consideration of the degree to which our life situation is our own creation and a recognition of how we avoid decisions. Change tasks are generally used to "hold up a mirror" for the client and thereby create a climate for self-confrontation. Victor Frankl (1905–1997) was known to use paradoxical tasks (prescribing the symptom), for example, by guiding clients to use self-distancing and humorous exaggeration to highlight the absurdity of how many of us live our lives (Frankl, 1946/1963). Other therapists may emphasize the time-limited nature of therapy in order to highlight the fact that life is finite so that issues of mortality can be addressed.

The existential therapist may use change tasks from other systems by using them in a manner consistent with an existential stance. Interpretations à la psychodynamic therapy (see chap. 2, this volume), for example, can be used to facilitate a deepening of an in-session experience or a fuller understanding of a significant life event, rather than to achieve insight into unconscious impulses. Existential therapists will often link the client's presenting complaints with his or her behavior within therapy by, for example, reminding a client who expresses scorn for others, "And you are lonely" (May & Yalom, 2005, p. 286).

Therapeutic Relationship

The therapist adopts a unique and challenging stance in existential therapy. Drawing on Martin Buber's (1878–1965) appreciation of how we tend to treat other human beings as objects—an "I–It" stance (Buber, 1970)—existential therapists attempt to be truly present with clients—an "I–Thou" relationship. This means that the therapist strives to be emotionally present and available to the client, to experience the client as a real person with hopes, fears, and insecurities like everyone else (including the therapist) and not as different or lesser because he or she is in need of help. The existential therapist thus strives to come to each session with an attitude of openness to that unique situation to allow the client's experience to unfold in its own right. The core of the therapeutic relationship is respect, faith in the client's potential, and the sharing of reactions with genuine concern and empathy as a coparticipant in a deeply personal process.

This focus on genuineness, authenticity, and awareness demands that therapists keep their vision as clear as possible by doing their own personal therapeutic work and engaging in continuing self-reflection. Existential therapists often have varied and rather intense life experiences behind them. This is because the approach does not tend to appeal unless one has first come to find out a bit about life the hard way. Existential therapists typically have a deep and intense understanding of their own experiences of crisis and distress, and a training therapy is generally considered a prerequisite to being effective. Indeed, part of the appeal of existential psychotherapy is that it invariably leads to self-discovery for the therapist as well as the client.

Although the existential therapist's relative lack of use of change tasks may appear to represent passivity in session, this is misleading. Being passive is not genuine. Existential therapists are very actively engaged in the therapeutic process as it unfolds and develops. Therapists must be willing to be brutally honest, challenging, sincere, and respectful. This type of relationship demands that the therapist be authentic. The therapist therefore works hard to understand the client's subjective experience as deeply as possible by staying attuned to the client's experiential state and bearing their struggle so that the client is not dissuaded from the daunting task of seeking self-awareness.

Evolution and Variations

Existential thought has informed and influenced most forms of psychotherapy practiced today, although, at the time of this writing, the intensely subjective nature of existential therapy is not congruent with the dominant empirically supported and evidence-based approaches to telling psychotherapists how to practice. Among practitioners, however, existential psychotherapy remains popular, with writers such as Irvin Yalom (1989, 1992, 2002, 2005, 2008) continuing to sell well and draw large crowds at conferences. Yalom is also responsible for providing a major unifying conceptualization (especially through the publication of *Existential Psychotherapy* in 1980) that has served to forestall the proliferation of variant schools as has occurred in many other therapeutic systems.

Logotherapy is the name that Victor Frankl (1905–1997) gave to his approach to existential therapy. Famous for barely surviving the Nazi concentration camps of World War II (in which all of his family members except his sister were killed), Frankl (1955) actually wrote his book *The Doctor and the Soul: From Psychotherapy to Logotherapy* while imprisoned. Shortly after his liberation, Frankl (1946/1963) wrote *Man's Search for Meaning: An Introduction to Logotherapy*, in which he detailed his death camp experiences in a profoundly moving way. He described how he found the will to live even in those most terrible of circumstances by finding meaning in helping others as best he could. Frankl's best-known contribution to therapy is the change task of *paradoxical intention*, whereby the client is invited to wish for the very thing he or she is trying to avoid. A young man who was mortally afraid of sweating in social situations, for example, was instructed to wish, "I only sweated out a quart before, but now I'm going to pour at least ten quarts!" (Frankl, 1955, p. 127). When subsequently faced with the opportunity to do so, he found he did not sweat at all. Another change task used by logotherapists is *dereflection*. Instead of reflecting inordinately on oneself, the client is encouraged to focus on others, such as trying to satisfy their sexual partner when they are having trouble experiencing an orgasm. Both of these tasks, like all tasks in logotherapy, are used within a Socratic dialogue intended to help clients abandon ineffective ways of making meaning and find new, more satisfying ones.

Existential humanistic therapy is the product of James Bugental (1915–2008), another popular existential therapist who wrote in an engaging personal style (Bugental, 1978, 1987, 1990). Bugental's approach retains the existential focus on choice, meaning, and the givens of existence, while incorporating humanistic goals of individual growth. A therapist working from an existential–humanistic approach draws change tasks from a number of theoretical approaches. From a psychodynamic approach (see chap. 2, this volume), interpretation is used as a means of promoting clients' insight into their potential. From a person-centered approach (see chap. 5, this volume), the therapist works to establish an accepting, supportive, responsive relationship. From a gestalt approach (see chap. 6, this volume), the client and therapist strive to have an authentic, challenging experience. In this way he presents a more optimistic, life-affirming rationale than what we might think of as "pure" existential therapy. What makes his approach fundamentally existential is that all of these change tasks are used to help each client face the implicit and often unrecognized contradictions in how he or she is living his or her life. The client's experience in therapy is still one of struggle and disappointment, from which new vigor can be found to take responsibility for his or her choices.

Existentialism and spirituality is an approach to existential therapy that has its roots in Kierkegaard's Christian-based writings and is concerned with spirituality as a means for making meaning in life. Emmy van Deurzen-Smith (1951–), in particular, explicitly added a spiritual dimension to existentialism in recognition that there is more to the human condition than the merely human (Deurzen-Smith, 1997). Thus, a consideration of the spiritual world is added to the personal world, the world of others, and the natural world. The existential therapist argues that resorting to believing in an omnipotent being that rescues us is yet another way to escape personal responsibility (Yalom, 1980). Instead, an existential appreciation of spiritual acceptance holds that because there is so much that we cannot understand, we ought to strive for humility in our lives. Our chaotic and ferocious human nature is acknowledged, and we seek forgiveness, healing, and strength in the recognition of our ultimate powerlessness. Rather than abdicating our personal responsibility, therapy is an opportunity to honor our capacity to make choices and to feel guilt and to surrender to that which we cannot control (Vaughan, 1985).

No Man's Meat

Shit, none of my friends would ever believe that I was talking to a shrink—okay, a social worker (whatever!). All I knew was if I had to see a shrink at this "school for pregnant and parenting teens" then that's what I'd do. Actually, Colleen wasn't so bad. Obviously, she didn't party much—I know I shocked her a few times. But she never looked down at me or made me feel bad just 'cause I worked the streets sometimes. "Promiscuous," my teachers said when they thought I couldn't hear. Screw them!

You'd be promiscuous too if your stepfather raped you at night and your mom didn't give a shit and you had to get the hell out of there as soon as you could. Then my boyfriend got me pregnant. Colleen says that that didn't make me who I am—that I can be who I want to. That almost made me cry. Something about who I am comes from how I live my life. I guess I kinda see what she meant, though.

So Colleen just kinda let me do most of the talking. But she really listened to me. And asked questions about what I wanted to do with my life and my daughter's—stuff like that. Not like I never got asked those questions before. But she really wanted to know what I thought—not tellin' me what I should think. She was really there, you know? Like a real person. I lived through more shit than most people, that's for sure. I could tell her life hadn't been a bed of roses either, even though she never actually said. Like she thought I was a good person inside, no matter what happens in your life—I can't explain it exactly.

The hardest thing was to decide that I would give my daughter up for adoption. Even though I love her so much, I know that being a mom is really hard 'cause of not having a dad around to share the load, and I've got to get my shit together. I want her to have a better life than I could give her. So talking to Colleen helped me sort out all that shit. Like how I have to trust my feelings and make choices that I can feel proud about. I sure learned the hard way that if I let someone else do it, it's still me that has to live with it. Maybe I don't always make the best choices—who does?—but they're my choices. And I feel stronger in myself.

I've just about finished my Grade 12 and applied for paramedic school. My marks are good enough to get me in. I may never be a doctor or like that—what I'd really like is to be a pediatrician—but I *am* making a better life for me, and my daughter. I sure miss her. . . .

Learning Task

Just to prove that I was not kidding when I said that existential therapists have an intense approach to life, complete the task provided in Exhibit 4.1. While you could obviously complete this task in a rather superficial way, you are encouraged to really think about what your life means and how your actions represent who you truly are as a person. If your psychotherapeutic training is part of an unbroken chain of years in schooling, you may find yourself noticing how difficult it is to reconcile the competing demands of the delayed gratification required of your training and your desire to do something meaningful with your life right away. Or you may have made major changes in your life in order to pursue your dream to become a psychotherapist such that you feel rather content with your life choices. In either case, use this task as an opportunity to think about how your day-to-day activities may or may not be congruent with who you want to be and what you want your life to stand for.

Your Reflective Journal

The existential approach to psychotherapy can represent something of a paradox. On the one hand, it is very philosophical and thus can seem somewhat abstract. On the other hand, it can be the most personally challenging of all of the theories you will encounter. Indeed, many find that completing the Learning Task can be rather unsettling. Take some time to consider and record how the Learning Task affected you. Did you find it difficult, irrelevant, or meaningful? What does your reaction tell you about your affinity for existentialism? How do you think the way

---

EXHIBIT 4.1

Your Obituary

Take as much time as you need to write two obituaries:

1. One that would be written about you now.
2. One that you hope would be written about you in the future when you are older and grayer.

After you have written them, read them over, take time to reflect, and consider the following:

1. How are the two different? Do the differences speak to your level of existential self-awareness and to the meaning that you make in your life?
2. To what extent do they reflect your personal world, the world of others, the natural world, and the spiritual world? What does the presence, absence, or prominence of one or more of these worlds tell you about how you are living your life?
3. How would you live differently today if you knew that you would not live long enough for the second one to be written? What does this tell you about how authentically you are living your life and how engaged you are in life?
4. How might you imagine using this technique in therapy? Do you have reservations about doing so? If so, what are they, and to what extent do they arise out of your own existential issues?

---

you live your own life has influenced your reaction to the Learning Task? What are your thoughts about how your clients might react to such an approach? What sort of person or circumstance do you suppose existentialism is most appropriate for? How could you confirm or disconfirm your supposition?

Summary

Existential psychotherapy applies the understandings of existential philosophy to helping people make sense of their lives and become fully alive. Existentialism provides a basis from which to address the truths of the human condition: isolation, concerns about freedom and responsibility, anxieties about death, and fear of meaninglessness. From this perspective, existence determines essence, not the other way around as in most therapeutic systems—what we do with our life gives it meaning or not. Thus, the therapist seeks to understand the experience of the client rather than attempt to identify essential parts. This understanding requires that the therapist be truly present as an authentic person, prepared to be genuine and respectful. Interventions therefore do not play an important part in this process. The existential therapist will use change tasks only as they arise out of a deep understanding of the clients' experience and to facilitate insight into their unique way of dealing with their ultimate concerns. From such an encounter we can emerge more aware, alive, connected, and with a renewed sense of purpose and meaning.

Further Resources

CASE READINGS

Bugental, J. F. T. (1990). *Intimate journeys: Stories from life-changing therapy.* San Francisco: Jossey-Bass.

Du Plock, S. (1997). *Case studies in existential psychotherapy and counselling.* New York: Wiley.

Schnieder, K. J., & May, R. (1995). *The psychology of existence: An integrative, clinical perspective.* New York: McGraw-Hill.

Yalom, I. D. (1989). *Love's executioner and other tales of psychotherapy.* New York: Basic Books.

RECOMMENDED READING

Cooper, M. (2003). *Existential therapies.* London: Sage.

Frankl, V. E. (1963). *Man's search for meaning: An introduction to logotherapy.* Boston: Beacon Press. (Original work published 1946)

May, R. (1969). *Existential psychology.* New York: Random House.

van Deurzen-Smith, E. (2002). *Existential counselling & psychotherapy in practice.* Thousand Oaks, CA: Sage.

Yalom, I. D. (1980). *Existential psychotherapy.* New York: Basic Books.

RECOMMENDED VIEWING

American Psychological Association (Producer). (2006). *Existential therapy with Kirk J. Schneider, PhD* [Motion picture]. (Available from the American Psychological Association, 750 First Street, NE, Washington, DC 20002-4242)

American Psychological Association (Producer). (2009). *Existential–humanistic therapy over time with Kirk J. Schneider, PhD* [Motion picture]. (Available from the American Psychological Association, 750 First Street, NE, Washington, DC 20002-4242)

Governors State University (Producer). (1997). *Existential–humanistic psychotherapy with James Bugental, PhD* [Motion picture]. (Available from Psychotherapy.net, 4625 California Street, San Francisco, CA 94118-1224)

Psychological & Educational Films (Producer). (1975). *Rollo May on existential psychotherapy* [Motion picture]. (Available from Psychotherapy.net, 4625 California Street, San Francisco, CA 94118-1224)

Yalom, V. (Producer). (2005). *Irvin Yalom: Live case consultation* [Motion picture]. (Available from Psychotherapy.net, 4625 California Street, San Francisco, CA 94118-1224)

Person-Centered   5

C arl R. Rogers (1902–1987; see Figure 5.1) has remained the most influential psychotherapist, even over Sigmund Freud, for over 25 years
(Smith, 1982; "The Top 10," 2007). Although the person-centered approach to psychotherapy may not currently be the most favored one
(Norcross, Prochaska, & Farber, 1993), many therapists assert that they
incorporate Rogerian principles into their practice, and Rogers's emphasis on the centrality of the therapeutic relationship has profoundly influenced all psychotherapies practiced today (Kirschenbaum & Jourdan,
2005).

Rogers filled his lectures and books with descriptions of his childhood, training, struggles, and therapeutic practice. He told of how he
reacted against the fundamentalist religious expectations of his parents,
of lonely teenage years surrounded by books instead of friends, and the
influence of a youth spent on his parents' farm, where he learned to
apply scientific methods to promote growth.[1] His original career aspira-
tion was to enter the clergy, and as part of his theological training he
served as the pastor in a small church. There he was exposed to "the
range of psychological and personal problems which exist in the ordi-
nary community" (Kirschenbaum, 2007, p. 46). After 2 years in the seminary he became dissatisfied with religion as a means for helping people

---

[1]In one of those wonderful synchronicities that so delight biographers, at age 13 Rogers col-
lected and raised moths through their life cycle from egg through cocoon to moth (Rogers,
1967).

FIGURE 5.1

Carl R. Rogers. Printed with permission of the University of California, Santa Barbara.

and turned instead to psychology. He subsequently obtained his doctorate in clinical and educational psychology in 1931. He later wrote of his discomfort in a graduate program that stressed an objective attitude toward patients and of his excitement when he first expressed his genuine feelings to a client (Rogers, 1967).

After graduation Rogers worked for 12 years as the director of a child guidance clinic, a position in which he developed the basic principles of what would eventually become person-centered therapy. During his time at the clinic, he credited attending a 3-day workshop presented by Otto Rank (1884–1939)—a neo-Freudian who argued for the importance of self-acceptance, self-reliance, and the client directing therapy (Raskin, 1948)—as a particularly important influence on his psychotherapeutic thinking (Rogers & Haigh, 1983).

Rogers reluctantly left clinical practice to accept what would become a series of academic and research positions (Kirschenbaum, 2007). Rogers (1942) very quickly established himself as both a visionary and rebel with the presentation of an article that became the classic book *Counseling and Psychotherapy: Newer Concepts in Practice*. In it he proposed a method frankly different from the prevailing psychoanalytic one: *nondirective therapy*. In the nondirective approach the client, not the therapist, was considered to be the expert on how therapy should proceed. Advice, persuasion, diagnosis, and so forth were not prized as helpful. Rogers later renamed his nondirective therapy *client-centered therapy* and finally *person-centered therapy* (Rogers, 1979) to reflect the application of his system to realms of human functioning outside of the therapeutic encounter.

Among Rogers's more notable writings was his foundational book, *Client-Centered Therapy: Its Current Practice, Implications, and Theory* (1951) and his classic and still controversial article, "The Necessary and Sufficient Conditions of Therapeutic Personality Change" (1957a). In these writings he established his epistemological position on therapeutic goals, change processes, and change tasks. He would eventually go on to write about the application of his person-centered system to a remarkable variety of situations: teaching, educational administration, encounter groups (small groups where person-centered change processes are facilitated), and marriage, among others. Late in his life he even applied his method to politics and the training of policymakers, leaders, and groups in conflict. He proposed that better political decisions are made when one has empathy for how others experience events. Well into his 80s he led huge workshops in countries such as Hungary, Brazil, South Africa, and the former Soviet Union. For his efforts he was even nominated for the 1987 Nobel Peace Prize (Kirschenbaum, 2007).

It is interesting to note that although he valued the subjective experience of the client in his therapy, Rogers insisted on testing his new approach by means of objective research. When he began his investigations in the 1950s, there were few usable methodologies that could be applied to what he was trying to do, and there were no exemplars of research in psychotherapy. In fact, such research was considered improper, if not outright impossible. Therapists had never let anyone listen in on the therapy session let alone try to measure and compare what they did. Rogers was undaunted, and proceeded to painstakingly record counseling sessions directly onto 3-minute disks, later using audiotape and then videotape. His group was the first—by some 20 years—to analyze transcripts and to measure outcomes by using psychometric tests and rating scales before and after therapy and to use control groups (Rogers, 1954).

One important finding that Rogers and others (e.g., Truax & Carkhuff, 1967) established was that being an effective therapist was associated with personal qualities unrelated to academic education. That finding led—and Rogers followed where it led—to the conclusion that professional designations and academic degrees are not prerequisites to being therapeutic. Why then not train church workers, nurses, mothers, teachers—anyone—to be a therapist? There was no inherent reason not to, so he did.

It is ironic that Rogers relied on research methodologies from the empirical tradition (see chap. 1, this volume) rather than qualitative methods consistent with his own humanistic epistemology. He never did fully explain this paradox, and some authors (e.g., O'Hara, 1995) have speculated that the disappointing empirical results of applying person-centered therapy to the treatment of hospitalized persons diagnosed with schizophrenia (Rogers, Gendlin, Kiesler, & Truax, 1967) may have prompted him to move more fully into a subjective epistemology. In an interview later in his life, Rogers suggested that he used the "language of empiricism" in an effort to persuade his objectively inclined colleagues of the validity of his approach (Barrett-Lennard, 1998). Perhaps, being as pragmatic and intellectually courageous as he was, he can best be understood as having used the empirical method because it is best suited to the task of finding out what works, and he followed his data to the conclusion that what works is attending to the client's subjective experience (e.g., Rogers, 1955). Whatever his motivations or epistemological inconsistencies, Rogers's therapeutic and research writings stimulated thousands of other research studies on the process and outcomes of psychotherapy and remain a seminal influence on the field of psychotherapy research (Kirschenbaum & Jourdan, 2005).

Without actually identifying it as such—and apparently without his awareness of being so—Rogers was primarily phenomenological in his approach to understanding. This can be seen in his liberal use of personal disclosure and the subjective titles he gave his articles: "A Therapist's View of the Good Life" (1957b) and "Some Social Issues That Concern Me" (1972), for example. For Rogers, his stories and personal references were more than simply appealing—they were the highest authority. Rogers disdained the objectivity of prediction and control (i.e., empiricism). Rather, he treasured subjective experience as the key, if properly nurtured, to promoting health. "Neither the Bible nor the prophets—neither Freud nor research—neither the revelations of God nor man—can take precedence over my own direct experience" (Rogers, 1961, pp. 23–24).

Person-Centered Rationale

Human beings have a powerful, innate capacity for growth that is constantly striving for expression. Everyone is capable of being fully human. Just like a plant will grow to its full potential if provided with the appropriate combination of sunlight, water, soil, and nutrients, our human potential will manifest itself under the right interpersonal circumstances. What prevents us from becoming the person we are capable of being are the expectations of significant people in our lives to be the kind of person that is incongruent with who we truly are. In our efforts to feel good about ourselves we tend to try to incorporate others' expectations—thereby denying our true selves and adopting instead a conditional self—resulting in feelings of disorganization and emotional pain.

If, on the other hand, we experience genuineness, nonjudgmental caring, and empathy in our relationships with others, then we can achieve our potential as persons. These conditions operate whether the relationship is between therapist and client, parent and child, leader and group, teacher and student, or administrator and staff—in fact, in any human situation. When we experience relationships where these qualities are present, we grow toward being fully functioning persons—open to experience and our feelings, able to live a meaningful and creative life. As Rogers (1980) summarized,

> As persons are accepted and prized, they tend to develop a more caring attitude toward themselves. As persons are empathetically heard, it becomes possible for them to listen more accurately to the flow of inner experiencings. But as a person understands and prizes self, the self becomes more congruent with the experiencings. The person thus becomes more real, more genuine. These tendencies, the reciprocal of the therapist's attitudes, enable the person to be a more effective growth-enhancer for himself or herself. There is a greater freedom to be the true, whole person. (pp.115–117)

Person-Centered Goals

According to the person-centered, humanistic worldview, we all have the capacity to become a *fully functioning person*, and achieving such a state should be our goal in therapy (Rogers, 1961, 1963). Being fully functioning is not an end state, however. It is, rather, a process state in which we are open to new growth experiences and feelings (rather than afraid of them), trust our own feelings and thoughts as guides to our choices and actions (rather than relying on the opinions of others), and have positive self-regard: "To be that self which one truly is" (Rogers, 1961, p. 163). When we are fully functioning we are then able to make healthy decisions and set goals for ourselves that are congruent with our personal possibilities.

The therapist, therefore, does not set goals for the client of solving or managing problems. Rather, clients who are able to become more fully functioning will decide for themselves how best to cope with problems and participate in a satisfying life.

Person-Centered Change Processes

In person-centered therapy, change occurs by shedding the self one is not and becoming one's true self. This change process begins with *self-*

disclosure; that is, clients disclose, or reveal, themselves, including their negative thoughts, feelings, problems, failures, inadequacies, and so forth. Freed from the need to please the therapist, clients can work with the disclosed material and explore strange, unknown, and dangerous aspects of their self-experience. Feeling heard and understood changes the client's experience to one that is more self-accepting (Gendlin, 1970). Efforts to gain acceptance from others that lock us into ingenuine roles can be relaxed, and we can consider our true thoughts, feelings, and beliefs. Phoniness and self-concealment can be gradually relinquished, and the false self can be gradually discarded. This genuine self-exploration leads to *self-discovery*—an awareness of what one is really like. Clients become aware of failures to actualize themselves and their potential. They are then able to accept themselves as they are and to commit themselves to becoming more like they can and want to be (Rogers, 1961). As more aspects of self are experienced fully and incorporated into their sense of self, clients gain a stronger, more complete, and more authentic *self-understanding*. Self-understanding results in an increase in self-regard that is independent of pressures to conform to the expectations and standards of others. Where previously clients experienced a state of incongruence between their sense of who they really were and what others valued (or devalued) about them, they can now feel congruence between their experienced self and ideal self.

Person-Centered Change Tasks

Person-centered therapy can be characterized as an *anti-intervention*. Like existential psychotherapy, person-centered therapy proceeds primarily through dialogue. Unlike existential therapy, however, the client is assumed to be motivated to tell the therapist what troubling problem in living has prompted him or her to seek assistance. The client, therefore, is given the opportunity—and responsibility—for directing the content of the therapeutic dialogue.

The therapist accepts the responsibility for striving to communicate in a way that establishes an optimal therapeutic relationship (see the Therapeutic Relationship section later in this chapter). An optimal therapeutic relationship particularly involves avoiding giving advice or providing interpretations of what the client "really" thinks. Instead, the therapist tries to communicate what the client has actually said—or has tried to say—at a deep, personal level. Paraphrasing of verbal and nonverbal messages, reflection of feelings directly and indirectly experienced, open-ended questioning, and self-disclosure—in the service of the client feeling understood—are used as genuine efforts to convey an empathic understanding of the client's experiencing. Although this may sound simple, it is not easy. To truly understand another person involves more than comprehending the literal meaning of what the client has said. It is a deep sharing of the client's subjective world.

Thus, therapists must be willing and able to listen without prejudice, judgment, or agenda if the client is to have any chance of feeling truly understood and accepted. Positive feelings, negative feelings, and silence must be acceptable to the therapist. The therapist strives to communicate to the client at every level, "I accept you as you are." Techniques or interventions cannot induce a state of feeling genuinely appreciated. Only the here-and-now participation of the therapist striving to understand the client's moment-by-moment experience will suffice. This is why person-centered therapy is often described as a *relationship-focused* approach.

Therapeutic Relationship

The therapist has a unique role in person-centered therapy. To be able to reflect the client's subjective experience, the person of the therapist is central. Because person-centered therapy is, at its heart, a highly collaborative approach, three qualities of the therapist must be evident in relationship with the client.

The first such quality is *genuineness*, realness, or congruence. Genuineness can be understood as a form of self-empathy (Barrett-Lennard, 1997)—paying close attention to one's experience, being aware of all that is going on inside one's self, and accepting it. It means being open to one's own experience. Genuineness requires a significant depth of self-knowledge. It is only a fully functioning person who can be totally genuine. The more the therapist is himself or herself in the relationship—putting up no professional front or personal facade—the greater the opportunity for the client to change and grow in a constructive manner. This means that the therapist is openly experiencing the feelings and attitudes that are present in the moment. The term *transparent* catches the quality of this condition: The therapist strives to be transparent to the client. In this way the client can experience who the therapist is in the relationship; the client experiences no holding back on the part of the therapist. What the therapist is experiencing is available to awareness, can be lived in the relationship, and can be communicated. Thus, there is a close matching—or congruence—between what is being experienced at the feeling level, what is present in awareness, and what is expressed to the client. The focus on genuineness, authenticity, and awareness requires the therapist to be emotionally present and available. The therapist must avoid hypocrisy at all cost—one's external presentation must match one's internal experience. The therapist must be able to openly express feelings and attitudes that are present in the relationship with the client. In many respects the therapist serves as a model of a human being struggling toward authenticity, which is not an easy task.

The second quality is an *unconditional positive regard*. It means that the client feels understood in a nonjudgmental way. In such an atmosphere the client can develop trust in the therapist and feel able to accept his or her own experience and feelings. When the therapist is experiencing a positive, accepting attitude toward whatever the client is at that moment, therapeutic movement or change is made possible. The therapist is accepting of whatever immediate feeling the client is experiencing—for example, confusion, resentment, fear, anger, courage, love, pride. Such caring on the part of the therapist prizes the client in a total rather than a conditional way.

Unconditional positive regard is sometimes misunderstood as behaving in an overtly and unreservedly positive manner toward the client—as expressing nothing but praise in response to whatever the client says or does. Such behavior on the part of the therapist, however, is a form of *conditional positive regard*, which says to the client, "I value what you have done, and if you want me to continue to value you, you must continue such behavior." Thus, conditional positive regard places clients in a position of having to question their own values, rather than fully experiencing their own self-worth. It may well be that something the clients had done that was praised by the therapist was not congruent with their true self, placing them in a growth-inhibiting circumstance.

The third quality of the therapist is *empathic understanding*. Many people believe that empathic understanding is the single quality that is most important in all forms of therapeutic listening. It means fully comprehending the subjective world of the client so that the client feels understood. This means that the therapist senses accurately the feelings and personal meanings that the client is experiencing and communicates this understanding to the client. The following two things are important about this: (a) that the empathy be accurate and (b) that the empathy be made known to the client. Both are learnable skills, and they do make a huge difference to the relationship between client and therapist. When functioning best, therapists are in tune with the private world of the other that they can clarify not only the meanings of which the clients are aware but even those meanings just beyond a client's awareness. This kind of sensitive, active listening is exceedingly rare in our lives. We think we listen, but very rarely do we listen with real understanding—with true empathy.

Evolution and Variations

Today, person-centered therapy is such an important influence on psychotherapeutic practice with respect to the importance of the therapeutic relationship that it has become integrated into most approaches (Kirschenbaum & Jourdan, 2005). This is particularly the case with training programs for counseling and psychotherapy (Egan, 2006; C. E. Hill, 2009; Ivey & Ivey, 2007). Although somewhat in decline in popularity in North America as a primary theoretical affiliation, active programs of research and practice are thriving in Europe and elsewhere around the world (Kirschenbaum & Jourdan, 2005).

Human technology is an integrative approach developed by Robert Carkhuff, on the basis of person-centered therapy that also incorporates psychodynamic and behavioral change tasks (Carkhuff, 1981; Carkhuff & Berenson, 1967). Carkhuff studied and worked with Carl Rogers and went on to articulate the core relationship conditions in more observable and measurable ways, so they might be applied to the training of therapists. What he found was that therapists who are in training do not necessarily become more effective. Although many do become effective, others do not—just as most clients improve with therapy whereas some do not. Carkhuff (1964) found that this is because clients tend to converge toward the level of functioning of their therapists, and trainees tend to converge toward the level of effectiveness of their instructors. To counter this tendency, Carkhuff trained therapists in the person-centered change tasks of *attending*, *observing*, *listening*, and *empathic responding*. Finding that these were necessary but not sufficient (cf. Rogers, 1957a), he introduced a modified form of *interpretation* from psychodynamic therapy in which therapists make an additive statement about their clients' desires for personal growth in the general form of, "You are here, and you want to be there." To this Carkhuff (1983) added having therapists work with clients to develop a behavioral (i.e., observable and measurable) *growth program* to help lead them toward their goals.

Nondirective play therapy was developed by Virginia Axline (1911–1988), a graduate student of Rogers, as an adaptation of the person-centered approach to helping children. Her well-known book *Dibs: In Search of Self* (1964) describes her work with a young boy named Dibs and is an inspirational introduction to the subject. In fact, much of current play therapy practice is based on Axline's work. Axline proposed that the therapist develop a warm and friendly relationship with the child, maintain a deep respect for the child's ability to solve problems, and not attempt to direct the child's actions or conversations in any way except as necessary to anchor the therapy in reality. Clark Moustakis (1997) described the process as one in which the child has an opportunity to enter into a significant personal relationship with an adult in which the child is free to express and play out usually forbidden impulses. Therapy ideally takes place in a room where one does not have to worry about damage to the floor and furnishings. Equipment may consist of paints and paper for creativity, dolls and puppets for fantasy play, clay for making and squashing things, a pan of water and a sand tray for being messy, and toys for release of aggressiveness—pounding boards, punching devices, and things for throwing or shooting without hurting. The therapist's role is to encourage free expression, to be available to relate as the child reaches out, and to enforce (only when necessary) the ground rules of "not hurting ourselves or others, or destroying property." These conditions allow the child's innate potential for growth to be unencumbered.

Virginia Satir (1916–1988), having worked with Gregory Bateson studying disorganized families (see chap. 8, this volume), instead applied person-centered—rather than systemic—principles to treating families (Satir, 1972). From the humanistic worldview Satir began with the idea that individuals are oriented toward growth, and from the collectivist worldview she incorporated the idea that each person's growth is constrained or nurtured by their family system. Like most systemic approaches, therapy takes place in the here and now of the session as current interpersonal patterns are manifested. Families that function to maintain the status quo are understood as *blocking* individual growth, whereas those that allow individual expression are understood as *facilitating* growth. It is the therapist's job to establish a genuine, valuing relationship with each family member so that they might feel safe to honestly self-disclose and relate to one another in an authentic manner. Sometimes a family chronology for each member is compiled so that the development of ingrained yet inauthentic qualities is highlighted. This allows the individual to see how family ideology, values, and expectations have influenced how they see themselves and to highlight how dysfunctional interpersonal patterns are maintained. By breaking out of fixed roles and relationships, the family can change their characteristic manner of relating to one another, and each person is freed to re-create him- or herself in healthy ways.

Focusing-oriented therapy was developed by Eugene Gendlin (1926–) —another student of Rogers—out of the observation that clients did better in therapy when they were able to articulate their subjective experience (Gendlin, 1996). So he set out to develop an approach to help clients do just that. Clients are asked to "clear a space" by imagining that they have set all their problems aside for the moment and then to pay attention to their inner experience. Then one problem is considered while the client is encouraged to pay attention to his or her *felt sense*. Our felt sense is holistic in nature and contains more than we can easily think or know about our situation—we can sense that something is there, but it is difficult to put words to it. It is more like what we typically call our *intuition*. By paying attention to this sense a process is stimulated that leads to a "felt shift" in the client's appreciation of the problem, from which new possibilities for its resolution can arise (Gendlin, 1981, 1996). Therapists use experiential empathic responding and sharing of their own immediate experience in session to further facilitate the client's ability to focus. Focusing is often used in gestalt therapy (see chap. 6, this volume).

The Committed Self

Diego sought counseling because he was having difficulty in making a commitment to his girlfriend. Diego and his girlfriend had been in a relationship for 3 years, and she was becoming increasingly frustrated with his reluctance to get married. He would become upset and angry when she asked about whether they had a future together.

He had heard of his therapist through a friend, who described the therapist as "friendly and understanding," which appealed to Diego because he felt so ashamed for having what he felt was such a stereotypically "macho" problem. In fact, he had resisted any sort of psychological help because of his shame. He was a bit surprised that she seemingly had no interest in assessing what was wrong with him. He also found it unsettling at first that she would not answer his direct requests for advice. Instead, she listened attentively to what he had to say and responded with subtle, emotionally astute comments.

He told her about how he loved his girlfriend and how the idea of settling down and having a family was appealing to him. He said, however, that he was worried that she was not going to "hang in there much longer" because he was so ambivalent about marriage. As he spoke, he came to realize that he saw himself as "a bad risk" as a husband because, even if they did marry, he would leave her eventually—if she did not leave him first. As he spoke these words, he became profoundly sad and began to cry. Embarrassed, he tried to stop himself, until his therapist responded sincerely to his emotional pain. He said that she was "like the parent I never had" and told her about his childhood in which he was expected to "be the man of the family" after his father abandoned them. He said he did not trust himself to "stay married when things got tough."

In response, his therapist said, "You want to be a good husband and father, but you're afraid you'll do what your father did when you were growing up. Have I got that right?"

"Yeah. He wasn't there for us, and I'm just like him," Diego replied passionately. "I hate him, and I hate myself!"

"You feel an intense hatred for yourself—that you are a bad person. I certainly experience you as a kind person," his therapist said. "It's almost like you want to protect your girlfriend from being hurt the way you and your mother were hurt by your father."

"I never had a chance to be a kid and grow up and learn how to be a good father," he said softly, while wiping away tears of sadness and anger. "I don't want to hurt my girlfriend. I love her."

After the session Diego had a long, heartfelt talk with his girlfriend. He told her about his childhood, his fears, and his hopes for their future together. He did not become angry, and he was surprised and pleased when she responded positively and lovingly. They became engaged a few months later.

Learning Task

To some, the person-centered concept of the therapeutic relationship seems too facile and thus could not possibly be the essential active ingredient in psychotherapy. To find out for yourself just how challenging it really is, try the task provided in Exhibit 5.1. After you have done so, record your experience. You will likely have noticed how difficult it was to do and to sustain for a whole day. You may also have noticed a variety of responses from others, especially those with whom you already have a relationship. What does this tell you about how trivial or potent an authentic relationship can be? Can you imagine yourself being this way all day every day as a therapist? What have you learned from this task about your ability to practice from a person-centered stance?

Your Reflective Journal

Take a few moments to think about a time in your life when an important relationship with someone (e.g., teacher, coach, counselor, neighbor) made a positive difference for you. Rather than focusing on what this person did, think about the kind of relationship that developed between the two of you.

1. Record what you remember about the nature of your relationship.
2. After you have done so, record your thoughts about the degree to which your experience is consistent with Rogers's rationale. Did you feel like you became more like yourself—that is, more authentic?
3. To what extent has your experience influenced your affinity for person-centered therapy?
4. Many people have difficulty accepting that clients will grow toward health under the permissive circumstances advocated by Rogers. What are your thoughts on this?

EXHIBIT 5.1

An Authentic Day

Try spending a day being fully available to everyone you meet. In every encounter, whether in line at the grocery store, over the dinner table, on the telephone, or wherever you are

1. Be truly engaged. Set aside distractions and pay attention to the other person.
2. Ask at least one question without being intrusive or judgmental that offers the other person an opportunity to go deeper into their own experience.
3. Avoid platitudes that deflect or belittle others' experiences. When you ask someone, "How are you?", for example, ask in a manner that tells them you are sincere.
4. If someone does or says something that upsets you, try being curious rather than furious. Attend to them and to your own experience with openness, acceptance, and compassion.

Summary

Person-centered therapy was developed by Carl R. Rogers, who observed and demonstrated that people have the personal resources to achieve health and their full human potential if they experience a growth-promoting relationship. This relationship is characterized by genuineness, unconditional positive regard, and empathy. Experiencing such a relationship will tend to promote self-acceptance, immediacy of experiencing, directness in relating, and an internal locus of evaluation. Person-centered therapists do not assess or diagnose pathology, instead directing their energies to creating a therapeutic relationship. Rogers was pioneering in his daring to actually record, transcribe, and publish complete cases of psychotherapy. He was also a leader in studying what was actually going on in therapy, whether therapy was helpful, and in proposing testable hypotheses about how therapy might work. By doing so, he heralded the entire field of psychotherapy research, which has, ironically, for the most part turned its back on humanistic therapies. Despite this, person-centered therapy continues to inform current psychotherapeutic practice in fundamental ways—most particularly by virtue of attending to the importance of the therapeutic relationship in bringing about positive outcomes.

Further Resources

CASE READINGS

Farber, B. A., Brink, D. C., & Raskin, P. M. (Eds.). (1996). *The psychotherapy of Carl Rogers: Cases and commentary*. New York: Guilford Press.

Rogers, C. R. (1942). The case of Herbert Bryan. In C. R. Rogers (Ed.), *Counseling and psychotherapy* (pp. 261–437). Boston: Houghton Mifflin.

Rogers, C. R. (1954). The case of Mrs. Oak. In C. R. Rogers & R. F. Dymond (Eds.), *Psychotherapy and personality change*. Chicago: University of Chicago Press.

Rogers, C. R. (1967). A silent young man. In C. R. Rogers, G. T. Gendlin, D. V. Kiesler, & C. Truax (Eds.), *The therapeutic relationship and its impact: A study of psychotherapy with schizophrenics* (pp. 401–406). Madison: University of Wisconsin Press.

RECOMMENDED READING

Barrett-Lennard, G. T. (1998). *Carl Rogers' helping system: Journey and substance*. London: Sage.

Bohart, A., & Tallman, K. (1999). *How clients make therapy work: The process of active self-healing*. Washington, DC: American Psychological Association.

Rogers, C. R. (1961). *On becoming a person: A therapist's view of psychotherapy*. Boston: Houghton Mifflin.

Rogers, C. R. (1980). *A way of being*. Boston: Houghton Mifflin.

RECOMMENDED VIEWING

American Association for Marriage and Family Therapy (Producer). (1984) *The lost boy with Virginia Satir* [Motion picture]. (Available from the American Association for Marriage and Family Therapy, 112 South Alfred Street, Alexandria, VA 22314-3061)

Center for Play Therapy (Producer). (1997). *Child-centered play therapy: A clinical session with Dr. Gary Landreth* [Motion Picture]. (Available from University of North Texas Center for Play Therapy, P.O. Box 310829, Denton, TX 76203-0829)

Center for Studies of the Person (Producer). (1981). *Carl Rogers interviews Phillip* [Motion picture]. (Available from Insight Media, Inc., 2162 Broadway, New York, NY 10024-0621)

Psychological & Educational Films (Producer). (1965). *Three approaches to Psychotherapy I: Part 1. Carl Rogers (client-centered therapy)* [Motion picture]. (Available from Psychological & Educational Films, 3334 East Coast Highway, #252, Corona del Mar, CA 92625-2328)

Psychological & Educational Films (Producer). (1978). *Three approaches to Psychotherapy II: Part 1. Carl Rogers (client-centered therapy)* [Motion picture]. (Available from Psychological & Educational Films, 3334 East Coast Highway, #252, Corona del Mar, CA 92625-2328)

<h1>Gestalt 6</h1>

Frederick Perls (1893–1970; see Figure 6.1)—known to all as "Fritz"—was the charismatic and controversial founder of gestalt therapy. Gestalt therapy—like person-centered therapy (see chap. 5)—flourished during the North American human potential movement of the 1960s and will probably always be associated with that historical period and the flamboyant Fritz. It endures as a therapeutic system, however, because of its unique incorporation of the "whole person" into therapy.

Fritz was born and raised in Berlin. After serving as a medical corpsman in World War I, he earned his doctor of medicine degree, specializing in psychiatry. He then moved to Vienna to undertake training in psychoanalysis, and he studied there with Karen Horney and Wilhelm Reich. Reich (1897–1957) was a student of Freud who was influential in introducing such central ideas to what would become gestalt therapy as *organismic self-regulation* and *character armor*, although he went on to have a controversial career.[1] Fritz later worked with Kurt Goldstein, a principal figure of the holistic school of psychology who is best known for coining the term *self-actualization* (Goldstein, 1939).

---

[1]Reich ultimately became best known for his unorthodox sex and energy theories and tragically died of a heart attack in Lewisburg Federal Penitentiary, Pennsylvania, where he was serving a 2-year term for distributing his invention, the *orgone energy accumulator*, in violation of a U.S. Food and Drug Administration injunction. This telephone-booth-size device purportedly gathered energy from the atmosphere to cure common colds, cancer, and impotence while the patient sat inside (Sharaf, 1983).

FIGURE 6.1

Frederick Perls. Printed with permission of The Gestalt Journal Press.

While working with Goldstein, Fritz met and later married Laura Perls (née Lore Posner; 1905–1990). Laura studied psychology at Frankfurt University and received a doctorate in science. Among her teachers were psychologists Kurt Goldstein and Max Wertheimer (one of the founders of Gestalt psychology) and existential philosophers Paul Tillich and Martin Buber (see chap. 4). Fritz and Laura later fled Western Europe, just ahead of the Nazis, to South Africa, where they established a psychoanalytic institute.

Fritz and Laura cowrote *Ego, Hunger and Aggression: A Revision of Freud's Theory and Method* (Perls, 1947)—although Laura was not given authorship credit—during this period of upheaval, and the book presaged many gestalt therapy concepts. In it they reevaluated the psychoanalytic conceptualization of aggression and suggested that Sigmund Freud had underestimated the importance of basic bodily functions like eating and digestion. They also discussed holistic and existential perspectives, and described therapeutic exercises designed to promote physical awareness rather than cognitive insight.

In response to the rise of apartheid in South Africa, Fritz and Laura immigrated to the United States and established the New York Institute for Gestalt Therapy in 1952. Several years of collaboration with members of this group resulted in a comprehensive formulation of the theory and practice for their approach. Paul Goodman (1911–1972) is generally credited with writing *Gestalt Therapy: Excitement and Growth in the Human Personality* (Perls, Hefferline, & Goodman, 1951), the seminal book on the theory and practice of gestalt therapy. Best known for his 1960 book *Growing Up Absurd: Problems of Youth in Organized Society*, Goodman was the prototypical starving artist, discouraged and marginalized, rarely making ends meet to support his wife and two children. During a period in his life when he was particularly distraught, he met Fritz and Laura and became a founding member of the New York Institute.

Half of *Gestalt Therapy* consisted of reports of the results of exercises in awareness that Ralph Hefferline (1910–1974) administered with his students at the Institute. The other half was a statement of their new approach. Although a rather dense read and not initially well received, *Gestalt Therapy* remains a cornerstone of the gestalt approach.

Fritz spent the rest of his life training, giving workshops, and establishing gestalt training centers. After the New York Institute, he established the Cleveland Institute of Gestalt Therapy in 1954; then the Esalen Institute in Big Sur, California, in 1962; and, finally, one on Vancouver Island, British Columbia, Canada, shortly before his death in 1970. Most of his writings from the latter part of his life were transcribed from his workshops. Laura remained in New York, where she continued to lead long-term training groups for gestalt therapists until the mid 1980s.

Gestalt therapy drew influences from a number of sources. First is psychoanalysis (see chap. 2), from which the rationalist concern with the inner life was drawn and adapted. As it is for the psychodynamic therapist, for the gestalt therapist the fundamental material with which to work is subjective phenomena—what is going on inside the client. Rejected were the construct-laden theory that Freud and his followers developed, and their reductionistic worldview. Gestalt therapy adopted instead the humanistic emphasis on holism and growth.

Existentialism (see chap. 4) also informs gestalt therapy. The existentialist view that Western societies have exalted intellectual reason over subjective experience is turned into the imperative used by Fritz to "lose your mind and come to your senses" (Perls, 1969, p. 69). Another influence from existentialism is the gestalt therapist's encouragement of individuals to make choices about how they will live on the basis of their own experience, rather than living according to established habits or unquestioningly accepting the norms of society. They also turned away from Freud's rationalist search for the reason *why* a person behaves a certain way and toward the existential *how* a person lives. Gestalt therapy is concerned with what *is*—the present, subjective experience. To gestalt therapists "why" the client is the way he or she is, is of no consequence to helping choose healthy behavior. What "caused" clients to become the way they are is assumed to be irrelevant.

Finally, Gestalt psychology gave to gestalt therapy more than its name. Although gestalt therapy is not directly an application or extension of it, Gestalt psychology's focus on interaction and process, and many of its important experimental observations and conclusions, informs gestalt therapy. In particular, gestalt therapy incorporates the Gestalt psychology concept of *homeostasis*. Needs are understood as disturbing of an individual's homeostasis. A healthy person, when aware of a need, acts to satisfy the need and thus returns to balance. Distress arises when a person is unable to act to regain homeostasis. For example, where displays of grieving are frowned on, emotions might be channeled into a psychosomatic illness. In this way, awareness is directed away from the grief and transferred onto concern about the illness—a concern the society will allow the person to take action to deal with.

Gestalt therapy also draws from Gestalt psychology language to describe this process of needs arising as *figure/ground* (gestalt) formation. The figure is whatever is the focus of attention for an individual within the entire *field*. The field encompasses other people, the environment, and the individual as a whole (i.e., mind, body, and emotions). The ground is everything else in the field except the figure. Whatever need is most disturbing an individual's homeostasis becomes figural for that person. With the need is satisfied, it merges back into the ground to make way for the next figure to emerge and so on.

Gestalt Rationale

A human being is a unified whole that cannot be reduced to a simple summation of physical, biological, psychological, or conceptual properties. We are different from the mere sum of our parts. We all have a heart, kidneys, lungs, and a brain, and also emotions, sexuality, memories, hopes, and dreams. Gestalt therapy strives to enlist our innate homeostatic tendency toward becoming a whole that is as healthy as we are able to be. Distress is understood as withdrawal from awareness of our experience of body, self, and environment. This withdrawal arises out of the lessons we learned in childhood when we were dependent on others for our survival. We learned to deny certain aspects of our experience because they were literally life threatening. Often clients who seek help through psychotherapy are in a state in which thoughts and feelings associated with distinct memories and fantasies about the past linger in the background of their experience. This state is associated with an inauthentic existence that results in preoccupations (e.g., worrying), compulsive behavior, wariness, and self-defeating behavior.

Because contact and withdrawal change from moment to moment as a need is met or an interest pursued and other needs and interests are allowed to arise, healthy functioning results from contact with our experience in the present. Answers to questions of how and why development may have been arrested in a client's childhood are not germane to current health. Instead, growth takes place as we let go of distractions that prevent personal growth from taking place. When these distractions are gone, a focused experience remains. With this uncluttered awareness, concentration is deepened, leading us into wholehearted functioning. In a world gone mad with complexity, the simplicity of immediate experience allows us to shed debilitating habits of mind that distract us from contact with our true selves. Life happens in the present—not in the past or the future—and when we are dwelling on the past or fantasizing about the future, we are not truly living. Our past informs our present, it does not determine it. Our future can inspire us, it need not dominate us. Through contact with our present experience, we are able to take responsibility for our actions and find the excitement, energy, and courage to live life fully and with intention.

Gestalt Goals

In gestalt therapy, the singular goal is *awareness*: awareness of the contact between our physical bodies, our environment, and our selves. Ideally, this awareness progresses to deeper levels as therapy proceeds and becomes a state that clients can experience more often in their life. This deepened awareness allows greater capacity for self-regulation and more opportunity for self-determination. Awareness allows clients to better accept responsibility for their actions and reactions, and to freely choose how to live their lives. Awareness also facilitates personal growth. Rather than attempting to help clients solve their problems, the gestalt therapist strives to show clients that awareness is a means for them to find their own solutions. Symptoms that prompt someone to seek therapy are understood as processes resulting from personal growth that has been thwarted. With awareness of how unacknowledged feelings are active in our experience, growth is released and symptoms resolve.

Gestalt Change Processes

From a gestalt perspective, change is paradoxical. This is because the more one tries to be who one is not, the more one stays the same (Beisser,

1970). If, instead, clients are encouraged to focus on the here and now of their experience, they will find that any point of contact becomes a portent of exciting new possibilities (Polster & Polster, 1973). Change then occurs spontaneously and without effort through awareness of what and how we are thinking, feeling, and doing—through awareness of the field of our present moment. The ensuing process leads to changes in the entire field that is the client's existence. It is this experience that is essential for change—not thinking or talking about the experience. Most of us tend to talk *about* ourselves, our past, our problems, our dreams, our ideas. The more aware we are of the full extent of our experience, the more able we are to integrate and accept all aspects of our self. In addition, the more thorough the exploration, the more intense the reorganization, allowing us to accept responsibility for our actions and reactions and thereby make choices that are based on a more authentic appreciation of environmental demands and of our true needs and desires.

Gestalt Change Tasks

Historically, Fritz discouraged preestablished techniques and encouraged therapists instead to design "games" or "experiments" that are individually tailored to each client (Levitsky & Perls, 1970). Yet the use of classic gestalt techniques has persisted, perhaps, because they are just so intriguing and in part because it is actually very difficult to propose unique change tasks for each client in each unique circumstance. Gestalt change tasks are called *games* to emphasize the interpersonal nature of the task and to highlight the "as if" quality of the undertaking. If the client experiences reluctance, this too is honored as an opportunity for learning. In fact, how we resist contact in the here and now can be a rich resource from which the therapist draws to propose original, individualized tasks.

The aim of gestalt exercises is to help clients learn about themselves from immediate experience—not from the therapist's conceptualizations. The exercises aim to heighten an individual's awareness of deadened feelings and sensations, reawakening knowledge of personal agency in shaping what is taken for granted as a fixed reality. Thus, the client is given a high degree of control over how and what is learned from psychotherapy.

Such experiments, properly undertaken, are part of the collaborative give and take between client and therapist in a psychotherapy session. The use of the present moment for therapeutic leverage is isomorphic of living in the here and now. When designing an experiment, the therapist pays particular attention to the client's nonverbal language and proposes a task designed to intensify the client's current experience in order to expand awareness of the here and now. Ideally, each individualized experiment grows out of the therapist's responsive interaction with the client. Because the experience can be very emotional and unsettling, it is best if clients are prepared for experiments (Greenwald, 1976) and a strong therapeutic relationship is established beforehand (see the Therapeutic Relationship section later in this chapter). The following paragraphs describe some of the games proposed by gestalt therapists.

Internal dialogue exercises are probably the most famous of the gestalt experiments. They are intended to address internal conflicts caused by uncritical acceptance of others' opinions and promote an integration of all aspects of self. The client plays each role and engages in a dialogue by moving back and forth between two chairs. From each chair, the client speaks directly to the imagined person–entity in the empty chair. The most common conflict is the *top dog–underdog*. The top dog is the inner dictator who tells us what we should do. The underdog plays the victim–rebel and schemes to thwart and avoid doing as the top dog demands.

Making the rounds is a group-based task that involves asking the client to speak to or do something with the other members of a group. Group members take turns giving the client feedback about what they have observed. This allows the client to take interpersonal risks, present newly owned aspects of the self, and confirm or disconfirm assumptions in relation to others.

Reversal exercises invite the client to behave in a manner opposite of his or her usual presentation, such as having a shy person behave in an extroverted way. This is helpful for denial of latent aspects of the self. The client is thrust into experiencing what at first feels strange and alien but eventually whole and authentic.

Rehearsal exercises have the client say aloud the inner thinking we all rehearse in preparation for behaving in expected ways. Our internal rehearsals tend to result in inhibitions of spontaneity and genuineness. By saying them aloud, the client can take ownership of his or her intentions to please others and consciously choose to meet those expectations or not.

Exaggeration exercises are used when the client appears to be unaware of some aspect of his or her experience. The client is invited to amplify a subtle behavior—such a vocal tone or a gesture—to heighten awareness. Exaggeration exercises can also be used with verbal statements in which some important experience is glossed over. This allows the client to experience something that he or she had been avoiding, thereby facilitating integration.

Dream analysis in gestalt therapy considers all parts of a dream to be parts of the dreamer. Dreams are seen as very useful because they are the most spontaneous and uninhibited expression a person can make. To work with a dream, the client retells the dream as though experiencing it here and now. The therapist then uses what is revealed by the dream to raise the client's awareness of self. This may mean the client acts out the dream's different elements—be they people or objects. Alternatively, dream analysis might involve finishing the dream in a different manner, or the therapist might ask the client to do an internal dialogue exercise with the dream to determine what it has to tell the person.

Using the *language of responsibility* involves encouraging clients to say what they mean and mean what they say. In other words, clients use language that injects real feeling into their words. The language of responsibility has three important aspects: (a) *directness*—talking directly to the therapist or another group member rather than alluding to matters by being indirect (e.g., "Smoking is harmful to the environment" may be replaced by "I cannot breathe properly, and you are killing me by smoking when I am with you!"); (b) *checking things out*—encouraging the client to ask directly, "How do you feel about that?" instead of guessing what another person thinks or feels; and (c) *first person, active speech*—allowing the speaker to own what is being said and imbue it with personal meaning and emotion (e.g., "It is not good for people to live alone," contrasts with "I do not like to live alone").

Therapeutic Relationship

Gestalt therapists strive to bring the full impact of their personality to the therapeutic encounter (Levin & Shepherd, 1974). This is not to say that the therapist dominates the session but rather that honesty, spontaneity, and direct engagement are modeled and valued in the session. Therapy is seen as an encounter between two people in which the conditions for change are made possible, in part, by the presence of a therapist who is committed to growth. The therapist therefore enters fully into the session in an active, assertive, engaged, confident, and creative manner. The therapeutic moment is prized as a precious, singular opportunity for change. If the client is fully present and aware, then the therapist will not interrupt their process. When the therapist observes withdrawal from experiencing, however, the client's attention is drawn to the phenomenon and an opportunity for growth is seized.

The gestalt therapist recognizes that change does not happen through coercion—it happens when a person is fully experiencing. Forced change is an attempt to actualize an idea—which is impossible—rather than to actualize the self. Awareness and self-acceptance are the conditions that make growth possible. Forced intervention inhibits this process. The gestalt therapist therefore tries to avoid speculation about what will emerge in session or what direction the client will or should take. Rather, the therapist pays close attention to the client's moment-by-moment experience and directs awareness toward truer expression of the client's real needs. In this sense, the therapist is an expert—an expert on the change process and skilled in removing obstacles to growth (Levin & Shepherd, 1974). Yet, the therapist cannot make discoveries for the client—ultimately, the client is responsible for his or her own actions, reactions, and decisions, and is the expert on his or her own life.

Evolution and Variations

Gestalt therapy suffered from the loss of the dominant (some would say domineering) presence of Fritz Perls after his death. Yet, gestalt therapy clearly is not dead yet; there are more than 60 gestalt therapy institutes throughout the world, and more continue to be established. A number of journals also continue to thrive: *International Gestalt Journal* (formerly *The Gestalt Journal*), *British Gestalt Journal*, *Gestalt Review*, and *Australian Gestalt Journal* are devoted primarily to articles on gestalt therapy. *Gestalt Theory* also publishes articles on Gestalt psychology, including some on therapy.

Earlier gestalt therapy practice tended to stress the clinical use of frustration and an abrasive attitude if the therapist thought the client was being manipulative. There has been a movement toward more interpersonal gentleness in gestalt therapy practice, largely influenced by the overwhelming empirical evidence of the importance of the therapeutic alliance (Wampold, 2001).

Emotion-focused—or *process-experiential*—*therapy* was developed by Leslie S. Greenberg (1945–), who, beginning his graduate studies with Laura Rice (Rice & Greenberg, 1984), has committed his career to understanding and testing gestalt therapy (Sloan, 2004). Emotion is understood as the primary adaptive motivator in human experience. By activating clients' emotions, their cognitions and behaviors will follow as their self-actualizing tendency is engaged (Elliot, Watson, Goldman, & Greenberg, 2004). The emotion-focused therapist strives for empathic attunement with the client to be able to propose change tasks that will facilitate healthy emotional processing. *Markers* of problematic emotional processing that occur in session, such as puzzling over an emotional reaction, feeling torn between alternatives, self-criticism, or ambiguous feelings toward a significant person, are used by the therapist as opportunities for introducing an experiential change task (L. S. Greenberg, 2002). These change tasks are designed to help clients identify, experience, explore, make sense of, transform, and flexibly manage their emotions in the present moment. As a result, clients become better able to access the important information and meanings about themselves and their place in the world around them that healthy emotional processing affords. Clients are then freed to use this information to live a full and vital life (L. S. Greenberg & Watson, 2006).

Body-oriented psychotherapy is currently quite a popular approach (e.g., R. Frank, 2001; Kepner, 1987; Kurtz, 1990). Originally developed primarily from the work of Wilhelm Reich, body-oriented psychotherapy assumes a functional unity between mind and body that contributes to the organization of the whole person. Thus, *body-oriented* does not merely mean the soma as separate from the mind, or psyche. These approaches draw from gestalt therapy and seek to facilitate the change process of heightened self-awareness of material remembered in bodily sensations and nonconscious patterns of behaving (Kurtz, 1995). The change tasks used in body-oriented therapies can involve physical movement, such as having a client who is afraid of men walk slowly toward the male therapist, or introspection of bodily experience in a manner much like traditional gestalt therapy. Body-oriented psychotherapists then typically draw on mindfulness-based psychotherapeutic tasks to help clients turn their awareness toward their present subjective experience with a calm and curious attitude (Kurtz, 1995). Unacknowledged material such as foundational memories, emotions, and implicit beliefs then naturally emerge into consciousness. Once this material becomes conscious, clients are able to consider how it influences their life and then choose how to think, feel, and act with greater self-determination.

Mindfulness-based psychotherapies help clients to pay attention to sensory experiences and mental contents in the present moment, deliberately and intentionally, in a nonelaborative and nonjudgmental way (Baer, 2006; Germer, Siegel, & Fulton, 2005). They also include attending to current activity, rather than functioning automatically without awareness of one's actions. Mindfulness can be contrasted with states of mind in which attention is focused elsewhere, such as on memories, plans, fantasies, or worries (Baer, 2003; K. W. Brown & Ryan, 2003). A variety of mindfulness-based interventions have been developed and applied to a variety of problems (Baer, 2006). Jon Kabat-Zinn (2005), for example, developed an 8-week group program of mindfulness-based stress reduction for up to 30 participants. Some mindfulness-based therapies involve rather formal traditional meditation practices of up to 45 minutes while sitting quietly, lying down, or practicing yoga poses. Others use briefer exercises that involve mindful awareness of everyday activities such as walking, eating, or washing dishes. Regardless of the activity, clients are typically encouraged to focus attention on a particular stimulus, such as an environmental sound, or a bodily process, such as breathing, often in conjunction with the rhythmic repetition of a word or phrase, such as "breath," "thought," or "sadness." This kind of attention facilitates greater awareness, clarity, and acceptance of present-moment reality, which in turn promotes well-being (K. W. Brown & Ryan, 2003).

A Heart Divided

Emma was successful in her career as a nurse and married to a man she loved. Yet she felt that she was her "own worst enemy." She wanted to work with a therapist who would help her "grow as a person" and heard that Dr. Smith worked from a gestalt perspective.

Emma liked how Dr. Smith was kind yet forthright. He took time to listen without interrupting, and he would then make penetrating observations about what she said, as well as how she spoke and behaved, inviting her to pay attention to these aspects as well.

Gradually, Emma became more aware of her body and tone of voice, and as she did so, she found herself increasingly anxious in session. Dr. Smith encouraged her to stay with this feeling.

"I can't. It's too painful."

"You mean you won't," replied Dr. Smith.

"That's so harsh. Can't you see I'm in pain?"

"You say you are in pain and yet you are smiling."

"Am I? I hadn't noticed."

"May I propose something? What do you notice around your mouth, your eyes, and your face? Try telling me what your smile is saying."

"You don't know pain. You don't know suffering. Don't you dare cry. There are plenty of things to cry about that are worse than what's happening to you."

"Oh, God! I haven't thought about this in years."

"About what?"

"About how I always had to take care of my younger brothers and I never had time to take care of myself. Argh! I just feel so angry!"

As Emma continued to talk about and pay attention to her feelings about her upbringing, this led to her feelings about her job.

"I know there are things I should be doing, and I want to do them. Yet, I put them off. I just can't seem to get around to them. I know! I know! *'I don't do them. I won't do them.'* But part of me just resents doing them."

"May I propose something else? Try sitting over there [*pointing to another chair*] and speaking from that part of you that resents doing those things."

"Why should I have to clean up after them just because they're incompetent? If I were as bad at my job as they are, no one would expect me to do it. It's not fair."

"Good. Now move over to that chair and speak from the other part of you."

"You'll damn well do it and do it well. No one gets ahead by slacking off. Those other nurses will never make anything of themselves with that attitude. And neither will you if you don't smarten up."

"God, I never realized how much my resentment has been festering on in me."

When it came time for Emma to terminate therapy, she described herself as "feeling grounded" and "more present" in her job. She was less resentful, while more assertive in her relationships with her colleagues. She also reported that her relationship with her husband had become "more loving and deeper, like we connect at more levels."

Learning Task

In gestalt therapy, a paradoxical experiment is often used to allow the issue of change to recede into the background and the experience of full engagement in the present moment to guide our growth. In this "anti-assignment," you are invited to read and attend to only those aspects of the Further Resources section at the end of this chapter, or even this task, that you are drawn to, that catch your eye, that you are curious about, that pique your interest, or that your heart desires—what you *feel like* exploring (Woldt, 2005).

As you do so, perhaps even as you think about or resist learning in this way, you may choose to pay attention to your inner processes and your awareness around not learning things you are told you "should" learn. You may notice bodily reactions (e.g., heart palpitations, tension, relaxation). Are these in any way related to the topic you are engaged in or considering?

You may also notice your mental response. Are there thoughts of resentment, anger, surprise, or relief? Finally, you may notice an urge to action. Perhaps consider sitting in one of two chairs and alternately changing seats, putting a voice to what you might like to tell me, the author, about this task.

After you have taken as much time as you need on this task, record your experience in your reflective journal.

Your Reflective Journal

The past is history, the future's a mystery, and today is a gift—that's why we call it *the present*. Take a few moments to pay attention to your immediate experience. Are you feeling stressed, harried, calm, or curious? Does this exercise seem silly to you? Does it seem meaningful, difficult, easy? How do you think it would be received by most clients? What do you notice about how you feel about gestalt therapy? What do your answers to these questions tell you about your affinity for the approach? How do you feel about it relative to the other approaches you have learned about so far? Record your thoughts and feelings in your reflective journal.

Summary

Gestalt therapy takes as its centerpiece the idea that the human condition is a unified whole different from the sum of its parts. Distress arises when we withdraw from awareness of our experience of body, self, and environment. If we focus on our experiential present moment, our innate homeostatic tendency toward health is activated. Gestalt therapy therefore focuses on the here and now of living in session and has as its goal awareness of the contact between our physical bodies, our environment, and our selves. Change is accepted as paradoxical in that the more one tries to be who one is not, the more one stays the same. By focusing on what is happening in the moment, change occurs spontaneously and without effort. Change is facilitated through the use of experiments individually tailored to facilitate awareness. In order to improve in this manner, the gestalt therapist must be active, assertive, engaged, confident, and creative in session and in relation to the client. Currently, gestalt therapy is enjoying a resurgence in popularity in the form of process-experiential, body-oriented, and mindfulness-based therapies.

Further Resources

CASE READINGS

Aylward, J., Bauer, R., Freedman, H., Harman, R., & Perls, L. (1986). A case presentation in gestalt therapy. *The Gestalt Journal, 9*, 16–35.

Feder, B., & Ronall, R. (1997). *A living legacy of Fritz and Lara Perls: Contemporary case studies*. New York: Feder.

Perls, F. (1969). *Gestalt therapy verbatim*. Moab, UT: Real People Press.

Watson, J. C., Goldman, R. N., & Greenberg, L. S. (2007). *Case studies in emotion-focused treatment of depression: A comparison of good and poor outcome*. Washington, DC: American Psychological Association.

RECOMMENDED READING

Greenberg, L. S. (2002). *Emotion-focused therapy: Coaching clients to work through their feelings.* Washington, DC: American Psychological Association.

Perls, F., Hefferline, R. E., & Goodman, P. (1951). *Gestalt therapy: Excitement and growth in the human personality.* New York: Dell.

Polster, E., & Polster, M. (1973). *Gestalt therapy integrated.* New York: Brunner/Mazel.

Woldt, A. J., & Tolman, S. M. (2005). *Gestalt therapy: History, theory, and practice.* Thousand Oaks, CA: Sage.

RECOMMENDED VIEWING

American Psychological Association (Producer). (2004). *Gestalt therapy with Gordon Wheeler, PhD* [Motion picture]. (Available from the American Psychological Association, 750 First Street, NE, Washington, DC 20002-4242)

American Psychological Association (Producer). (2007). *Emotion focused therapy over time with Leslie S. Greenberg, PhD* [Motion picture]. (Available from the American Psychological Association, 750 First Street, NE, Washington, DC 20002-4242)

Milton H. Erickson Foundation (Producer). (1990). *Erving Polster, PhD: Humanization of technique* [Motion Picture]. (Available from the Milton H. Erickson Foundation, 3606 N. 24th Street, Phoenix, AZ 85016-6500)

Psychological & Educational Films (Producer). (1965). *Three approaches to Psychotherapy I: Part II. Frederick Perls (gestalt therapy)* [Motion picture]. (Available from Psychological & Educational Films, 3334 East Coast Highway, #252, Corona del Mar, CA 92625-2328)

Psychological & Educational Films (Producer). (1973). *Gestalt dream analysis with Frederick Perls* [Motion picture]. (Available from Psychological & Educational Films, 3334 East Coast Highway, #252, Corona del Mar, CA 92625-2328)

Cognitive | 7

ognitive therapy traces its development to at least three sources: the success and limitations of behaviorism (see chap. 3), the computer as a metaphor for human information processing, and dissatisfaction with psychoanalysis (see chap. 2).

By the 1960s, behaviorism was slipping out of favor, both among academics and behavior therapists, who looked to researchers for guidance in developing new therapeutic tools. Valuable as they had been, classical conditioning and operant conditioning were seen as not going far enough in explaining the human condition. As a result, behavior therapy could not go far enough either. Too much was unaccounted for. In particular, what were missing were cognitive processes such as thoughts, beliefs, assumptions, attitudes, memories, mental imagery, and fantasies that people brought to therapy. The study of memory, for example, was pointing to how people are not passive receptacles of new information, but rather how they are actively engaged in processing strategies (Dember, 1974). Also, behavior therapy could only be applied to behavioral problems or at best to the behavioral aspects of problems that also appeared to have cognitive aspects. Practitioners found that not all of the problems that clients presented with could be understood this way.

The original foundations of behavior therapy were seen to focus too narrowly on interactions between people and their environments—on stimuli in the environment and on those aspects of the person's responses that could be observed and therefore measured. This focus was very useful and productive as far as it went. In fact, focusing on observable events has the advantage of discouraging speculation about inner, covert processes that need to be inferred because they cannot be directly observed. The subjectivity that many felt had led psychoanalysts astray was thus avoided. Eventually, behavior therapists came to accept that the conditioning paradigm was leaving out too many important aspects of the human condition.

Those who endorsed behaviorism were not about to abandon the worldview on which their approach to treatment was based, however. What behaviorism lacked could still be supplemented by using established empirical principles. All that was needed was a theoretical model that could do a better job of accounting for the existing data and guide the search for more and better data (Kuhn, 1962). The "cognitive revolution" (Dember, 1974) appeared to provide just such a theory.

A 1956 symposium on information processing at Massachusetts Institute of Technology (Whorf, 1956) is usually credited with ushering in the cognitive paradigm in psychology. The growing familiarity with computational information-processing models just fit so well with empirical methods. Computers do not, after all, have subjective experiences. Yet they can be observed to process information according to reliable, linear rules. The metaphor of the computer for human cognition suggested a model in which human thought could be considered objective—or at least measurable—rather than merely subjective. Indeed, a number of theoretical formulations based on behavioral principles were proposed. Lloyd Homme (1965) and Joseph Cautela (1966, 1967) were notable for conceptualizing cognitions as covert behaviors subject to the laws of conditioning, although satisfactory evidence was not forthcoming and this line of reasoning petered out.

It was Albert Bandura (1925–) who presented a truly revolutionary new theory. His *social learning theory* (Bandura, 1969) was built from the phenomenon of observational learning and empirical demonstrations of behaviors being acquired solely through cognitive processes (Bandura & Walters, 1963). Bandura showed that behavior is not determined solely by environmental stimuli and consequences (Bandura, 1977a). He then went on to explain how cognitive processes can mediate between the individual and his or her environment (Bandura, 1977b). Most important to note, Bandura used information-processing principles in explicating his social learning model. This allowed behaviorists to consider nonbehavioral topics that clients present with to therapy, such as choice and self-control. With an information-processing model, these topics could be understood as problem-solving and self-regulation processes that followed reliable rules (Bandura, 1974).

Meanwhile, in psychotherapeutic practice the relevance of cognitions to psychological disorders and personal problems was also being explored. Aaron T. Beck (1921–; see Figure 7.1) was trained in psychoanalysis and

FIGURE 7.1

Aaron T. Beck. Printed with permission of Aaron T. Beck.

sought to empirically validate Freud's theory that depression was the result of anger turned against the self (S. Freud, 1917/1957). Beck found that people who sought treatment for depression did not appear to be angry with themselves, however (A. T. Beck & Hurvich, 1959). They seemed to him, rather, to have a pervasive negative bias in their thinking about themselves, the world, and the future—what Beck termed a *negative cognitive shift* (A. T. Beck, 1967).

Furthermore, people who were depressed experienced specific types of cognitions in the form of *automatic thoughts* that tended to arise quickly, as though by reflex (A. T. Beck, 1976). They were not "unconscious" or strange and primitive, as Freud described them. Rather, they were treated as perfectly plausible by the sufferer and appeared to be reliably associated with subsequent unpleasant affect. These automatic thoughts were conceptualized as part of an internal information-processing system. If changes were made such that this internal system was less negatively biased, then depressive affect was found to lessen as well.

What really brought Beck into favor with empirically minded therapists was his use of scientific rigor in the form of testing his hypothesized change processes, operationalizing his change tasks, and evaluating the efficacy of his approach. In other words, Beck behaved like a good empiricist and made it possible for those who felt limited by a strictly behavioral approach to broaden the scope of their practice.

Albert Ellis (1913–2007) was similarly trained in psychoanalysis. His dissatisfaction, however, was with the passivity of its methods (Ellis, 1957a, 1957b). Ellis felt that he could speed up the process of psychotherapy by taking a more active role—interjecting advice, making direct interpretations, confronting irrationality, and persuading clients to adopt rational beliefs (Ellis, 1962). His *rational emotive behavior therapy* and *ABC* (activating events are mediated by irrational *b*eliefs in determining inappropriate *c*onsequences) *theory* (Ellis & Whiteley, 1979) presaged many later ideas in cognitive therapy.

Although Beck and Ellis developed their approaches independently from one another, there are numerous similarities. Both approaches try to help clients learn to pay attention to the occurrence of maladaptive cognitions, recognize their disruptive impact, and replace them with more realistic and adaptive thought patterns. Most important, both approaches are based on an information-processing rationale that is empirically testable and therefore able to be subjected to scientific scrutiny.

Before long, treatment studies were produced that provided empirical support for the effectiveness of cognitive therapy. Of particular note are studies that show cognitive therapy to be as effective as drug treatment for depression—or, actually, more effective, when posttreatment relapse rates and the uncertain consequences of long-term drug use are taken into account (Dobson, 1989). Other studies, chiefly of panic attacks, obsessive–compulsive disorder, and other problems of excessive fear and anxiety, have produced similar empirical results in favor of cognitive therapy over other nonempirical therapies. In today's political and intellectual climate of (empirical) evidence-based practice, cognitive therapy is right at home.

Cognitive Rationale

Cognitive therapy is based on the idea that the way human beings make sense of situations influences how we behave and feel emotionally. In particular, when we misperceive situations—for example, by seeing them more negatively than they really are—we make ourselves unhappy for no good reason. Misinterpretations of situations or sensations and negative expectations just make us unhappy without serving any useful function. These distortions in our thinking have been shown to be important in the development and maintenance of a variety of psychological disorders. In contrast, by seeing situations more objectively and rationally, we experience a substantial shift in thinking and subsequently in mood and behavior.

For example, one person hearing about cognitive therapy might think, "This sounds good; it's just what I've always been looking for." This person feels pleased and optimistic. Another person hearing the same information might think, "I would like to do cognitive therapy, but I don't think I can." This person feels sad and discouraged. How we feel emotionally, therefore, is not purely a reaction to a situation. Rather, it is our thoughts about the situation that influence our response. These thoughts are not like the obvious surface level of thinking, such as focusing on understanding something someone is saying. The thoughts that influence our behavior and mood tend to be evaluative, brief, and spring up automatically. We notice them when someone says, "What was going through your mind just then?"

When we are upset, it is the automatic thoughts that are causing our negative mood. Cognitive therapy helps people to identify the thoughts that are distressing them and to evaluate how realistic they are. Then they learn to change their distorted thinking. When we think more realistically, we do not suffer unnecessarily.

Cognitive therapy consists of a combination of strategies and tasks that have been designed and rigorously demonstrated to effectively modify cognitive distortions that cause psychological problems. The appropriate application of these tasks enables us to rid ourselves of the source of our emotional difficulties. In fact, a substantial body of research exists documenting how correcting dysfunctional thinking provides relief from, and subsequently remission of, a wide variety of psychological conditions.

Cognitive Goals

Cognitive therapy is based on an educational model—on the assumption that the cognitive distortions that cause most emotional and behavioral problems are learned. Therefore, the goal of therapy is to help clients identify unhelpful thought processes and to learn new ways of thinking. The logic is that if clients learn what the therapist has to teach them, they will not have the personal problems they are experiencing. The educational emphasis of cognitive therapy has an additional benefit: When people understand how and why they are doing well, they can continue doing what they are doing to maintain gains and adapt when faced with new challenges. The ideal healthy person from a cognitive therapy point of view is not unlike a scientist—someone who thinks, judges, analyzes, decides, and acts carefully, methodically, and logically.

Cognitive Change Processes

The mechanism of change in cognitive therapy is the sequential alteration or replacement of cognitive processes from irrational or distorted to rational or realistic. For such changes to take place, clients are encouraged to (a) become aware of the cognitive content or stream of thought of their reaction to an upsetting event, (b) view their thoughts as hypotheses—rather than facts—so that they can recognize what thoughts are dysfunctional or irrational, (c) substitute accurate judgments for inaccurate judgments, and (d) gather feedback to inform them whether the changes made have resulted in the desired outcome. Emotional and behavioral change—and thereby most difficulties that prompt people to seek therapy—will necessarily follow from these cognitive changes. Once clients have achieved this kind of learning, self-management and problem-solving skills can be brought to bear on future problems.

Sometimes clients will discover that their thoughts are organized around themes or core beliefs that form *cognitive schemas*. These schemas are underlying cognitive structures that are not as readily accessible as automatic thoughts. The process by which they are changed is fundamentally identical to more circumscribed cognitive distortions. The process does tend to take longer, however, as the client and therapist explore the multitude of ways and circumstances in which they are active.

Cognitive Change Tasks

The cognitive therapist draws from a range of empirically tested interventions to correct errors and biases in information processing and modifying thoughts that result in faulty conclusions and emotional distress. Most focus on identifying the client's beliefs or automatic thoughts; correcting them if they fail an empirical, logical, or adaptive test; and then teaching more accurate and functional beliefs.

Identifying and testing automatic thoughts is the central task of cognitive therapy. Clients are encouraged to engage in a behavioral experiment by gathering data on what types of automatic thoughts they have and how often they occur. They are then invited to test the validity of their beliefs. So people who think, "No one likes me," might record how often anyone treats them nicely. Even a smile from a stranger forces them to at least modify their beliefs to "Not everyone likes me," with much different resulting emotional consequences.

Decatastrophizing involves helping the client prepare for feared consequences by imagining "what if" (A. T. Beck & Emery, 1979, 1985). If anticipated consequences are indeed likely to happen, problem-solving strategies can be learned and used. If feared consequences are actually exceedingly unlikely, then alternative, more adaptive cognitions can be substituted. Decatastrophizing can be particularly helpful when a client is avoiding doing things he or she ought to be doing.

Reattribution involves testing automatic thoughts and assumptions by considering the plausibility of alternative explanations. Rarely do we actually know—or can we ever know—what causes events in our lives. Blaming ourselves or others for events is a common source of misery that can be overcome by making more realistic and appropriate attributions.

Redefining a problem can help us to find opportunities to make changes in our lives when our conceptualization of it was preventing action (A. T. Beck & Emery, 1985). Making a problem more concrete and specific is one way of redefining it that is often very helpful. Stating a problem in terms of behaviors over which we have control is another way.

Decentering was developed primarily for dealing with anxiety (A. T. Beck & Emery, 1985). Believing that one is the center of others' attention is a common cognitive error and can be addressed by undertaking behavioral experiments to test it. More often than not, clients find that they are not the center of others' lives.

Thought stopping involves breaking a chain of thoughts that tend to escalate into distress, particularly anxiety. The client is helped to identify the sequence of thoughts and then attend to those that occur early in the process. A thought or image is then consciously elicited, or an engrossing activity undertaken, to interrupt the chain.

Distraction is similar to thought stopping, but here the client is taught to focus on complex thoughts, such as number sequences or the periodic table of the elements. The rationale is that distressing thoughts and nondistressing thoughts cannot be maintained simultaneously.

The *three-column technique* is usually assigned as homework to assist clients in identifying automatic and irrational thoughts. There are a number of variants of the technique. One variant (A. T. Beck, Rush, Shaw, & Emery, 1979) is to have the client identify the triggering situation, automatic thought, and the logical error the automatic thought represents (see the three left-hand columns in Table 7.1). Another variant (Ellis & Dryden, 1997) is to identify the illogical thought, the logical error it represents, and an appropriate rational response (see the three right-hand columns in Table 7.1). Under the pressure of rational thought, illogical thoughts tend to lose their hold, and the absence of these distorted thoughts results in the negative feelings they generate falling away or never arising in the first place.

Other variants include having the client (a) identify and list the emotions aroused in each situation as a result of the influence of the automatic thought and (b) attend to and record the outcome of identifying a rational alternative thought (A. T. Beck et al., 1979).

TABLE 7.1

Three-Column Technique

Situation	Automatic–illogical thought	Logical error	Rational response
Wearing a new outfit	"People will laugh at me."	No evidence	"I like my new outfit."
Orally presenting a report	"I froze before therefore I'll freeze again."	Overgeneralization	"I can be successful."
Lost my job	"I'll never find another job."	Arbitrary inference	"I will have to try."
Family moved away	"They don't love me."	Personalization	"They had their reasons."
Date rejects me	"My life is ruined."	Magnification	"I can meet someone new."
Got a *B* on a paper	"I have no grasp of the material."	Polarized thinking	"I can do better."

Therapeutic Relationship

For cognitive therapists, a positive therapeutic relationship is necessary for effective therapy, although it is not the focus. With some forms of therapy, the therapists assume that the main reason people get better is because of the relationship between them and the client (see chap. 4, this volume). Cognitive therapists attend to the psychotherapy process research literature and therefore know that it is important to have an emotional bond with the client and to collaborate on therapeutic tasks and goals (Horvath & Greenberg, 1994). They also know that this same literature shows that a good therapeutic alliance is not sufficient to bring about positive outcomes. Research on the effectiveness of cognitive therapy has revealed (e.g., Dobson, 2001) that clients' problems change when their thinking changes. The therapist therefore takes a more active role in the relationship—not unlike the behavior therapist (see chap. 3, this volume). The cognitive therapist's role is to listen, teach, and encourage, whereas the client's role is to disclose private thoughts, learn new ways of thinking, and implement that learning.

The manner by which the cognitive therapist teaches tends to be *Socratic*. That is, the therapist asks questions intended to elicit the distorted quality of clients' thinking and to assist in identifying more rational alternatives. The therapist is like a catalyst and guide to logical thinking.

As cognitive therapists work to identify problems and generate solutions, they tenaciously challenge clients to use specific, concrete, and measurable descriptions. In this way, the faulty information processes and assumptions that are the cause of clients' problems can be specified, then systematically eliminated or modified. Therapist and client collaborate like coinvestigators seeking to test the validity of the client's hypotheses.

Cognitive therapists take the principle of collaboration very seriously. Given that the therapist recognizes the need to be active in the therapeutic process, so too must the client. Clients are expected to not only actively participate in session but also to carry out homework assignments and implement new skills in their everyday lives.

Evolution and Variations

Cognitive therapy has been absorbed into behavioral therapies, with "cognitive–behavioral therapy" (CBT) being the second most common self-description of current therapists after "eclectic" (see chap. 1, this volume). Cognitive therapy has expanded tremendously, although primarily on a plane of breadth, rather than depth (Dobson & Pusch, 1993). This is to say that the basic rationale has been proven to be applicable to a broad number of personal problems. Less advance has taken place in "deepening" its epistemological foundation, however. This is not to say cognitive therapy is in any way stagnant, and there have certainly been a number of innovative developments.

Structural psychotherapy is part of an integrative trend in cognitive therapy as theorists and therapists incorporate the rationalist worldview by way of a constructivist rationale (see chap. 10, this volume). Drawing on a decade of research and experience, Vittorio Guidano and Giovanni Lotti (1983) concluded that the full complexity of emotional difficulties could only be understood if the active role of an individual's knowledge of self and the perceived world was taken into account. The *validity* of knowing processes is thereby replaced with the idea of their *viability* (Guidano, 1991). Guidano and Lotti drew heavily from Bowlby's (1977) attachment theory (also based on the rationalist worldview) to explain that our understanding of ourselves and the world is influenced by significant childhood relationships. Guidano (1987, 1991) expanded on the therapeutic implications of this rationale by arguing that the change processes of therapy are to have clients disengage from perturbing beliefs and reject old views of the self and world. Change tasks used by the structural therapist are the same as those of other cognitive therapists. Given that objective reality is not taken for granted, however, the goal of therapy becomes a "personal revolution" in which the client adopts new, more functional views of the self and world, which may or may not be "realistic" (Guidano, 1991).

Dialectical behavior therapy (DBT), despite its name, is a predominantly cognitive therapy. Developed by Marsha Linehan (1943–; Linehan, 1987) for the treatment of suicidal behavior, it has been empirically demonstrated to be effective for borderline personality disorder (Linehan, 1993a), dissociative disorders (Barley et al., 1993), and drug abuse (Linehan, 1993b). DBT involves an extensive program of cognitive skills training to enable the client to tolerate previously intolerable emotions such as guilt, shame, and anger. Problem behaviors are analyzed in great depth for precipitants and consequences that lead to, elicit, maintain, or reinforce them. Solutions are then developed that address impediments to skillful behavior by changing reinforcement patterns, overcoming inhibitions through exposure, cognitive modification, and direct teaching of skills. Once self-destructive behaviors are reduced or eliminated, behaviors that interfere with the client's quality of life are targeted. Individual therapy is typically augmented with group therapy to address interpersonal, emotional regulation, and distress tolerance skills. The groups are structured around weekly didactic skills training modules. DBT is somewhat unique in addressing how difficult the therapeutic work is for therapists by encouraging the formation of consultation teams to help therapists problem-solve treatment strategies and remain faithful to the treatment protocol, empathic, and psychologically healthy.

Cognitive–analytic therapy (CAT) was developed by Anthony Ryle (1949–) and integrates psychodynamic and cognitive therapies (Ryle, 1989, 1995, 2005). CAT focuses on identifying how personal problems are made worse by the habitual reliance on the very strategies enlisted to cope with them. These problematic coping strategies are understood as arising out of solutions to clients' early life experiences. The focus of treatment is on recognizing how these solutions originated and how they can be adapted and improved to enable effective coping in the present. After an assessment of the client's personality structure and difficulty, the CA therapist develops a contract with the client for a set number of sessions and concrete goals. Once the therapist has a clearer sense of the client's problematic coping strategy, a reformulation letter is drafted and given to the client. This letter describes the client's persistent negative patterns and how the client is responsible for the problems that prompted them to seek therapy. It then becomes the template for the treatment goals to be achieved by using a variety of cognitive and behavioral change tasks in the remaining sessions. The therapeutic relationship is understood as both a manifestation of the client's difficulties and a means for challenging the client's interpersonal expectations. Thus, the psychoanalytic concepts of transference and countertransference are reconceptualized in observable, procedural terms (Ryle, 1994).

Schema therapy was developed by Jeffrey Young (1950–) for treating personality disorders and other chronic problems as an adaptation of Beck's cognitive therapy (Young, Klosko, & Weishaar, 2003). When dealing with these entrenched problems, the schema therapist does not assume that the client will present with specific difficulties or goals, participate fully and actively, be able to use tasks independently, or readily establish a therapeutic relationship. Schema therapy instead addresses core cognitive schemas that are the product of early childhood interpersonal relationships. These tend to be stable and elaborated throughout a lifetime of self-fulfilling relationships. In addition to the typical cognitive change tasks, therefore, schema therapy places greater emphasis on the therapeutic relationship as an opportunity for the client to alter maladaptive schemas. Assuming that these schemas developed because core needs were not met in childhood, the schema therapist attempts to create a therapeutic relationship in which the client's unmet emotional needs are met. Clients who were traumatized by others in childhood, for example, are provided a relationship in which the therapist strives to be completely trustworthy, honest, and genuine. Likewise, a client who was deprived in childhood is given an engaged, connected, and guiding experience where advice is provided when requested (Young et al., 2003).

The Successful Underachiever

Danielle was married with one child, owned and operated her own travel agency, and was unhappy with her life. Although she had all of the outward signs of success, she felt as if she would never really lived up to her potential. Her friends told her that she was experiencing "empty-nest syndrome" because her son was grown up and on the verge of leaving home, but she thought such ideas were silly excuses. She did think something was wrong, however, and wanted to get rid of or at least control her unpleasant feelings, so she decided to see a therapist. Danielle was concerned that most psychotherapists would have ideas as silly as her friends' or worse ("If crystals or past lives are involved, I'm out of there"), so she did some research and found one who described his methods as scientifically proven.

Danielle was impressed with how astutely her therapist focused on what was concerning her. She liked the precision he brought to what had felt like vague feelings and how he explained that they were linked to her thinking. She left the first session feeling optimistic and was even glad to have some "homework" to do; she was finally doing something about her unhappiness. She spent the next week keeping track of her "automatic thoughts" and even developed a few ideas about how to test their accuracy.

During the course of her therapy, Danielle came to see how errors in her thinking were making her unhappy. At first she felt foolish as she discovered how illogical she could be and considered dropping out to avoid further embarrassment. However, when her therapist reminded her of how she successfully made the transition in her business from storefront to Internet based and that she could apply the same talents to learning new ways of thinking, she felt deeply validated and encouraged.

Danielle came to understand that she tended to see any failures and even minor successes as indicative of her being fundamentally inadequate. She learned to identify these distortions (her therapist called it "dichotomous thinking") and to replace them with more reality-based interpretations, such as "Nobody's perfect, and mistakes don't mean I'm a failure as a person; I can fix them or learn from them and do better next time." She observed that as she became more adept at thinking adaptively, she felt more content more often in her work and in her relationships.

Therapy ended once Danielle could see that she had achieved the goals she and her therapist had established early in therapy. She returned for two planned "booster sessions" 3 and 6 months after termination, in which she and her therapist reviewed her continued progress and developed a few new strategies for managing her feelings of loss as her son prepared to go away to college.

Learning Task

Cognitive therapies are exquisitely sensitive to language as a reflection of how we think. In an effort to begin to sensitize yourself to the ways that people express themselves with language that reflects dysfunctional thinking, try the exercise described in Exhibit 7.1. Be careful not to point the dysfunctional thoughts out to people too often, if at all, as you will probably find they become annoyed with you. Rather, use the task as an opportunity to educate yourself about how common distorted cognitions are. At the end of each day, review your notes and consider whether any themes are present and what effective language you might substitute for the distorted thoughts you have identified. Can you think of any clients you have worked with who had similar distortions?

Your Reflective Journal

A useful idea from cognitive therapy is the *thought–feeling–behavior cycle* that can occur in particular personal and interpersonal situations. For example, take a few moments to relax and think of a situation in which you were criticized. Try to remember everything you can about the situation: who was there, where you were, and so forth. Now remember

EXHIBIT 7.1

Tracking Dysfunctional Language

Keep a small notebook (or other recording device) and record dysfunctional thoughts as expressed in your language and the language of others. For example,

- *arbitrary inference*—drawing a specific conclusion without supporting evidence;
- *selective abstraction*—conceptualizing a situation based on a detail taken out of context;
- *overgeneralizing*—abstracting a general rule from an isolated incident and applying it to unrelated situations;
- *magnification–minimalization*—treating something as far more or less significant than it actually is;
- *personalizing*—inaccurately attributing events to oneself; and
- *dichotomous thinking*—categorizing events in terms of extremes, such as "all or nothing."

what your thought or thoughts were in response to that criticism, followed by what your feelings and behavior were in response to that thought. Next, pick an alternative, more positive thought and imagine the cycle through. In your reflective journal, record how easy or difficult you found this exercise. Do the results of this exercise inform you about your affinity for the cognitive approach? Why or why not? What might it take to convince you of the merits of cognitive therapy?

Summary

The intellectual environment of the early 1960s was fertile ground for the growth of cognitive considerations in psychotherapeutic practice. The limitations of focusing solely on behaviors and the influence of information-processing models derived from computing science were prompting researchers and practitioners to consider cognitions. Aaron T. Beck and Albert Ellis had been independently developing their cognitive approaches to therapy in response to their dissatisfaction with psychoanalysis and found a welcoming audience. With its rational and objective underpinnings, cognitive therapy readily gathered empirical support, further solidifying its popularity. Cognitive therapy is based on the belief that people perceive, interpret, and assign meanings to life events through cognitive processes. Problems in living and emotional distress are understood as being the result of misperceptions, misinterpretations, or dysfunctional interpretations of situations. The cognitive therapist attempts to help clients recognize and then replace their faulty information processes with adaptive ones. After integrating with the behavior therapies, today cognitive–behavioral therapy is the most popular system of psychotherapy practiced.

Further Resources

CASE READINGS

Beck, A. T., & Young, J. E. (1985). Cognitive therapy of depression. In D. Barlow (Ed.), *Clinical handbook of psychological disorders: A step-by-step treatment manual* (pp. 206–244). New York: Guilford Press.

Ellis, A. (1971). *Growth through reason: Verbatim cases in rational–emotive therapy.* Hollywood, CA: Wilshire Books.

Ellis, A., & Dryden, W. (1996). Transcript of a demonstration session, with comments on the session by Windy Dryden and Albert Ellis. In W. Dryden, *Practical skills in rational emotive behavior therapy* (pp. 91–117). London: Whurr.

Freeman, A., & Dattilio, E. M. (Eds.). (1992). *Comprehensive casebook of cognitive therapy.* New York: Plenum.

RECOMMENDED READING

Beck, A. T., Rush, A. J., Shaw, B. F., & Emery, G. (1979). *Cognitive therapy of depression.* New York: Guilford Press.

Beck, J. S. (1995). *Cognitive therapy: Basics and beyond.* New York: Guilford Press.

Burns, D. (1980). *Feeling good.* New York: Morrow.

Ellis, A., & Dryden, W. (1997). *The practice of rational emotive behavior therapy.* New York: Springer.

Freeman, A., Simon, K., Buetler, L., & Arkowitz, H. (Eds.). (1989). *Comprehensive handbook of cognitive therapy.* New York: Plenum Press.

RECOMMENDED VIEWING

American Psychological Association (Producer). (2006). *Cognitive therapy with Judith S. Beck, PhD* [Motion picture]. (Available from the American Psychological Association, 750 First Street, NE, Washington, DC 20002-4242)

American Psychological Association (Producer). (2007). *Schema therapy with Jeffrey E. Young, PhD* [Motion picture]. (Available from the American Psychological Association, 750 First Street, NE, Washington, DC 20002-4242)

Beck Institute for Cognitive Therapy and Research (Producer). (1979). *Cognitive therapy of depression: Interview #1 (patient with hopelessness problem) with Aaron T. Beck, MD* [Motion picture]. (Available from the Beck Institute for Cognitive Therapy and Research, One Belmont Avenue, Suite 700, Bala Cynwyd, PA 19004-1610)

Psychological & Educational Films (Producer). (1965). *Three approaches to Psychotherapy I: Part 3. Albert Ellis (rational–emotive therapy)* [Motion picture]. (Available from Psychological & Educational Films, 3334 East Coast Highway, #252, Corona del Mar, CA 92625-2328)

Psychological & Educational Films (Producer). (1986). *Three approaches to Psychotherapy III: Part 3. Aaron T. Beck (cognitive therapy)* [Motion picture]. (Available from Psychological & Educational Films, 3334 East Coast Highway, #252, Corona del Mar, CA 92625-2328)

Systemic 8

The idea that the family is an important determinant of psychological well-being is certainly a very old one. The role of family factors in psychotherapeutic treatment planning and delivery has been recognized at least as far back as Sigmund Freud (1909/1959a) and Alfred Adler (1931). The profession of social work, in particular, has long considered the family to be the primary unit of concern. Indeed, social workers have played a central role in the expansion of systemic therapy, having provided family life education since the early 1900s.

It was during the 1960s, however, that a number of social movements coalesced into a ground swell that would ultimately produce systemic therapy. The momentum of the established family life education movement, the growing dissatisfaction with the medical–psychiatric approach that would eventually become the psychiatric survivors movement, and the optimism of the burgeoning North American human potential movement all looked to improve the lives of individuals through changes in society. Direct action, public protests, and other methods of social change were being used on a large scale, with encouraging results. There was a palpable sense of excitement and of participating in something truly innovative.

Caught up in the enthusiasm of the day, psychotherapists sought to incorporate a broader interpersonal context into their approach to therapy. They began to invite families into session, producing dramatic changes in how therapy was practiced and conceptualized (Guerin, 1976). Problems that were previously attributed to the individual were now apparent as symptoms of a systemic disorder—often but not necessarily the family—and a truly collectivist rationale (see chap. 1, this volume) gradually developed.

It was perhaps inevitable that systemic therapy grew out of the work of a number of different individuals and groups: Gregory Bateson and those working within his communication project, Norbert Weiner's cybernetic theory, and Ludwig von Bertalanffy's general systems theory.

Gregory Bateson (1904–1980; see Figure 8.1) came to psychotherapy through his research into paradoxical communication patterns in animals and humans (Bateson, 1972). As an anthropologist, he was looking for evidence that could be experienced by observing the lives of others. Bateson began his communication project in 1952 and employed Jay Haley and John Weakland—both also anthropologists—to join him in studying unique modes of communication: children in groups, training of Seeing Eye dogs, and the speech of people diagnosed with schizophrenia. In 1954, Bateson shifted focus exclusively to schizophrenic communication, and Don Jackson joined the project as a consultant psychiatrist.

The most significant—and infamous—result of their work was the development of the concept of the *double bind* (Bateson, Jackson, Haley, & Weakland, 1956). Bateson et al. (1956) proposed that the disordered speech common to individuals diagnosed with schizophrenia is a response to conflicting messages in the communications from family members. They gave the example of a mother who, made anxious by closeness and affection, says, "Don't you love your mother? Come and give me a hug." Yet when her son approaches her she recoils and stiffens. Her child is thus placed in a double bind. If he refuses the hug, he will be criticized for not responding to the overt request. If he complies, he fails to respond to the nonverbal message that his mother does not actually want a hug. His resulting speech appears to be illogical.

Bateson et al. (1956) did not—as is commonly criticized—restrict their explanation of the causes of schizophrenia to mothers. They also described how hospitals are rife with double binds:

> Since hospitals exist for the benefit of their personnel as well as—
> as much as—more than—for the patient's benefit, there will be
> contradictions at times in sequences where actions are taken
> 'benevolently' for the patient when actually they are intended to keep
> the staff more comfortable. We would assume that whenever the
> system is organized for hospital purposes and it is announced to the
> patient that the actions are for *his* benefit, then the schizophrenogenic
> situation is being perpetrated. (Bateson et al., 1956, p. 263)

The idea that psychological problems as bizarre and dramatic as schizophrenia could be the result of relationships with other people rather than something disturbed within the individual was a radical one. Bateson's theory of the double bind thereby established an objective and experien-

FIGURE 8.1

Gregory Bateson. Courtesy of the Institute for Intercultural Studies, Inc., New York. Photograph by Fred Roll.

tial understanding of psychiatric symptoms, which was then applied to other human activities such as humor, art, and psychotherapy.

Cybernetic theory was developed by the mathematician Norbert Weiner (1894–1964) during World War II to understand the process of information exchange in machines such as missile guidance systems. One of the major contributions of cybernetic theory was the idea of *homeostasis*, whereby machine systems regulate themselves through feedback loops to maintain a steady state (Weiner, 1948).

Human beings are a particular type of system with both internal homeostatic processes (e.g., body temperature, emotional distress) and external ones (e.g., environmental demands, interpersonal relationships). Of particular interest to budding systemic theorists was the role of feedback loops in an individual's interpersonal environment. They began to see how interpersonal relationships—such as the double bind—could be understood as feedback processes that maintain the system's status quo. Communications between individuals were seen as a form of feedback that could also provide the stimulus for change. If there is a change in the process or content of communication within a system, then the individuals who are a part of that system will vary their internal homeostasis in response to this new feedback.

General systems theory was not the product of any one individual, although Ludwig von Bertalanffy (1901–1972) is generally credited with much of its development. Von Bertalanffy began his theorizing around systems in the physical sciences and later proposed a theoretical model to explain all living systems.

In his book *General Systems Theory: Foundations, Developments, Applications*, von Bertalanffy (1968) suggested that a system comprises many elements that interact together as part of a whole structure. Each element cannot be considered or examined individually; it must be viewed within the context of its interactions. All systems are understood as tending to restore themselves after disturbances, resulting in a state of equilibrium. This process fit nicely with the cybernetic concept of homeostasis. It is easy to understand when considering a chemical reaction or some other such simple physical system that contains identical elements isolated from their environment.

Human systems are much more complex, however. Unlike molecules in a chemical reaction, a human being is a system within a system of other human beings. Human systems are constantly maintaining themselves in a two-way exchange of information internally and externally with other systems. This results in a *circular causality* whereby any cause is an effect of a previous cause and in turn becomes the cause of a later event, and so on. This means that a human system cannot achieve a state of total equilibrium (Buckley, 1967). It also creates a circumstance in which systems can change toward lower or higher levels of organization and function (von Bertalanffy, 1968). The systemic therapist's role then becomes one of introducing new information into the system that will set in motion change toward more organized functioning at a higher homeostatic level.

The net result of these influences (i.e., 1960s social optimism, Bateson, cybernetic theory, and general systems theory) was an approach to psychotherapy quite unlike any that had been practiced before. Systemic therapy shifted the focus away from the individual and toward the social context, and the repercussions were nothing short of revolutionary.

Systemic Rationale

Systemic therapy is based on the idea that a change in the complex, repeating sequences of an intimate group will result in the creation of more alternatives and greater variety in people's lives. This implies that how a problem persists is much more relevant to therapy than how the problem originated, and that problem persistence depends mainly on social interaction, with the behavior of one person both stimulated and shaped by the response of others. Moreover, the duration and continuation of a problem are dependent on what people persistently and currently do (or do not do) to control, prevent, or eliminate the problem.

Systemic therapy thus focuses on observable (i.e., objective) patterns of communication between individuals in the present (i.e., experiential) who are related to each other in some significant way. Not unlike their epistemological cousins, the humanists, systemic therapists assume that systems—of which families are typically but not necessarily the most important—are inherently self-correcting and self-actualizing. Individual problems are assumed to be byproducts of attempts to respond to pressures on the system and persist only if they are maintained by ongoing current interactions between the person with the problem and others. In a corresponding manner, if such problem-maintaining patterns are changed or eliminated, the problem will change, be resolved, or vanish, regardless of its nature, origin, or duration.

A personal problem, then, can be thought of as the product of a vicious cycle that involves a negative feedback loop between a behavior or quality someone considers undesirable and an action intended to solve or eliminate it. The solution makes perfectly good sense to the participants, yet its consequences serve only to confirm each person's unsatisfying reality. How such a cycle began is likely to remain obscure, and what caused it is a more-or-less arbitrary matter. Given that problems persist because of people's attempts to solve them, therapy consists of identifying and deliberately altering these well-intentioned solutions, thereby breaking the feedback loops that are actually maintaining the problems. If this can be done—even in a small way—less of the solution will lead to less of the problem, leading to less of the solution, and so on.

Systemic Goals

Systemic therapy strives to promote clearer and more constructive interactional patterns within the system, thereby allowing individual members of the system to become fully functioning. Ideally, therapy will result in *second-order change* (Fraser & Solovey, 2006). First-order change involves improvements in symptoms expressed by an individual, without changing the organization of the system itself. First-order change usually involves logical solutions to problems attributed to qualities possessed by individual members. Negative feedback is used in an attempt to do the opposite of whatever the problem is. Such changes are not expected to endure, however. Second-order change involves fundamental changes in the system's organization and function through positive feedback. The system, in effect, is changed. Communication patterns and transactional rules are changed so that the presenting problem is no longer necessary to the system's functioning. If interactions and roles are too rigid and restrictive, the goal will be for them to become more growth promoting. If the system is too chaotic, the goal of therapy will be to have the system become more supportive.

Systemic Change Processes

Systemic therapy works to interrupt dysfunctional feedback loops to unbalance the homeostatic processes of the individual's social system. The individuals within the system will first try to solve problems by doing what they have always done (i.e., negative feedback). The systemic therapist strives to introduce new information (i.e., positive feedback) into the system that thwarts the members of the system from doing more of the same. This information is introduced in session or as homework so that change takes place in the present functioning of the system. As the members experience the struggle of this challenge, the rules of interaction change, viewpoints are altered, and old experiences are seen in a new light. A revised context emerges in which new patterns are made possible. These new patterns create opportunities for the system's inherent self-correcting and self-actualizing processes to be mobilized. Although the precise nature of the resulting change is unpredictable, if it involves the rules of interaction of the system, the individual members will experience a more satisfying reality.

Note that insight is not required or even particularly desirable. In fact, change through systemic therapy can be retarded if the therapist explains the rationale of the interventions. Better that the members of the system struggle together to incorporate and accommodate the new information introduced by the task.

Systemic Change Tasks

The systemic therapist draws from a wide range of interventions designed to interrupt social interactions. Sharing an experiential orientation with their humanist cousins, systemic therapists favor a spontaneous, individualized approach. Some of the more commonly used types of tasks are described in this section.

Reframing presents the family system with new, unpredictable information in which undesired symptoms are described as being a function of desired family processes (Coyne, 1985). For example, in a family in which an adolescent complains about having her privacy invaded, the therapist might describe the parents as wanting to make sure she is safe, and not knowing how to, given that she is now older and more mature. The family is thus invited to change communication and relationship patterns in light of this new understanding. The focus of intervention is not on changing the facts of the behavior; it is rather that new responses to it are made possible.

Therapeutic double bind involves prescribing the symptom to interrupt feedback loops (Watzlawick, Weakland, & Fisch, 1974). For example, a person with excessive worrying is asked to worry at certain times for a specific period of time, or a quarrelling couple is instructed to argue under circumscribed circumstances. Families have the choice of (a) continuing to manifest the behavior, thus demonstrating that it has at least some voluntary component that can be enlisted for change, or (b) not manifesting the behavior, in which case the problem is gone. A variant of the therapeutic double bind is an *ordeal*, in which an unpleasant task is prescribed that clients must perform when they show symptomatic behavior to interrupt feedback loops (Haley, 1984). Another variant is *reductio ad absurdum* (Whitaker, 1975), in which the family is instructed to exaggerate a communication pattern to highlight the absurdity of the feedback loops within the system.

Enactments involve directing the family to role play important activities to introduce new information about structural dysfunction. The emphasis is on acting out difficulties to emphasize observable patterns and avoiding talk about conflicts or complaints. The therapist—and the family—can thereby "see" that problems and interventions can be proposed immediately and tried out. A famous enactment example is Salvador Minuchin asking a family with an anorexic daughter to bring lunch to the session and enact a family meal (Minuchin, Rosman, & Baker, 1978). The therapist can then use such tasks as *exaggeration*, in which the therapist makes prominent the family's communication pattern to highlight structural dysfunction; *blocking*, in which family interactions that maintain dysfunctional structures are prohibited to unbalance homeostasis; and *marking boundaries*, in which the therapist prescribes activities that establish functional structures such as the parents collaborating to discipline children.

Family sculpting is a form of therapeutic drama in which family members take turns "directing" the other members into a physical arrangement in the room (Papp, Silverstein, & Carter, 1973). It introduces new information about each individual's perception of his or her relationship with each family member, particularly with respect to boundaries, subsystems, roles, and alliances. Each individual's experience of altering these sculptures can then be processed to introduce new ways of relating. Family sculpting can be particularly useful for eliciting information about family processes not readily available through verbal report.

Circular questioning is used to help families focus on connections and possibilities rather than symptoms and blame. Several members of the family are asked a question about their perception of some aspect of same family event or relationship. So if a parent says, "Our child won't listen," the therapist might ask, "Who gets most upset when your child doesn't listen?" and "What does mom do when dad gets upset?" and then ask the child, "How would your parents get along without you?" (Penn, 1982). This enables the pattern of underlying conflicts to be elicited without directly confronting the family's homeostatic processes and highlights the circular causality within the system.

Therapeutic Relationship

The systemic therapist relates to the family/system as an ally who has to "join with" them not unlike how an anthropologist does with a culture. Once the therapist has successfully negotiated an engagement with the family/system, strategies for change can then be designed. Minuchin and Fishman (1981) described the situation as like being in the same boat with the family, with the therapist at the helm. The family's role is to follow the therapist's directions and alter their transactions without much explanation by the therapist. The therapist strives for accurate empathy, warmth, and caring, not unlike the humanistic therapist. The systemic therapist is more of an authoritative leader, however, who challenges, confronts, blocks, and disrupts the homeostatic processes within the system out of a belief in the objective reality of the family's functioning. "Less talk, more action" is the systemic therapist's credo. The therapist's verbal contributions to the session are understood as information entered into the family system and thus are understood as and designed to be interventions. This emphasis on the impact of the therapist's verbal contributions, rather than the content, gives the systemic therapeutic relationship a distinctly different quality than most other systems of therapy.

Evolution and Variations

The boon and bane of systemic therapies has been their expansion beyond the family system to appreciate the larger social systems and their influence on the family and individuals, particularly gender expectations (Goodrich, Rampage, Ellman, & Halstead, 1988; Silverstein & Goodrich, 2003) and culture (McDaniel, Lusterman, & Philpot, 2001; Mikesell, Lusterman, & McDaniel, 1995). The feminist critique in particular (see chap. 9, this volume) attacked the systemic approach for ignoring gender power inequalities and thereby fostering them (Hare-Mustin, 1978). The net result has been a splintering of the field and a dispersion of practitioners. Where once there was a feeling of camaraderie (Framo, 1996), there is now a steady decrease in memberships of family therapy associations and of attendance at family therapy conferences. In addition, almost all of the freestanding family therapy institutes and clinics have closed. Why this is the case is difficult to say. A systemic explanation would be that times have changed and the social zeitgeist is no longer one in which the power of the collective is dominant. Indeed, most social commentators describe current Western social and political orientation as much more individually focused, conservative, and even somewhat anticollective than it was in the 1960s and 1970s. This does not mean that family therapy is dead, however. In fact, although much reduced from its heyday, there remains an enthusiastic and committed—albeit small—following of what is still a unique and valuable approach to therapy.

All major systems of psychotherapy—psychodynamic (Bowen, 1990), behavioral (N. Jacobson & Margolin, 1979), existential (Kempler, 1981), person-centered (Satir, 1988), gestalt (S. M. Johnson, 1996), cognitive (Dattilio, 1998), feminist (Silverstein & Goodrich, 2003) and constructivist (White & Epston, 1990)—have been applied to families. All but feminist are not true systemic approaches, however, in that they are not grounded in collectivism. Most are, rather, variations of individual therapies delivered with more than one member of a family present.

Structural family therapy was developed by Salvador Minuchin (1921–) and colleagues in a residential institution for boys from Philadelphia's ghettos. *Families of the Slums: An Exploration of Their Structure and Treatment* (Minuchin, Montalvo, Guerney, Rosman, & Schumer, 1967) was revolutionary for arguing that the behavior of these boys was not the result of individual pathology but was survival based. Minuchin later expanded his work to helping families with eating disorders and other presenting problems. The structural family therapist works to correct dysfunctional structures within families. The most important of these structures are the *boundaries* or rules that define who participates and how they participate in various organizations (e.g., parent–child, husband–wife), thereby regulating the amount and type of contact between family members. Overly rigid boundaries result in *disengagement*, whereby family members act as if they have little to do with one another, leaving individual members disconnected. Overly permeable boundaries result in *enmeshment*, whereby family members intrude into the domains of others, leaving individual members disorganized. The structural therapist attempts to create powerful in-session experiences that prompt moments of crisis. These efforts usually take the form of exaggeration of the family's habitual patterns of relating to one another. Taken to their extreme, such patterns are obviously nonfunctional, and in these moments family members are often open to considering alternative methods of relating to one another.

Strategic therapy is a direct offspring of Bateson's communication project. Paul Watzlawick (1921–2007), John Weakland (1919–1995), and Richard Fisch (1926–) and others formed the Brief Therapy Center at the Mental Research Institute in Palo Alto, California, to apply what they had learned to psychotherapy (Watzlawick, Weakland, & Fisch, 1974). They also incorporated the uncommon therapeutic techniques of Arizona psychiatrist Milton Erikson into an approach that sometimes, although not always, involves entire families in therapy. Strategic therapists aim to use expedient, focused interventions to bring about change in the system. The problems that prompt help seeking are understood not as problems in and of themselves but rather as the result of the family's efforts to deal with the normal disquietudes that are the natural part of family life. Families who seek help typically have become stuck in a pattern of repeating unsuccessful solutions to everyday problems. The strategic therapist seeks to discover the family rules that underlie these problem-solving-maintaining behaviors and then introduce new rules. These new rules are created by helping the family to adopt a different understanding of the problems that they are trying to solve, so that a different solution is evoked or no solution is necessary. *Reframing* (see the Systemic Change Tasks section earlier in this chapter) and *paradoxical directives*—instructions to not change or to intentionally produce symptoms (Haley & Richeport-Haley, 2003)— are the primary change tasks of the strategic therapist.

Milan systemic therapy was developed by Mara Selvini Palazzoli (1916–1999), Luigi Boscolo, Gianfranco Cecchin (1932–2004), and Giuliana Prata (Selvini Palazzoli, Boscolo, Cecchin, & Prata, 1978). They were influenced by the work of Gregory Bateson and unlike the strategic therapy group have remained true to Bateson's original focus on communication. In the classic version of Milan systemic therapy, sessions were conducted with a team of therapists who observed the therapist in session with a family from behind a one-way mirror. The team would formulate a treatment strategy and provide it to the therapist during a break in the session. These strategies usually involved a *positive connotation*—a positive reframe (see the Systemic Change Tasks section)—or a *therapeutic ritual* similar to the strategic paradoxical directive. The group has since split into two, with Boscolo and Cecchin adopting an approach in which the family's ability to grow and change is facilitated by *circular questioning* (see the Systemic Change Tasks section) and the presentation of a systemic hypothesis that provides the family with a new way of viewing their problems

(Cecchin, 1987; Tomm, 1987). Selvini Palazzoli and Prata have gone on to develop an *invariant prescription* intervention in which the parents join in a secret coalition against the other family members to develop a stable alliance from which to alter pathogenic family interactions (Prata, 1990).

Life Is Short

Janie, 20 years old, was all but physically dragged into the clinic by her mother. She clearly did not want to be there. Her mother said that Janie spent her time "doing nothing" except "getting stoned with her friends." She did, in fact, look rather vacant.

Janie said that she did not know what all the fuss was about: She was not getting into any trouble, she "worked hard to stay out of her parents' way" (said with a subtle, ironic smile), and she was happy with her friends. She felt that her mother was too bossy and should just leave her alone. After all, she was just "doing what [her] friends were doing, and their parents weren't giving them grief," and neither was her father.

They agreed that mornings were the worst. Her father typically left for work before Janie was awake. Then she and her mother would almost always get into a shouting match, with her mother "nagging" her to do something productive with her day and her life. This usually occurred as her mother rushed off to work. Janie would be so upset that she would feel the need to "toke up" to calm down.

Janie's mother expressed frustration with her daughter's lack of initiative and helplessness over her inability to get her to "do something with her life." She also said she was disappointed with her husband's indifference. She said she felt very alone and unsupported, with no time to live her own, very full, life.

The therapist instructed them to return with Janie's father for another session. They both expressed doubt that he would attend. The therapist remained firm, stating that she had every confidence that they would find a way to get him to come in.

When Janie returned with her mother and father, the therapist listened to his version of Janie's situation, observed how he positioned himself in the room, and noted how and when he spoke. The therapist saw that he was indeed uninvolved with his daughter and prescribed that for the next 2 weeks he arrange to have breakfast with Janie while her mother left for work on her own schedule. Her mother was instructed to refrain from making any comments about Janie's day or her lack of motivation.

When Janie and her parents returned, Janie was happier and more animated. She said that she was fascinated to learn from her father over breakfast that he had a "checkered past." When he was her age, he had nearly flunked out of school before finally finding what he wanted to do with his life. They talked about her not necessarily wanting to do what others thought was best for her, and he said he understood because he had felt the same way. She was surprised to find him quite supportive of her interest in electronic music. Her parents reported with obvious pride that she had been accepted into a school for video game music composition.

The therapist asked whether they had any more concerns, to which they replied they did not, and everyone said their goodbyes.

Learning Task

It is generally accepted that to properly practice systemic therapy, one has to be aware of the interpersonal patterns and social meanings that one takes for granted. Although there are a number of in-class exercises available that are wonderfully facilitative (e.g., Kane, 1996), you can also undertake an individual task (see Exhibit 8.1) designed to highlight your own family-of-origin influences. Once you have completed the task in Exhibit 8.1, record your reactions in your reflective journal: Was it difficult to ask your family member about certain aspects? Do you feel different about yourself or the person you interviewed? Do you now have questions you would like to ask other people in your family? How do you think your psychotherapeutic practice might change in light of what you have learned?

Your Reflective Journal

Most people find systemic therapy, with its emphasis on the collective rather than the individual, to be rather different from their ideas about what psychotherapy should be. Do you feel similarly, or not? How so? Can you imagine yourself working with a group of individuals toward a collective goal and not toward individual goals? Take some time to record how the systemic rationale is congruent with or discrepant from your assumptions about how therapy ought to work. Are there other aspects of systemic therapy that are salient for you? What do they tell you about your affinity for the approach? What are the social or familial expectations of you around being a therapist? Are these expectations facilitative or hindering of your personal goals in regard to becoming a therapist? That is, do important other people in your life want you to become a therapist? If they do, is this what you want? If they do not, how does this impact your becoming one?

Summary

Systemic therapy was developed by theorists who were not from an individualist tradition and is based on principles from outside of the human sciences. Gregory Bateson, an anthropologist, drew on cybernetic theory

EXHIBIT 8.1

A Family of Origin Exercise: Interview a Family Member

Interview someone important in your family of origin—usually your mother or father, or perhaps a sibling or relative who played a pivotal role in your life as you were growing up. If your family member is geographically close enough, perform the interview in person. If your family member is too far away, arrange a telephone interview. Try to approach this person as if you know almost nothing about him or her. Ask your family member about his or her own childhood and events that shaped his or her life. Ideally, record the interview for later review. Even if you do, make sure to take notes.

You will probably notice that your interviewee leaves out important information, such as long periods in his or her life, or fails to talk about a parent. Be persistent. Ask your family member to elaborate or fill in missing facts. Notice how difficult this can be.

and general systems theory to understand the patterns of communication in schizophrenia. The enthusiastic adoption of systemic thinking was fueled by dissatisfaction with existing psychotherapies that looked for the source and solution to problems within individuals. True systemic therapy—as opposed to individually based therapies delivered with one or more family member present—understands individual problems to be the product of dysfunctional processes of the social (usually family) system. Change comes about by altering the manner in which individuals relate to one another so that the system is forced to reconfigure its processes. Reframing, double binds, enactments, circular questioning, and family sculpting are among the tasks used to stress the system. Systemic therapy is much less practiced today than during its heyday, although the importance of the individual's social system is arguably now a generally accepted clinical fact.

Further Resources

CASE READINGS

Haley, J., & Hoffman, L. (Eds.). (1967). *Techniques of family therapy*. New York: Basic Books.

Lawson, D. M., & Prevatt, F. F. (Eds.). (1998). *Casebook in family therapy*. Pacific Grove, CA: Wadsworth.

Napier, A. Y., & Whitaker, C. A. (1978). *The family crucible*. New York: Harper & Row.

Walsh, W. M. (1991). *Case studies in family therapy: An integrative approach.* West Nyack, NY: Allyn & Bacon.

RECOMMENDED READING

Bateson, G. (1972). *Steps to an ecology of mind.* New York: Ballantine Books.

Boscolo, L., Cecchin, G., Hoffman, L., & Penn, P. (1987). *Milan systemic family therapy: Conversations in theory and practice.* New York: Basic Books.

Hoffman, L. (1981). *Foundations of family therapy: A conceptual framework for systems change.* New York: Basic Books.

Liddle, H. A., Santistebaun, D. A., Levant, R. F., & Bray, J. H. (2002). *Family psychology: Science-based interventions.* Washington, DC: American Psychological Association.

Minuchin, S. (1974). *Families and family therapy.* Cambridge, MA: Harvard University Press.

Whitaker, C. A., & Blumberry, W. M. (1988). *Dancing with the family: A symbolic-experiential approach.* New York: Gardner.

RECOMMENDED VIEWING

American Association for Marriage and Family Therapy (Producer). (1984). *Unfolding the laundry with Salvador Minuchin* [Motion picture]. (Available from the American Association for Marriage and Family Therapy, 112 South Alfred Street, Alexandria, VA 22314-3061)

American Association for Marriage and Family Therapy (Producer). (1989). *Mad or bad? with Paul Watzlawick* [Motion picture]. (Available from the American Association for Marriage and Family Therapy, 112 South Alfred Street, Alexandria, VA 22314-3061)

American Association for Marriage and Family Therapy (Producer). (1994) *Minuchin, in person* [Motion picture]. (Available from the American Association for Marriage and Family Therapy, 112 South Alfred Street, Alexandria, VA 22314-3061)

Blumberry, W. M., & Tenenbaum, S. (Producers). (1986). *A different kind of caring: Family therapy with Carl Whitaker* [Motion picture]. (Available from Brunner/Mazel, 19 Union Square, New York 10003-3304)

Triangle Press (Producer). (2000). *Compulsory therapy: A case of violence with Jay Haley* [Motion picture]. (Available from moreFOCUS Group Inc., 5928 Geiger Court, Carlsbad, CA 92008-7305)

Feminist 9

F eminist scholars like to say that instead of a founding father, feminist therapy has many mothers (L. S. Brown, 1994): no leaders or gurus; no Freud, Rogers, or Perls. That is, feminist practice has developed out of the work of many theorists—predominantly women—who have attempted to apply feminist sociopolitical theory to psychotherapeutic practice. Having said this, Laura S. Brown (1952–; see Figure 9.1) stands out as a theorist who presents feminist therapy as a valid, viable approach to mainstream psychotherapeutic practice.

Feminism emerged in North America out of the civil rights and social change movements of the 1960s that also spawned systemic therapy (see chap. 8, this volume). Although seemingly every aspect of society was being scrutinized for its effect on the quality of individuals' lives, women began to question the particular influence of gender-role socialization (L. W. Sherman & Denmark, 1978). Feminists started to look for ways to take action to effect social changes to institutional forms of sexism and patriarchy that undermine women's rights, human dignity, and health. Prior to this time, the unique distress that women experienced was "the problem that has no name" (Friedan, 1963, p. 15). This conceptualization of women as an oppressed group opened up new ways of thinking about helping individual women through systemic remedies. Male violence against women in particular was reconceptualized as an (extreme) expression of societal values that favor men dominating and controlling women, rather than the product of individual men's psychopathology or women's masochism (Caplan, 1984). This early women's movement es-

FIGURE 9.1

Laura S. Brown. Printed with permission of Laura S. Brown.

tablished battered-women's shelters and rape crisis centers (Worell & Johnson, 2001)—institutions that are still part of our society today.

One of the first women to give form to feminist therapy was Phyllis Chesler (1941–). From her experience as an intern on a psychiatric ward and at a psychoanalytical institute, she saw firsthand how harmful attitudes toward women were ingrained in the training and practice of psychotherapy. She also saw how these attitudes resulted in disastrous consequences for women patients. During the 1950s and 1960s, therapists were taught that women suffer from penis envy, were morally inferior to men, and were innately masochistic, dependent, passive, heterosexual, and monogamous. In her now-classic book *Women and Madness*, Chesler (1972) traced the systemic and often horrific abuses of female patients by male doctors and institutions back to the 16th and 17th centuries. She argued that in a patriarchal mental health system women are often falsely labeled as being "mad" simply because they do not conform to stereotypical feminine roles. She described how women were delivered into treatment by their husbands or families not just because they were depressed, anxious, or schizophrenic but also because they were sexually unresponsive, lesbian, unwilling to marry, victims of sexual molestation, or generally nonconformist. In addition, Chesler noted that most women display psychiatric symptoms that are exaggerations of what society expects of them, such as depression, frigidity, paranoia, psychoneurosis, self-harm, and anxiety. Most men, on the other hand, display diseases consistent with societal expectations of masculinity, such as alcoholism, drug addiction, personality disorders, and brain diseases.

Although the main thesis of her book was not completely new in 1972 (Wilkinson, 1994), Chesler wrote powerful prose backed with unassailable data. Her book electrified a burgeoning feminist consciousness among many of its readers. Women, Chesler (1972) argued, constitute a greater number of psychiatric patients than men not because they are appreciably more ill, but because they are socially identified as the weaker sex—both physically and mentally. Their inferior social role and lack of socially acceptable outlets for personal development lead to long "careers" as psychiatric patients. She established a sound objective basis for the argument that social limitations are inextricably linked to personal health. This rationale remains a central tenet of feminist therapy. As the cofounder of the Association for Women in Psychology and the National Women's Health Network, Chesler became an advocate for the rights of women to voice their experiences.

Miriam Greenspan (1947–) was one of those women who were inspired by Chesler's book. Greenspan channeled that inspiration into writing another groundbreaking book. In *A New Approach to Women and Therapy*, Greenspan (1983) drew particular attention to oppressive myths that therapists labored under that limited women's growth. Most harmful is the myth that problems are located in the client rather than in society's gender role expectations. That is, a failure to appreciate that problems common to women are actually healthy reactions to an unhealthy system. The second myth is that emotional pain can be treated in the same manner as physical pain. Emotional pain—from a feminist perspective—is a symptom of systemic dysfunction and therefore is not in need of being "cured" through medicine. It is the system that is need of a cure. The third myth is that the doctor is the expert and the woman–patient needs to be told what to do or have something done to cure her. Instead, Greenspan proposed that social action and empowerment are the appropriate means by which to help women overcome the systemic forces that are the real cause of their difficulties (Geenspan, 1983).

Jean Baker Miller (1927–2006) was another early pioneer in feminist therapy and theory. In her 1986 book, *Toward a New Psychology of Women*, she presented a view of human development that included a consideration of the distinctly different psychological challenges that women typically face in a patriarchic society. In particular, she described the central role that relationships play in women's development and how women are socialized to adopt negative conceptions of femininity.

Miller argued how concepts of mental health such as autonomy, individuality, and independence are associated with masculinity (J. B. Miller, 1986). These concepts are also embedded in psychotherapies that are—not coincidentally—developed and practiced by men. Traditional psychotherapy is understood as devaluing women's experiences as pathological, rather than addressing how our society neglects and distorts women's true needs (H. Lerner, 1988). The patriarchal view of women's mental health is that women should strive to be an object of desire for a future husband, get married, and subjugate their needs and wants in the service of a husband (Wolowitz, 1972). Being unhappy in this role or rejecting it is seen as pathological, as is the failure to achieve it.

Psychotherapy as viewed from a feminist point of view is seen as being biased by the conceptualization of gender roles as biologically determined, rather than as the product of social forces. The idea that gender roles are innate serves to limit the possibilities and opportunities for women (American Psychological Association, 1975, 1978). This discrimination on the basis of gender is seen as causing oppression of women, rendering them more vulnerable to mental health problems (Walker, 1989).

Feminism, therefore, is based on a collectivist worldview (see chap. 1, this volume) and emphasizes the impact of society in creating and maintaining the problems and issues that women bring into therapy. To behave in a manner congruent with this worldview, feminist therapists challenge assumptions, traditions, professional practices, and societal structures that limit the understanding, treatment, and responsible self-determination of women (Feminist Therapy Institute, 2000).

Feminist Rationale

Feminist therapy is based on feminist political philosophy and analysis, and grounded in the scholarship of the psychology of women and gender (L. S. Brown, 1994). The basic tenets of feminist therapy include recognizing that each individual's personal experiences and situations are reflective of society's attitudes and values. This is captured in the famous feminist slogan, "The personal is political" (Gilbert, 1980). That is, individuals do not possess attributes or flaws that cause their suffering. Emotional distress is not necessarily considered a symptom of pathology, therefore. Rather, the social forces that shape individual experience are at the root of suffering. The most important of these forces for women are gender expectations that restrict opportunities to achieve their full potential. The individual is not seen as the source of distress, even though distress is experienced individually. Instead, if unhealthy, patriarchal social factors are removed or changed, the major source of women's distress will be eliminated, and they will be able to grow as human beings. By changing societal structures, individuals are free to actualize their true selves. This is why feminist therapists engage in social change activities in addition to their work in consulting rooms. While varying in scope and content, such activities are an essential aspect of a feminist perspective (Feminist Therapy Institute, 2000).

In keeping with an objective, experiential—collectivist—epistemology, feminist therapy recognizes that power cannot be given to someone. Power can only be taken away or the individual thwarted in their efforts to express their personal power.

Feminist theory holds that our very sense of self is a product of societal expectations based on our gender. A clear sense of who we are is discouraged to the extent that it conflicts with maintaining the status quo. Thus, feminist therapists are committed to political and social change that equalizes power among men and women and to recognizing and reducing the pervasive influences and insidious effects of oppressive patriarchal attitudes and institutions in society.

Feminist Goals

Feminist therapy has as its goal creating the awareness in women that they belong to a subordinate group that has suffered wrongs, that this condition is not natural but determined by society, and that they must join with other women to remedy these wrongs (G. Lerner, 1993). The development of this *feminist consciousness* allows women to become personally empowered to acquire a wide range of behaviors and an individual identity that is freely chosen rather than determined by societal gender-role expectations.

The client's goals are accepted prima facie—so as not to interfere with her expression of personal power—whereas the means of achieving them are negotiated in a manner consistent with feminist consciousness development. It is not assumed, however, that a goal of therapy will be to soothe the client's distress. Instead, consciousness raising is very likely to result in a disruption of the client's life as she takes action to change the social systems of which she is a part, rather than adjusting to them (Perkins, 1991). Over the course of therapy, the client may well experience an increase in subjective distress where there was previously acceptance and calm (Brabeck & Brown, 1997). Ultimately, she will be free to choose how to respond to the realities of society's expectations.

Feminist Change Processes

Personal change through feminist therapy involves first becoming aware of one's gender-role socialization process. Individual understanding about oneself then forms the basis for understanding the oppression of all women. As long as problems are understood as products of individual deficits or excesses, solutions will be directed toward the individual, rather than toward the appropriate target: changing social circumstances.

Once awareness has been achieved, clients can learn to differentiate between what they have been taught is socially acceptable and what is actually healthy for them. Always, therapists honor clients' distress as efforts to resist the pathological dominant system, rather than symptoms of individual pathology.

Next, therapists help clients to acquire skills to bring about change in their lives and circumstances. Typically, these changes involve how power is accessed among the people in the clients' interpersonal spheres (e.g., intimate and career partners).

Finally, therapists help clients to acquire skills to bring about change in society, to understand the need to continue fighting for their rights, and to be positive role models for feminist social involvement.

Feminist Change Tasks

Feminist therapy is a technically eclectic approach in which the therapist's feminist epistemology guides the choice of tasks to promote feminist change processes and goals (Worell & Remer, 2003). The one caveat is that clients must be aware of the task's purpose and agree to its use, making many of the strategic tasks from systemic therapy (see chap. 8, this volume), such as paradoxical interventions, unacceptable.

Gender-role analysis is synonymous with doing feminist therapy. Clients are helped to identify and understand the impact of gender-role expectations and societal structures in their lives. The origins of troubling or problematic behaviors in clients' lives are explained in terms of social norms and oppressive circumstances. The possible consequences of acting counter to expectations and in opposition to oppression are discussed as a context for exploring alternatives and making individual choices.

Power analysis is another uniquely feminist change task. Power differences between men and women in society and how these can be used toward destructive and productive ends are explored. Clients are assisted in recognizing different kinds of personal and institutional power they have access to and how they do and can exercise such power. Also, the circumstances and people in the client's life that affect her use of power are discussed along with the risks and benefits of using alternate types of power.

Consciousness-raising group work is a product of the women's movement that has been incorporated into feminist therapy. Women share information about their individual lives to identify commonalities in their experience so that thinking shifts toward a more collectivist understanding and away from individual pathology. Most of the other tasks of feminist therapy work as well or better in groups as women learn from one another. Consciousness-raising groups are generally leaderless, egalitarian, growth-oriented, and focused on working toward social advocacy and change.

Bibliotherapy is the use of extra-session reading to learn coping skills, gender-role stereotypes, gender power differentials, gender inequality, and ways sexism is promoted (e.g., society's obsession with women's thinness). Bibliotherapy is used in particular because it equalizes the power differential between therapist and client by sharing the therapist's privileged knowledge.

Assertiveness training was adopted from behavioral therapy (see chap. 3, this volume) to teach women how to act counter to their culturally entrenched passivity to make changes in their lives. *Assertive behavior* is a direct, honest expression of one's thoughts, feelings, and beliefs that respects others' rights and one's own rights. Patricia Jakubowski (1977) has written extensively on the topic and identified four components: (a) teaching the distinctions between assertive, nonassertive, and aggressive behaviors; (b) teaching a philosophy of respect for individual rights; (c) removing or reducing the factors that inhibit assertive behavior, such as negative beliefs; and (d) learning assertive skills through practice.

Therapy-demystifying tasks are used to establish an egalitarian therapeutic relationship to minimize limits placed on women accessing their personal power. Therapist self-disclosure, for example, can model the therapeutic work clients are expected to undertake. As the client is deciding whether to undertake therapy, feminist therapists describe their therapeutic approach, the change tasks they are likely to propose, relevant professional and personal values they hold, expectations of therapy in general and for the client in particular, and the client's rights as a consumer of therapy. Therapy will usually begin by collaboratively establishing a therapeutic contract that articulates the circumstances of therapy (e.g., fees, times) and the therapeutic goals (Worell & Remer, 2003).

Reframing and relabeling are tasks adopted from systemic therapy (see chap. 8, this volume) that change the frame of reference for understanding an individual's behavior from an intrapersonal to an interpersonal description. Reframing is often used to promote clients' awareness of how their distress is an expression of their struggle with oppressive forces in their lives. Relabeling refers to describing characteristics and behaviors that have been understood as weaknesses or maladaptive as strengths or adaptive efforts. Anorexia, for example, can be relabeled as a "hunger strike" (Orbach, 1986).

Therapeutic Relationship

Certainly any therapy developed since 1970 will focus on the therapist–client relationship as an important aspect of fostering positive outcomes. Feminist therapy adds something unique to the consideration of the therapeutic relationship, however. Because social relationships and the power embedded in them is the focus of feminist therapy, the power imbalance in the therapeutic relationship comes under scrutiny. The feminist therapist sees therapy as a deep, personal, two-way communication regarding feelings, ideas, and how to start solving problems. From a feminist point of view, the traditional conceptualization of the therapeutic relationship can be destructive because it does not include how the relationship can mirror oppressive patriarchal relationships.

Feminist therapists thereby acknowledge the inherent power differential in therapy and work to minimize it. The goal of equality may be a theoretical ideal that can never be realized, however, because the therapist decides much of the form and content of therapy: when and where to meet, for example. An egalitarian relationship, however, is one that is structured to strive for equality of power and the elimination of barriers to equality. The feminist therapist uses self-disclosure, for example, to minimize the power imbalance created when therapists avoid being vulnerable by withholding personal information. By striving to be clear about their values and biases, therapists attempt to facilitate clients who are making informed choices about undertaking therapy and what goals will be pursued in what manner. Similarly, much time is taken to educate the client on the therapeutic process to minimize the therapist's power arising out of knowing versus not knowing.

The feminist therapist strives to *empower* clients by not oppressing their efforts to exercise their own power. Clients' experiences are honored, as is the belief that they know what is best for their lives and they are the expert on their lives.

Evolution and Variations

Prior to the 1990s, many therapists—and theorists (e.g., Brody, 1984)—thought of feminist therapy as women treating women for "women's issues" such as incest, eating disorders, and assertiveness (L. S. Brown, 1994). Feminist therapy has evolved to include the understanding of power as well as all forms of societal oppression based on gender, race, culture, religion, class, physical ability, sexual orientation, and age. Feminist therapy theory has expanded to include consideration of the effects of racism, classism, ableism, and heterosexism on men and women (Greene & Sanchez-Hucles, 1997).

Because feminist therapy has its roots in political, sociological, and philosophical perspectives on feminism, the feminism of the therapist has a greater influence on practice than any specific psychological theories of therapy (L. S. Brown, 1990). Carolyn Enns (1992) described four different forms of feminist philosophy that inform practice: liberal, cultural, radical, and socialist. All of these approaches draw from a technically eclectic approach to therapy, although they differ in their understanding of the causes of gender oppression and therefore the appropriate goals and solutions for women's suffering (Enns, 1992, 1993).

Liberal feminism is the most mainstream feminist approach and has as its goals individual freedom, dignity, equality, autonomy, self-efficacy, and self-fulfillment. It is more closely aligned with the humanist worldview of personal growth, the expression of emotions, and overcoming social conditioning than the other feminist approaches. A liberal feminist therapist will draw on change tasks from other systems in an effort to help clients achieve their goals, although those from the cognitive–behavioral approach are most commonly used (M. Hill & Ballou, 1998). The behavioral change task of assertiveness training (see the Feminist Change Tasks section earlier in this chapter), for example, can be enlisted to help a client learn to change how she relates to others so that she might access more interpersonal power. When teaching skills to bring about change in society, the liberal feminist therapist focuses on legal structures and legislation to promote access for women to opportunities denied them because of gender discrimination. In this way social power is redistributed more fairly, rather than seeking to question the basic assumptions of major social institutions (Enns, 1992).

Cultural feminism seeks to bring about social change through incorporating feminine values such as cooperation, altruism, and connectedness into existing societal structures. As such, a number of fascinating efforts have been made to reformulate traditional psychotherapies—because they are, after all, reflections of existing social structures—from a feminist perspective. Systemic therapy (Goodrich, Rampage, Ellman, & Halstead, 1988; Silverstein & Goodrich, 2003), cognitive–behavioral therapy (Allen, 1995), and even psychodynamic therapy (Eichenbaum & Orbach, 1983) have been recast in cultural feminist terms. Most of these approaches discuss how women's "feminine" selves develop—particularly in the dynamic of the mother–daughter relationship—and how the human experience is essentially one of interpersonal relationship (J. B. Miller, 1986). Even therapists who do not seek to adopt a feminist approach to therapy would do well to read a cultural feminist critique and reinterpretation of their preferred approach. The primary goal of cultural feminist therapists is to raise the client's consciousness by appreciating the role of culture in women's difficulties, identification of women's relational strengths, discovery of an authentic self free of cultural biases, and mutual empowerment through association with other women (Enns, 1992). Ultimately, when women's values come to permeate the larger culture, greater flexibility of behavior will be accorded to both women and men.

Radical and socialist feminism is the "purest" collectivist approach to feminist therapy. The patriarchal values inherent in social systems—of which psychotherapy is another expression—and their influence on women's experiences are the foci of radical and socialist feminism. Radical feminist therapists tend to reject or drastically alter traditional forms of psychotherapy. Some have even gone so far as to view *feminist* and *therapy* as mutually exclusive concepts because therapy tends to focus on the individual and places the therapist in a position of power over the client, thereby discounting societal factors as the source of women's suffering (e.g., Perkins, 1991). These theorists argue for the exclusive use of self-help modalities such as consciousness-raising groups (Tennov, 1973). The radical feminist therapist often incorporates creative expression into therapy, using tools or techniques such as touch therapy, poetry, photography, and storytelling (Laidlaw & Malmo, 1990) as alternatives to inherently oppressive traditional change tasks. For the socialist feminist therapist, psychotherapy is a useful but incomplete means for altering harmful social structures. Community organizations, social advocacy, and coalition building are the essential methods for helping individuals live a healthy and productive life. Socialist feminist therapists will therefore tend to use a multiservice approach that includes psychotherapy as well as educational, health, child care, and social services.

Feminist therapy and *men* used to be incompatible ideas, with men being considered inappropriate as recipients or providers of feminist therapy (Chesler, 1972). The logical conclusion of the collectivist epistemology underlying feminist therapy, however, is that men's experience is just as influenced by societal gender expectations as women's and not always to their advantage (Levant, 1996). Men's gender role strain occurs when their essential nature conflicts with society's expectation that they be aggressive, uncaring, and self-reliant. Problems arising for men from masculine gender role socialization include domestic violence, homophobia, objectification of women, and neglect of their health (Levant, 1996). Feminist therapy for men involves gender-role and power analysis with the goal of increasing men's awareness of gender stereotypes and problem behaviors and reducing unhealthy values (Good, Thomson,

& Brathwaite, 2005). Feminist therapy provided by a man is theoretically possible if he is willing to use his experience of power, privilege, and anger in the service of feminist understandings, analysis, and social change (DeVoe, 1990).

Her Own Mind

Francis's family physician had prescribed medication for her "depression," but Francis didn't think that she was depressed. Her life just felt so unreal that she worried she was losing her mind. So she made an appointment to see Jan, a feminist therapist.

Francis found Jan pleasantly approachable, particularly in how she took so much time to explain her therapy and to listen to Francis describe her life as "a movie in which the voice-over didn't match the plot." She expected Jan to tell her what was wrong with her and how to fix it. Instead, she was asked about her life and what she had learned growing up about being a woman. Jan even shared how her career choice to become a therapist was influenced by what other people thought it was proper for a woman to do. Francis certainly was unhappy about how motherhood had derailed her career plans, but her husband was supportive, and she loved her children, so what was there to talk about?

Jan said that she thought the real Francis was hidden behind the kind of person society expects a good wife and mother to be. By conforming to a tightly prescribed feminine role, the full range of her attributes—good and bad—had to be suppressed. This might be why her life didn't feel like her own. Jan wanted her to attend a therapy group with other women so that she could learn how to make her own choices for her life. This explanation made sense to Francis, so she agreed to try it.

She found it difficult at first to talk intimately about herself with the other women in the group, but as she listened to their experiences, she was struck by the similarities with her own. She liked feeling close to other women in a way she had not experienced since she was a little girl, and gradually, she shared her thoughts and feelings. She recalled how her mother had once told her with intense regret that she had wanted to be a writer but her family discouraged her because a woman could not make a living that way. Francis followed the example and encouragement of others in the group and made some changes in her life. They were not big changes—asking her family to contribute to more of the housework and taking the few courses needed to finally finish her degree—but she felt much better about herself. Even when she was sad (or angry!), her experience was more "real," and her feelings felt right. She came to see herself as an intelligent, talented person.

Francis continued in the group for just over a year—even after she felt she had addressed her own issues—because she wanted to help some of the women who joined after her, and she had made a commitment to take part in a demonstration to lobby for affordable housing that the group had been planning for months.

Learning Task

Feminist theory asserts that prevailing systemic social forces—particularly gender role discrimination—profoundly influence our sense of self and our relationships. To help you understand the influence of these forces in your life, try the exercise described in Exhibit 9.1. Once you have done so, record your reactions in your reflective journal: What have you learned from this task about your openness to practicing from a feminist orientation? Can you imagine proposing a gender-role analysis as a change task for a client? If not, why not? If so, under what circumstances?

Your Reflective Journal

How might you approach the issues presented in the case illustration given the underlying philosophy, assumptions, and goals of the feminist approach? Do you find yourself thinking that you would prefer to do things rather differently? If so, what system of psychotherapy does your preference represent? Does your preference represent a real commitment to one approach over another? Are there aspects of the feminist approach that you prefer over other approaches? Could you imagine yourself practicing psychotherapy from a feminist perspective? Why or why not? Is there anything else you would like to know about feminist therapy before you make up your mind?

Summary

The origins of feminist therapy are rooted in the North American women's movement of the 1960s, when existing approaches to psychotherapy were understood as perpetuating the traditional role of women in society and blaming women for their problems. The goals of feminist therapy revolve around heightening the awareness of women as to how they are oppressed by societal systems and assisting them to acquire freely chosen, individual identities. These goals are achieved through becoming aware of one's gender-role socialization, differentiating what is socially acceptable from what is actually healthy, acquiring skills to bring about social change, continuing to fight for one's rights, and being a positive role model for empowerment. Typical feminist change tasks include gender-role analysis, power analysis, consciousness-raising group work, bib-

EXHIBIT 9.1

Personal Gender Analysis

Take some time to think about and record what you learned in your childhood about females and males. For example,

1.   How were you treated differently than opposite-gender siblings or other relatives?
2.   What behaviors were acceptable or unacceptable in school and other public situations on the basis of your gender?
3.   What did you learn from each parent about gender expectations?
4.   Make a list of *shoulds* and *shouldn't*s you learned about your gender.

After recording your answers to these and any other similar questions that may occur to you, consider how your personally gendered frame of reference might affect your therapeutic practice. For example,

1.   What positive and negative expectations for growth in therapy might you have of male and female clients?
2.   In what ways might your expectations of personal agency be different for male and female clients?
3.   Are there personal qualities that you now consider healthy, or unhealthy, that you might once have thought about differently?
4.   How might your empathy be differentially available to female and male clients?
5.   Are there topics commonly dealt with by feminist therapy that you would not be comfortable helping someone in therapy to deal with?

liotherapy, assertiveness training, therapy-demystifying techniques, and reframing and relabeling. The therapeutic relationship in feminist therapy is focused primarily on attempting to reduce the power differential inherent in the therapeutic circumstance through self-disclosure and sharing of information about therapy. Feminist therapy has evolved to incorporate aspects of societal oppression beyond gender roles such as race, class, and sexual orientation.

Further Resources

CASE READINGS

Cantor, D. W. (Ed.). (1990). *Women as therapists: A multitheoretical casebook*. New York: Springer.

Goodrich, T. J., Rampage, C., Ellman, B., & Halsted, K. (Eds.). (1988). *Feminist family therapy: A casebook*. New York: Norton.

Meth, R. L., Pasick, R. S., Gordon, B., Allen, J., Feldman, L., & Gordon, S. (1990). *Men in therapy: The challenge of change*. New York: Norton.

RECOMMENDED READING

Brown, L. S. (1994). *Subversive dialogues: Theories in feminist therapy*. New York: Basic Books.

Chesler, P. (1972). *Women and madness*. Garden City, NY: Doubleday.

Enns, C. Z. (2004). *Feminist theories and feminist psychotherapies: Origins, themes, and diversity* (2nd ed.). New York: Haworth.

Miller, J. B., & Stiver, I. P. (1997). *The healing connection: How women form relationships in therapy and in life*. Boston: Beacon Press.

Worell, J., & Remer, P. (2003). *Feminist perspectives in therapy: Empowering diverse women* (2nd ed.). New York: Wiley.

RECOMMENDED VIEWING

American Psychological Association (Producer). (1994). *Feminist therapy with Laura S. Brown, PhD* [Motion picture]. (Available from the American Psychological Association, 750 First Street, NE, Washington, DC 20002-4242)

American Psychological Association (Producer). (2005). *Working with women survivors of trauma and abuse with Laura S. Brown, PhD* [Motion picture]. (Available from the American Psychological Association, 750 First Street, NE, Washington, DC 20002-4242)

American Psychological Association (Producer). (2006). *Working with men survivors of trauma and abuse with Laura S. Brown, PhD* [Motion picture]. (Available from the American Psychological Association, 750 First Street, NE, Washington, DC 20002-4242)

Governors State University (Producer). (1998). *Feminist therapy with Dr. Lenore Walker* [Motion picture]. (Available from Pearson Education, One Lake Street, Upper Saddle River, NJ 07458-1813)

Yalom, V. (Producer). (1996). *Effective psychotherapy with men with Ron Levant, EdD* [Motion Picture]. (Available from Psychotherapy.net, 4625 California Street, San Francisco, CA 94118-1224)

Constructivist 10

onstructivist therapies are a loosely affiliated group of therapies with a rather short, and somewhat contested, history. Although there are a number of theorists who can be said to presage constructivist psychotherapy, it has been only in the last 20 years that anyone has called themselves a constructivist. From an epistemological perspective, constructivism has its roots in the rational worldviews (see chap. 1, this volume) of Giambattista Vico (1668–1744), Immanuel Kant (1724–1804), and Hans Vaihinger (1852–1933). These philosophers argued that human beings cannot know reality directly. Rather, the nature of the human experience is an active, meaning-making one, and we can only construct a subjective model of reality (Mahoney, 1988).

Alfred Adler (1870–1937) may have been the earliest constructivist therapist. A contemporary of Sigmund Freud (see chap. 2, this volume) and trained in psychoanalysis, Adler differed from Freud by not accepting that people's lives are determined by past experiences. Adler argued instead that it is our subjective appraisal of experiences that determines how we adjust to our circumstances. Adler was influenced by Vaihinger in his consideration of how clients' fictional life goals shape how they seek and find personal satisfaction (Neimeyer & Stewart, 2000). Adler posited that individuals actively reconstruct their past and anticipate their future in light of their unique personal goals, resulting in an individual "lifestyle" (A. Adler, 1992). Problems in life reflect the degree to which these goals are not met or are blocked in some way. His approach to psychotherapy was to help individuals recognize and change self-defeating constructions.

Adler encouraged clients to behave differently in their day-to-day life—to behave "as if" their problem was solved or they could do the things they always wanted to do (A. Adler, 1963). Therefore, a depressed patient, for example, was instructed to "only do what is agreeable to you" or "at least, do not exert yourself to do what is disagreeable" (A. Adler, 1964, p. 25).

More recently—though still not quite fully constructivist yet—George Kelly (1905–1967) developed his *fixed-role therapy* in Kansas during the American economic depression of the 1930s and 1940s (Neimeyer, 2000). Kelly, as did Adler, drew on Vaihinger's philosophy of personal construc-tions for the development of his own theory of personality known as *personal construct psychology* (Kelly, 1955). Kelly characterized people as continually constructing, testing, and revising their own personal theo-ries of themselves in the world. These theories allow us to anticipate recurring themes in our lives.

In fixed-role therapy, the therapist first evaluates the client's con-structed theory system by having him or her write a self-characterization from the perspective of someone who knows him or her well. Then the therapist writes a script of an alternative fictional identity and coaches the client to enact it for a 2- or 3-week period to experiment with a different way of living. The client practices the new role in session with the therapist and then performs it between sessions in increasingly inti-mate relationships. This make-believe activity is designed to loosen the client's identification with unsatisfying constructs and prompt the devel-opment of a more flexible and adaptive construct system.

Milton Erickson (1901–1980) had the most direct influence on constructivist therapies. He was the object of much observation and specu-lation throughout the 1960s until his death, and for some time after-ward. Famous for his unorthodox methods and unique successes, Erickson eschewed theory and said that he drew on his patients' own strengths to be used in new ways. Erickson used a remarkable variety of techniques in the service of "the development of a therapeutic situation permitting the patient to use his own thinking, his own understandings, his own emotions in the way that best fits for him in his scheme of life" (Erickson, 1965, p. 65). He defied established psychotherapeutic conventions, par-ticularly with respect to how the process of eliminating problems has to be protracted and difficult. His approach continues to defy easy descrip-tion, and most constructivist theorists embrace him as the definitive constructivist therapist for this very reason.

Steve de Shazer (1940–2005; see Figure 10.1) was the first therapist to develop a system of psychotherapy fully based on constructivist prin-ciples. He came from a strategic systemic approach grounded in Bateson's communication model (see chap. 8, this volume) and was also influ-enced by Milton Erickson's work. Along with a number of other thera-

FIGURE 10.1

Steve de Shazer and Insoo Kim Berg. Printed with permission of the Brief Family Therapy Center.

pists—most notably his wife, Insoo Kim Berg (1934–2007; see Figure 10.1)—he established the Brief Family Therapy Center in Milwaukee, Wisconsin, in 1978 with the intention of replicating the work of Watzlawick, Weakland, and Fisch's (1974) Brief Therapy Center at the Mental Research Institute (see chap. 8, this volume). De Shazer's group became dissatisfied with the systemic worldview of objective patterns of interpersonal relationships as "real," however. They came to believe that a shift in the client's subjective experience is what is necessary for therapeutic change (de Shazer, 1985; Nunnally, de Shazer, Lipchik, & Berg, 1986). It is interesting to note that by rejecting the objective reality of systems and adopting subjective constructions of the world they have very little in common—epistemologically—with the systemic therapies from which they originated. In fact, the newest system of psychotherapy has brought us full circle back to the worldview of the oldest system— rationalism.

It was the increasing popularity of *postmodernism* as a way of understanding knowledge construction that finally gave constructivist therapies a means to break away from their systemic roots. (Some commentators have suggested that constructivism is the only practical application of postmodernism to date.) *Modernism*, from a postmodernist perspective, has been recast as an approach to understanding the world based on a belief in the accumulation of truth. Postmodernism, on the other hand, does not accept that we can be certain about the "truth" of "facts." Postmodernists argue that "truth" (they use a lot of quotation marks) is not universal. Rather, knowledge represents a linguistic consensus among people who are socially accepted as "experts." In other words, truth is a social construction. De Shazer took the position that seeking the truth of why individuals were unhappy is, therefore, ultimately fruitless. He proposed that therapists would be more effective if instead they helped people seek (i.e., create) the truth of how they can solve their problems. By having done so, he is generally credited with founding the application of postmodernism to psychotherapy.

Constructivist Rationale

Constructivist therapy is based on the understanding that human beings actively construct meaning from experiences that could be understood in an almost infinite variety of ways. We link certain events together in a particular sequence across a time period—while disregarding other events and linkages—in an effort to make sense of our lives. These linkages form the plot and content of the story of our lives. An individual may understand him- or herself as being successful or a failure, competent or a loser, crazy or eccentric. Although all of these understandings could be occurring at the same time, we tend to adopt one and interpret new events according to the understanding that is dominant for us at the time. In this way constructions become self-fulfilling. The plot of these stories is constructed through the manner in which we have linked select events together in a sequence and the meaning we have attributed to them. Because we cannot incorporate all of the events that happen in our lives and all of their possible linkages, there are many possible stories occurring at the same time.

Constructivist therapists assume that we construct realities that are more or less useful for us depending on our situation, not more or less true in any absolute sense. "Mental disorders" of one form or another are similarly understood as social constructions. They are problems only because they are sustained by social behavior and coordinated in language (Goolishian & Anderson, 1987), not because they are "real" in the way that a broken bone is. For those who suffer from problems in life, it is assumed that their constructions of reality are not functionally adaptive—they are not getting the job done of living well.

Because speculation about the origin of problems is just another form of construction and is not real in any helpful way, constructivist therapists focus on solutions. Past mistakes, misfortune, or trauma only have meaning through our constructions. It follows then that solutions are not necessarily directly related to problems. Similarly, change can be understood as being inevitable—whether we notice changes depends on our constructions. Therefore, noticing and paying attention to small positive changes can set in motion more positive changes by changing our constructions of ourselves from problematic to productive.

Constructivist Goals

The overall goal of constructivist therapies is to have clients replace problem constructions with more functional and satisfying ones, in whatever way the client perceives them. De Shazer made the interesting argument that therapists accept clients into therapy on the basis of their self-perceived need, so why do therapists tend not to accept their perception of that need being satisfied? Building from this collaborative attitude, the constructivist therapist and client can coconstruct new possibilities.

Beyond this broadly defined goal, constructivist therapists work to help clients clarify their own goals in ways that are specific, action oriented, and positive (de Shazer, 1988; O'Hanlon & Weiner-Davis, 1989). Absence goals—getting rid of something—are avoided, and clients are encouraged to specify what they would like to have be present. Therefore, rather than the goal of "not being depressed," a client might have the goal of "being more happy," which could then be elaborated as "spend more time with my friends," "smile more often," and so forth.

Constructivist Change Processes

So much of the talk that takes place in nonconstructivist therapies, and in people's lives in general, centers on how things go wrong. Indeed, it can be argued that by spending so much of our time talking about problems and limitations, we keep them alive. We might even say that the nature of the dialogue we have gives life to abstract ideas that make us unhappy. Constructivist therapists suggest that when people spend time talking about how and when things go right—or even go wrong in a way inconsistent with their preconceptions—they nourish their strengths and create new possibilities.

The first step in constructivist therapy, therefore, is to deconstruct problems. That is, to pay very careful attention to the ways that we treat as real what are actually just ideas. If we carefully talk about and ask questions about lives and problems in a manner that challenges dominant conceptualizations and is open to alternative ones, we begin to see that there are many different perspectives about who we are. This insight, or changed consciousness, thus allows us the opportunity to imagine options, strengths, selves, and lives that had been unacknowledged.

Once these previous solutions and exceptions to the problem have been talked about, the client can experience new and multiple possibilities that they might like to pursue. The therapist can then encourage the client to do more of what has previously worked or to implement changes he or she has previously refrained from doing.

Constructivist Change Tasks

Constructivist therapists focus on proposing change tasks that are based on the client's previous solutions or exceptions to his or her problems. Only in rare circumstances are therapist-generated solutions proposed.

Patient questioning is an attitude that the language of problems tends to be different from the language of solutions. Usually problem language is negative, past-oriented, and often suggests permanency. The language of solutions, on the other hand, is usually more positive, hopeful, future oriented, and often suggests a transience of problems. Because language is the primary tool of therapeutic interventions, all questions are viewed as potential interventions. For example, asking a mother, "What would your daughter say she hates about your being drunk?" elicits a very different response from asking, "What would your daughter say she likes about your being sober?" Questions are thus asked very carefully and in a patient manner to invite the client to engage in a shared enquiry (Anderson, 2001).

Finding exceptions is based on the assumption that problems are not always occurring or do not always unfold in the same way every time. Attending to those times when exceptions occur communicates to clients that the therapist is confident of their ability to find solutions. Finding exceptions also helps the client to feel that problems are not monolithic. Exceptions can also highlight what can be done to create desired solutions. This may be done in a number of ways, but the simplest is to ask for them directly: "Tell me about times when you dealt with this problem in a way that you felt good about." "When did the problem not happen?" This can then begin an exploration of the influence of the client over the problem. By finding historical antecedents of any kind, and by linking exceptions to the client's conscious intentions, values, commitments, hopes, and dreams, the exception can be more richly elaborated. "Who from in your life would not be surprised by the exception(s) that you have described?" "What did these people, such as teachers, aunts or uncles, neighbors, past lovers, and so on, know about you such that they were not surprised?" "What planning or preparation did you do that enabled you to perform this exception?" "How does this exception fit with what it is you want and what does it say about you as a person?"

The miracle question can be helpful when clients have difficulty articulating clearly defined criteria for successful outcomes. The therapist asks the client, "Suppose that one night, while you were asleep, there was a miracle and this problem was solved. How would you know? What would be different?" The client's answer to the miracle question can construct a vision of what the solution would look like. The answer can help to define the initial steps toward solutions if the client is able to describe concrete changes such as, "My husband would smile at me and say 'good morning' instead of frowning and grumbling." It can be useful to convey the therapist's respect for the immensity of the problem while at the same time leading the client to come up with small, realistic, concrete steps. Therapists must be careful that the miracle question is not used cavalierly such that the client feels that his or her problem is being belittled, which is a very real risk. It is also important to follow up and expand on this beginning of the solution and help to build on this so that it can be transformed into manageable, doable beginning steps.

Scaling can be adapted to elicit useful information that will help negotiate and assess numerous things that matter to the client. The client is asked, "On a scale of 1 to 10, how would you rate your problem before coming to therapy. How would you rate it right now?" Any difference, however small, can be deconstructed by asking, "How did that happen?" Because of its simplicity and subjective nature, scaling can readily provide both therapist and client with useful information about experiences that are not easily observed. Numbers are so simple to use that even 4- or 5-year-olds can respond by showing visual aids or toys that indicate what their own assessment of the situation is on a number of issues.

Reauthoring is a task associated with narrative therapy (see the Evolution and Variations section later in this chapter) in which clients are encouraged to describe their experiences of their life and of the problem. Therapists help their clients to give a name to the problem story that reflects their experience, such as "My Big Fat Geek Wedding" for a client who felt humiliated at his wedding. It is often useful to explore the history of the problem story. It may emerge that it is the result of historical circumstances, such as an abusive parent who systematically undermined the client's confidence. The problem story is also often connected to societal or cultural stories against which clients judge themselves, such as the idea that intellectuals can't be romantically desirable. Once these factors are named, it is possible to invite clients into a critique of these factors and of the effects that they are having on their lives. Following this, therapists look for exceptions to the problem story. These can then be incorporated into an alternative preferred story, often finding a new name that reflects clients' experiences, such as "Prince Charming."

Externalizing is another narrative task that is intended to emerge naturally from the naming of problem stories and from the assumption that problems are not an intrinsic part of the person but, rather, external to them. At its simplest, to externalize is to take any quality that is cast as being internal to a person and casting it as external. Thus, "I am weak" becomes "I get overwhelmed by a feeling of weakness," or "I am anorexic" may become "My fear of food has taken control of my life." By casting the problem as outside of the client, it becomes possible for the person to enter into a relationship with the problem and to take responsibility for revising the relationship. When the problem is internal, a person can only attack the problem by attacking him- or herself. In families, externalizing the problem also opens the way for everyone to join together against the problem instead of attacking the person who is the subject of the problem. Externalization thereby reduces the experience of blame and shame.

Therapeutic Relationship

The constructivist therapist takes an active role in therapy and assumes responsibility for what happens in session. Direct challenges or confrontations of the client are rarely made, however. Instead, gentle and persistent questions are used as both the primary communication stance and as change tasks to have a conversation about strengths and construct solutions. Unlike many other systems of psychotherapy, the therapist strives to adopt a "not knowing" conceptual stance—keeping preconceptions at bay to avoid categorizing the client and thereby restricting possibilities. Clients are prized as experts on their lives and as capable of achieving their own personal goals. The therapist serves as a participant–observer and accepts what the client says at face value without making any assumptions about underlying pathology. The therapist accepts the role of expert in facilitating change by focusing on client resources and noticing exceptions to problem constructions. The therapist also brings a sincere and deeply held sense of optimism, compassion, and respect for the client.

Compliments are another way of conceptualizing what is unique about the constructivist therapeutic relationship. Rather than focusing on what is going wrong in the client's life, genuine compliments can validate what the client is already doing right. Compliments can acknowledge how difficult the client's problems are, while communicating the therapist's belief in the client's capacity for change.

Each client (and indeed each therapist) is not seen as possessing a static identity or immutable traits. Therefore, each therapeutic relationship can be a unique, mutually respectful collaboration toward the coconstruction of a shared solution. If the uniqueness of this relationship is acknowledged, then clients will have an opportunity to be free to explore, reflect upon, feel excited about, and create new possible selves that are more satisfying than their previous problematic selves.

Evolution and Variations

Constructivist therapies encompass a number of similar approaches that prize clients' subjective experience and trust that their personal realities develop out of healthy efforts to live within their unique life circumstances. Although many still use concepts derived from their systemic forebears, all now work primarily with individuals. The optimistic nature of constructivist therapies—in contrast with Freud's Victorian pessimism— seems to strike a chord with many contemporary therapists, and most current therapies have a distinctly "constructivist" flavor.

Narrative therapy was developed independently by two social workers— Michael White (1948–2008) of Australia and David Epston (1944–) of New Zealand—who then came together to write their seminal book *Narrative Means to Therapeutic Ends* (White & Epston, 1990). As such, they tend to have a more systemic (see chap. 8, this volume) flavor to their rationale and emphasize cultural, familial, and historical influences on how people come to make sense of their place in the world. Criticism of the pathogenic influences of the dominant "truths" in society is thus an important aspect of how the narrative therapist makes sense of the problems that clients bring to therapy. In this regard they share much with feminist therapy (see chap. 9, this volume). Rather than focusing on how people have problems, the narrative therapist looks at how problems come to dominate people's sense of who they are. Our sense of ourselves can thus be understood as being *problem saturated*, which in turn results in more—and more entrenched —problems. Narrative therapists use *externalizing conversations* to help people reconceptualize themselves as separate from their problems and work to coconstruct *alternative stories* that run counter to problem-saturated ones, thereby creating new possibilities for change. The power of words to shape our reality is very important from a narrative perspective, and positive words such as *survivor* are used instead of *victim*, for example, to help construct a strength-based rather than deficit-based personal reality.

Solution-oriented therapy was developed by Bill O'Hanlon (1952–) at around the same time that Steve de Shazer and his colleagues were developing solution-focused therapy (de Shazer, 1985). O'Hanlon (1986) was a student of Milton Erickson and even worked as Erickson's gardener because he did not have the funds to pay for supervision. As would be expected given the similarity of their names, solution-oriented therapy shares much with solution-focused therapy. Solution-oriented therapists assume that clients have the resources and strengths to resolve their problems, that small changes can lead to bigger ones, and that the therapist's job is to identify and amplify what is possible and changeable (O'Hanlon & Weiner-Davis, 1989). The solution-oriented therapist seeks to negotiate a solvable problem with the client so that once a small positive change is made, the client can feel optimistic and more confident about undertaking further changes. When one member of a couple makes a small gesture that pleases their partner, for example, that person reciprocates, which in turn stimulates the other to respond in kind, and so on. If the client has difficulty identifying a well-formed goal, then the therapist might ask them to observe an aspect of their life between sessions that they want to continue to have happen.

Collaborative therapy was developed by Harlene Anderson (1942–) and Harry Goolishian (1924–1991) at the Houston Galveston Institute (Anderson & Goolishian, 1988). It is based on the idea that therapy is a collaborative conversation in which new possibilities can be generated through shared inquiry (Anderson, 1997; Anderson & Gehart, 2006). Similar to narrative therapy, people who seek collaborative therapy are assumed to be embedded in conversations (i.e., stories) that maintain the problem and limit alternatives. By conversing with clients in a collaborate manner, collaborative therapists can present an opportunity for a transformation of clients' reality into one that allows them to live well. The therapist will frequently ask—and almost always be wondering—whether the client is talking about what he or she wants to talk about and whether therapy is progressing as the client would like. The collaborative therapist adopts a nonexpert, not-knowing, caring, *being-with* stance in an effort to set aside preconstructed knowledge about the client, thereby allowing for new possibilities. The therapist communicates to the client that he or she is worth listening to and not a member of a class of persons or diagnostic category (Anderson, 2001). Thus, the therapist is always striving for the therapy to be a good process for the client. Goals are established by the client, then clarified, elaborated, and refined through conversation with the therapist as therapy progresses.

Cognitive constructivism was developed by Michael Mahoney (1946–2006) by integrating constructivist epistemology into cognitive therapy (see chap. 7, this volume) through assuming an interdependence of thinking, feeling, and behavior, rather than accepting the supremacy of cognition (Mahoney, 2003). Emotions are valued as another way of knowing and as functional in human information processing, not as problems to be controlled or modified. Depression, for example, is not understood as a consequence of maladaptive cognitions but as another way of "knowing." The value of cognition, therefore, is in its coherence, order, and usefulness for making sense of our experience. Instead of assuming that there is an objective reality that individuals understand accurately (in the case of health) or inaccurately (in the case of psychopathology), cognitive constructionists see people as active creators of their own personal realities. The primary task of the therapist then becomes collaborating with the client in such a way that comfort and challenge are paced according to changing personal needs (Mahoney, 2001). The change tasks of cognitive therapy are retained, as is the voluminous empirical base of support for their effectiveness, and are implemented in the service of a constructivist rationale.

The Exceptional Bully

Josh was referred to the school counselor because he was bullying his Grade 6 classmates. The therapist adopted a sincere not-knowing stance to honor Josh as the expert of his situation and patiently sought out exceptions to Josh as the problem:

> *Therapist:* So, why are you here to see me today?
> *Josh:* My teachers said I have to come.
> *Therapist:* Okay. So, why did your teachers say you have to come?
> *Josh:* They want me to stop picking on other kids. But it's not my fault.
> *Therapist:* Okay. So what do you want?
> *Josh:* I wish I wasn't so big.
> *Therapist:* Big?
> *Josh:* Yeah. They tease me because I'm the biggest kid in my class. They call me Shrek [a movie ogre] and make farting noises. Stuff like that. It's mean. I fight back.
> *Therapist:* Do you always fight back?
> *Josh:* No. Lots of times I do nothing.
> *Therapist:* Oh? How do you not fight back, even when they tease you?
> *Josh:* I just ignore them. They're ignorant.
> *Therapist:* So, you see that what they're doing is ignorant, and you show them that you are smarter than that?
> *Josh:* Yeah. You know, if I were small and they were teasing me about being small, they would be the bully, not me. I get teased because I'm big, and

then I get in trouble for being a bully because
I'm big. I can't win!

Therapist: Wow, that is smart. I don't think many people
would see things as clearly as that.

Josh: Yeah, well, a lot of good it does me.

Therapist: Hmm, good point . . . I wonder if you've noticed
whether it's *all* the kids in your class who tease
you, or just some, or one?

Josh: Well, there is this one guy who usually gets them
going.

Therapist: So he starts, and the rest join in?

Josh: Yeah.

Therapist: Have you noticed times when he isn't teasing
you?

Josh: Well, it's not like he's always goin' after me. Most
of the time we're just doing school stuff. Sometimes we just goof around.

Therapist: Goof around?

Josh: You know—tellin' jokes and stuff.

Therapist: When you're goofing around and telling jokes,
he's not teasing you?

Josh: Yeah.

Therapist: And then the rest don't join in, and you're not
fighting back?

Josh: Yeah. You know, he's always jokin' around.
Tryin' to get other kids to laugh. It's not like it's
just me—he teases other kids, too.

Therapist: Really?

Josh: Yeah. I guess I'm not a freak. [*Smiles.*] He's just
tryin' to get laughs. If he doesn't get 'em from
me, he just goes at someone else until he gets
them laughing. Huh, I never thought of that.

Josh attended one more session in which he and the counselor talked
about how he was resisting his classmate's teasing. His teachers
reported a marked reduction in his bullying to the extent that they
were no longer considering transferring him to a school for students
with behavior problems.

Learning Task

Most people find the idea that we construct stories about ourselves, and
that these stories may or may not be the ones we want to live our lives
by, rather appealing. To help you gain an appreciation of this idea, reread
the autobiographical sketch you wrote in your reflective journal for chapter 1. After doing so, complete the task provided in Exhibit 10.1. Once
you have completed the task, record your reactions in your reflective

EXHIBIT 10.1

Authoring Your Therapeutic Identity

Begin by creating a comfortable circumstance for quiet reflection by taking a long walk, a soothing bath, or whatever else works for you. Think about times when your actions have resonated with how you aspire to be a therapist. When have you acted in ways congruent with your preferred therapeutic identity? Incongruent? What was different about them? What was involved in your acting in a manner that was incongruent with your therapeutic self? External demands? Other reasons? Have there been particular clients, or certain client problems that particularly resonate with you? What events are currently unfolding that are significant for your therapeutic self? What do your actions and reactions in relation to these events tell you about the therapist you want to be? Take some more time to record these thoughts.

Next, write a letter to yourself explaining how you intend to act in a manner congruent with your preferred therapeutic self. Try to specify those aspects of who you are that are most in accord with what you value as a therapist. Identify how you will know that you are acting in harmony with your values. Describe what others will see you do that will show them that you are the kind of therapist you want to be

Note. Data from Sax, 2006.

journal: Did you notice a change in how you think about yourself as a therapist? How convinced are you that your therapeutic identity is a constructed one? Can you imagine working with clients to reauthor their problem-saturated identities?

Your Reflective Journal

What do you like best about the constructivist approach to therapy? What aspects of the approach do you find amenable? What aspects do you dislike about it? Be specific—what rationale, tasks, or goals can you commit to using in your practice, if any? If none, describe how your approach to therapy will not be like constructivist therapy. How would you rate your affinity for it relative to the other approaches? What does your rating tell you about where you feel situated within the taxonomy of systems of psychotherapy presented in chapter 1?

Summary

Constructivist therapies arose out of the systemic therapies, buoyed by the postmodern zeitgeist that rejects an objective reality and instead accepts a subjectively constructed reality. Problems that prompt people to seek therapy are not accepted as real in the objective sense nor is the therapist seen as the expert who knows what is really wrong with the client. Rather, people are understood to be experiencing problems that can be deconstructed and replaced. Given that there are many—equally valid—ways to understand the client's reality, constructivist therapists choose to understand clients as healthy, competent, and resourceful. Constructivist therapists strive to establish a collaborative relationship in which the client is an active participant, while adopting a stance of not knowing, which allows a participant–observer and process-facilitator role. The goal of constructivist therapy is to assist clients in replacing problem constructions with more functional and satisfying ones. Therapists enter into a dialogue with clients to elicit their perceptions, resources, and experiences that can be incorporated into new constructions. Common change tasks are exception questions, the miracle question, scaling questions, externalizing, and reauthoring.

Further Resources

CASE READINGS

Berg, I. K., & Dolan, Y. M. (Eds.). (2001). *Tales of solutions: A collection of hope-inspiring stories.* New York: Norton.

Eron, J. B., & Lund, T. W. (1998). Narrative solutions couple therapy. In F. M. Dattilio (Ed.), *Case studies in couple and family therapy: Systemic and cognitive perspectives* (pp. 371–400). New York: Guilford Press.

Hogan, B. A. (1999). Narrative therapy in rehabilitation after brain injury: A case study. *NeuroRehabilitation, 13*(1), 21–25.

Penn, P., & Frankfurt, M. (1994). Creating a participant text: Writing, multiple voices, narrative multiplicity. *Family Process, 33,* 217–231.

Rhodes, J., & Jakes, S. (2002). Using solution-focused therapy during a psychotic crisis: A case study. *Clinical Psychology and Psychotherapy, 9,* 139–148.

RECOMMENDED READING

Angus, L. E., & McLeod, J. (2004). *The handbook of narrative and psychotherapy: Practice, theory and research.* Thousand Oaks, CA: Sage.

Bertolino, B., & O'Hanlon, B. (2002). *Collaborative, competency-based counselling and therapy.* Needham Heights, MA: Allyn & Bacon.

De Jong, P., & Berg, I. K. (2001). *Interviewing for solutions* (2nd ed.). Pacific Grove, CA: Brooks/Cole.

Lieblich, A., McAdams, D. P., & Josselson, R. (Eds.). (1995). *Healing plots: The narrative basis of psychotherapy.* Washington, DC: American Psychological Association.

Neimeyer, R. A., & Mahoney, M. J. (Eds.). (1995). *Constructivism in psychotherapy.* Washington, DC: American Psychological Association.

White, M., & Epston, D. (1990). *Narrative means to therapeutic ends.* New York: Norton.

RECOMMENDED VIEWING

American Association for Marriage and Family Therapy (Producer). (1989). *Escape from bickering with Michael White* [Motion picture]. (Available from the American Association for Marriage and Family Therapy, 112 South Alfred Street, Alexandria, VA 22314-3061)

American Association for Marriage and Family Therapy (Producer). (1997). *Brief therapy: Constructing solutions with Steve de Shazer* [Motion picture]. (Available from the American Association for Marriage and Family Therapy, 112 South Alfred Street, Alexandria, VA 22314-3061)

American Psychological Association (Producer). (1994). *Narrative therapy with Lynne Angus, PhD* [Motion picture]. (Available from the American Psychological Association, 750 First Street, NE, Washington, DC 20002-4242)

Governors State University (Producer). (2001). *Solution-focused therapy with Insoo Kim Berg, MSSW* [Motion Picture]. (Available from Psychotherapy.net, 4625 California Street, San Francisco, CA 94118-1224)

Governors State University (Producer). (2002). *Solution-focused child therapy with John J. Murphy, PhD* [Motion Picture]. (Available from Psychotherapy.net, 4625 California Street, San Francisco, CA 94118-1224)

Adapting Your Approach 11

T he whole point of adopting a theory of psychotherapy that you believe in is to help you become an effective therapist. As discussed in chapter 1 of this volume, theory serves as a guide to formulating tasks that will facilitate change processes in order to promote client goals. We, therefore, need to adopt a theory if we want to be effective therapists. Adopting a theory is only one—albeit very important—aspect of a process, however. Becoming an effective therapist depends on adapting your approach over the course of your career so that it is congruent with who you are as a person. Being effective is also, of course, not just about you. Effective psychotherapy depends on establishing a common rationale for change in which you and your client believe. Theory can provide a basis from which to do so if you adapt your approach over the course of each therapeutic encounter to be congruent with who your client is as a person. Scott D. Miller (1958–; see Figure 11.1) has been the most vocal proponent of this view that theory is for therapists and therapy is for clients (Duncan & Miller, 2005; Duncan, Sparks, & Miller, 2005; S. D. Miller, 2004; S. D. Miller, Duncan, & Hubble, 1997).

We know that the variation in outcomes among therapies is much, much smaller than the variation in outcomes among therapists (Crits-Christoph et al., 1991; W. P. Henry & Strupp, 1994; Orlinsky, Rønnestad, & Willutzki, 2004; Wampold, 2001b). This means that it makes a bigger difference who the therapist is than which therapy is being delivered. Therefore, attending to your own personal and professional development is a crucial aspect of becoming an effective therapist. Most people think

FIGURE 11.1

Scott D. Miller. Photo printed with permission of Scott D. Miller.

of professional development as the circumstance of accruing experience. Although experience is positively correlated with psychotherapeutic outcomes, the strength of this correlation is weak and accounts for little of the variance (Beutler et al., 2004; Crits-Christoph & Mintz, 1991; Stein & Lambert, 1995). This is because, although experience can be a great teacher, too many therapists practice for years and, Sisyphus-like, only gain 1 year of experience over and over again. This limits opportunities for learning, and therapists' development is stunted, leaving them with only the knowledge and skills they retain from their formative training. As any well-seasoned therapist will tell you, if your approach to psychotherapy does not change over the course of your career, you are just not learning from your experience.

Highly effective therapists engage in an ongoing process of professional development in which their personal and professional values, beliefs, and behaviors are integrated into a unified therapeutic self (Goldfried, 2001; Nevels & Coché, 1993; Orlinsky & Rønnestad, 2005; Skovholt & Jennings, 2004; Skovholt & Rønnestad, 1992). As a result, they are able to cultivate and express their therapeutic selves through their psychotherapeutic practice. They accomplish this by maintaining an attitude of openness to new learning—an active, searching, exploratory stance (Rønnestad & Skovholt, 2003). Gradually, over time and with the lessons learned from experience, they "throw out the clutter" (Rønnestad

& Skovholt, 2003, p. 20) and become congruent, confident, and effective therapists. As an added bonus, they also have longer and more satisfying careers (Dlugos & Friedlander, 2001; Vasco, Garcia-Marques, & Dryden, 1993).

Adapting your approach to become one that maximizes your psychotherapeutic effectiveness involves a process of continuous development through (a) learning a theory of psychotherapy in which you believe; (b) learning from your personal and professional experience; (c) learning and assimilating rationales, tasks, and goals from other theories; and (d) learning to be responsive to your clients' experience of therapy to establish a shared rationale for change.

Learn a Theory of Psychotherapy

As discussed in chapter 1, once you have identified your own preferred epistemological worldview and become knowledgeable of the major theories of psychotherapy, you can choose a theory that is amenable to you (Hansen & Freimuth, 1997). A particular theory of psychotherapy will feel right in a logical, intuitive, and aesthetic way if it captures the essence of your way of making sense of the human condition (Freimuth, 1992; Guy, 1987; Vasco et al., 1993).

Most therapists say that personal values and philosophy are very important when selecting a theoretical orientation, although their choice was largely determined by accidental factors such as the theoretical orientation of their training program, mentor, or therapy supervisor, and not a deliberate one (Prochaska & Norcross, 1983). Leaving such an important choice to accident, of course, may well result in adopting a theory that is inconsistent or in conflict with your personal worldview (Cummings & Lucchese, 1978; Halgin, 1985; Vasco et al., 1993). Remember that you will be a more confident, contented, and effective therapist if your practice is based on a system that is compatible with your epistemological worldview.

Therapists who have no salient theoretical allegiance are more likely to feel ineffective, dissatisfied, and stagnant, and less likely to feel skillful and efficacious or experience professional growth (Orlinsky & Rønnestad, 2005; Vasco et al., 1993). As Yann Martel (2001) said in *Life of Pi*, "To choose doubt as a philosophy of life is akin to choosing immobility as a means of transportation" (p. 31). Effective therapists are committed to and positively influenced by a theory of psychotherapy; therefore, devote sufficient time and energy to finding one that suits you.

Once you have found "your" theory, you can learn about the variety of theorists associated with it. Theorists tend to differ in their emphasis or explanation of a theory's governing rationale and in their style of presentation such that you will probably find one or another more to your liking. You can then intensively study one theory or theorist. You can learn and understand fully the rationale and goals and master the proper application of the attendant change tasks. You can delve into their writings and attend workshops to learn the approach in depth. There are also discussion and supervision groups of therapists of similar persuasion that you can join in person or online.

You may find it helpful to think of this aspect of your professional development as one of *secure attachment* (Bowlby, 1969) or *earned security* (Siegel & Hartzell, 2003), whereby from the secure base of your preferred theory you gain the confidence to explore the rich variety of psychotherapeutic opportunities that are available to you and your clients.

Learn From Your Own Experience

Personal values undergo significant change during the careers of psychotherapists (Dryden & Spurling, 1989; Goldfried, 2001; Guy, 1987; Skovholt & Rønnestad, 1995; Vasco et al., 1993). Life experiences—of which the practice of therapy is an important one—contribute significantly to these changes. Sometimes our beliefs change such that they conflict with the core assumptions of our therapeutic worldview. When they do, some therapists respond by curtailing professional growth (Rønnestad & Skovholt, 2003; Vasco et al., 1993), whereas others expand their approach to one that is more flexible and responsive to the varieties of the human experience. Those who profit from this crisis do so by maintaining an attitude of openness to new learning (Dlugos & Friedlander, 2001; Rønnestad & Skovholt, 2003).

The practice of psychotherapy is usually a commitment to a lifestyle—rather than merely an occupation—that merges the personal and professional dimensions of life into a unified perception of self and practice (W. E. Henry, 1966; Kottler, 1986; Rønnestad & Skovholt, 2003). Thus, unresolved dissonance between one's theoretical and personal beliefs can result in a powerful and pervasive crisis with negative consequences for therapeutic effectiveness and professional satisfaction, and it can even prompt the abandonment of the profession altogether (Cummings & Lucchese, 1978; Vasco et al., 1993). For this reason, it is important for therapists to engage in regular self-care practices so that any dissonance can be resolved in a growth-promoting manner (Baker, 2003).

Students face particular growth-limiting challenges in the form of the achievement orientation of the academic culture and the misuse of the power differential between professor or supervisor and student (Rønnestad & Skovholt, 2003). These challenges can result in a stagnant approach to professional development that, obviously, should be mitigated as much as possible. The best means for maintaining a developmental focus is having a supportive supervisory relationship or, where this is not forthcoming, turning to supportive peers.

In particular, as you begin to practice independently, disillusionment can result from learning that your preferred theory does not work with all clients (Rønnestad & Skovholt, 2003). If we cling to our preferred theory in an inflexible way to avoid facing the conflicts that arise out of accepting its limitations, we risk being less responsive to our clients' worldviews. This can become a vicious cycle of stagnation in which learning decreases, professional satisfaction suffers, and our effectiveness is diminished (Skovholt & Rønnestad, 1992; Vasco et al., 1993). One way to address this is to cultivate referral relationships with other therapists. In particular, seek out therapists who practice from a different theoretical orientation from your own. This will allow you to refer clients who have a worldview different from that on which your personal theory is based or who otherwise are not benefiting from therapy with you. This can give you the freedom to more fully develop your own approach to practice and gradually broaden your therapeutic repertoire at a pace that is right for you.

Effective psychotherapists are particularly adept at responding in a growth-promoting way to the lessons of their experience (Dlugos & Friedlander, 2001; Drapela, 1990; Dryden & Spurling, 1989; Goldfried, 2001; Skovholt & Rønnestad, 1995). These practitioners make use of their experience to adapt their therapeutic approach to be more of an expression of their individuality (Drapela, 1990; Dryden & Spurling, 1989; Goldfried, 2001; Skovholt & Rønnestad, 1995). This then tends to result in an increase in therapeutic responsiveness, flexibility, and effectiveness (Beitman, Goldfried, & Norcross, 1989; Vasco et al., 1993). Recognizing personal expressions in professional functioning is an important aspect of becoming a confident, satisfied, and effective therapist (Rønnestad & Skovholt, 2003). You would do well to consider, therefore, striving to adapt your evolving personal approach to your evolving personal strengths, weaknesses, values, attitudes, and interests through self-reflection, self-care (including personal therapy), continuing education, consultation, and supervision with well-experienced therapists (Orlinsky, Geller, & Norcross, 2005).

This personally integrative focus can inform one's external circumstances for the better as well. After all, work roles and work environment can be more or less compatible with one's worldview and therapeutic approach. Just as a personal congruence facilitates therapeutic effectiveness, so too does compatibility between the values of one's place of work and one's personal values (Rønnestad & Skovholt, 2003). Ultimately, learning from your own experience provides you with an opportunity to practice more authentically and competently.

Learn From Other Theories

Effective therapists modify their practice and expand their therapeutic repertoire by assimilating change tasks and goals from other theories into their evolving personal approach (Dryden & Spurling, 1989; Goldfried, 2001; Orlinsky & Rønnestad, 2005; Skovholt & Jennings, 2004) in a process of "shedding and adding" (Rønnestad & Skovholt, 2003, p. 17). This *pluralist* stance does not assume that there is one "true" theory of psychotherapy waiting to be discovered, just as none have consistently demonstrated superior results (see chap. 1, this volume). Well-seasoned therapists appreciate that there are many ways of making sense of our world—that no theory or system can preempt or preclude another (Koch, 1981). They assume that the best way of approaching truth is through an ongoing consideration of multiple, divergent theories and diverse types and sources of evidence (Safran & Messer, 1997). Objective, subjective, rational, and experiential sources of evidence are seen as "pieces of the puzzle" that is the human condition. Each theory of psychotherapy is accepted as relatively adequate and sufficiently valid, without being definitive.

In response to the dissonance that invariably results from personal and professional growth, effective, well-seasoned therapists continuously revise their approach to therapy by decreasing the exclusive influence of a single theory on their practice. Over time, they incorporate change processes and tasks from other theories and systems into their therapeutic approach. In this instance dissonance functions as an impetus to actualization in therapeutic and personal development by signaling a need for revision of one's epistemological assumptions and helping therapists accept that incongruities are an inevitable part of the human condition (Rønnestad & Skovholt, 2003; Vasco et al., 1993).

This *assimilative integration* strategy for growth as a therapist allows you to incorporate elements from other therapies into your own, taking meaning from the theory of origin and giving them additional meaning from the structure of your preferred theory of practice (Messer, 1992). Assimilative growth can be accomplished through reflective critique of your practice, continuing study, ongoing consultation, and supervision. It is most important to note that assimilation of other theories of psychotherapy requires an attitude of curiosity, openness, and acceptance of alternative constructions of the human condition. Therapeutic change tasks are viewed as deriving meaning and value from the theory from which they were developed, not as being inherently valid or invalid. Through assimilative integration, the beliefs and practices of your preferred theory are not discarded—they are supplemented and augmented by additional ones. Gradually, your preferred theory becomes a personal approach that is more inclusive as you incorporate and accommodate, in considered fashion, new perspectives and practices.

As J. D. Frank and Frank (1991) stated,

> The success of all techniques depends on the patient's sense of alliance with an actual or symbolic healer. This position implies that ideally all therapists should select for each patient the therapy that accords, or can be brought to accord, with the patient's personal characteristics and view of the problem. Also implied is that therapists should seek to learn as many approaches as they find congenial and convincing. (p. xv)

Initially, you will find it easiest to learn from theories that share a common axis with your personal theory (see Figure 1.2, chap. 1, this volume). Therefore, cognitive therapists, for example, will probably find it relatively easy to incorporate constructivist notions of the importance of subjective constructions of reality (Ramsay, 2001). Psychodynamic therapists have already incorporated humanistic ideas around empathy in the therapeutic relationship as well as some cognitive and behavioral change tasks (Gold & Stricker, 2001).

Ideally, new change tasks should be assimilated gradually to give you time to fully learn and understand them and so that you do not subject your clients to unsettling swings in their experience of psychotherapy with you. As professionals we are expected to introduce new techniques in a thoughtful way to achieve particular goals for a client or to address a gap in our scope of practice, not just because we are excited about them.

New rationales from other theories should probably be assimilated even more gradually than change tasks, so that you do not subject yourself to dramatic and unsettling shifts in your psychotherapeutic—or personal—worldview. It may help to think of this aspect of assimilative integration as evolutionary rather than revolutionary (Messer, 1992).

Learn to Be Responsive to Your Clients

Probably the most powerful learning for well-seasoned therapists comes from responding to their clients' experience of therapy (Dryden &

Spurling, 1989; Goldfried, 2001; Guy, 1987; Skovholt & Rønnestad, 1995). Becoming an effective therapist involves going beyond the limits inherent in your preferred theory and adapting it to each and every client. Your client's worldview will often be different from yours and from the worldview that underlies your approach to psychotherapy. If you are guided by the rationale of your preferred theory and adapt it to each client's experience of how congruent therapy is with his or her personal worldview, you create an opportunity for harnessing the power of psychotherapy. Highly effective therapists do this by using their preferred approach as a basis from which to establish a therapeutic rationale in which they and each client can believe. These master therapists paradoxically manage to maintain a "beginner's mind" despite—or perhaps because of—being so well-experienced (Skovholt & Jennings, 2004). In this way their theory provides a base from which to be helpful, not a Procrustean bed that they force their clients to fit into.[1]

Therefore, as you work at becoming an effective psychotherapist, strive also to provide effective psychotherapy. This means treating every session as an opportunity to collaborate through activities consistent with a shared therapeutic rationale toward goals that are meaningful to your client. To do this, you must remain mindful of the assumptions of your preferred theory in relation to the uniqueness of each client as a person and be willing to adapt your approach to be congruent with your client's assumptions and expectations.

The uniqueness of each client can be understood in an infinite number of ways, including diagnosis (e.g., Clarkin & Levy, 2004; Wampold & Brown, 2005), culture (e.g., Atkinson, Thompson, & Grant, 1993; Marsella & Yamada, 2007), gender (e.g., Orlinsky & Howard, 1980), and religion (e.g., Propst, Ostrom, Watkins, Dean, & Mashburn, 1992), among others. Yet, not one of these attributes has been reliably associated with even a small amount of the variance in psychotherapeutic outcomes (Clarkin & Levy, 2004). What we want to do is avoid taking an overly reductionistic approach whereby we arrive at so many different combinations of attributes that the number of possible categories is bewildering. Each client, even if categorized on the basis of only a few possible attributes, essentially becomes a member of a category of one, thereby evidencing no variance and rendering prediction impossible. Even if it was possible to develop such a system of categorization, the task of articulating ration-

---

[1] Procrustes (whose name means "he who stretches") kept a house by the side of the road and offered hospitality to passing strangers. The strangers were invited in for a pleasant meal and a night's rest in his very special bed. Procrustes described it as having the unique property that its length exactly matched whoever lay down upon it. What Procrustes did not volunteer was that because it fit him, he concluded that everyone should fit it. Therefore, as soon as a guest lay down, Procrustes went to work stretching those who were too short for the bed and chopping off the legs of those who were too long.

ales and interventions for each of these categories would be overwhelming. This system would then create an impossible situation for therapists, who would have to master as many different variants of psychotherapy as there are clients seeking their services. Rather, we want to keep in mind the words of Harry Stack Sullivan (1947), who reminded us that "we are all simply much more human than otherwise" (p. 7). That is, if we start from the premise that each client is similar to us in a fundamentally human way, and different from us in important ways, we can begin the process of effective collaboration.

To use one particularly important example, *culture* is the set of shared meanings about the nature of the world and our place in it that we adopt through our association with a particular group (Markus, 2008). These meanings inform the structure of social interactions by providing members a set of norms for acceptable behavior and lifestyle (Fowers & Richardson, 1996). These norms create expectations about how to think, feel, and behave to remain a member of the group and also about who is not a member of the group. The meanings and norms derived from your client's cultural identity are therefore usually an important influence on what they expect of and from psychotherapy.

The degree to which one's worldview is shaped by cultural norms is highly individual, however. Some of us are unaware of the extent to which we live by cultural norms, others consciously choose to belong and behave in accordance with the norms of certain groups, and we are all influenced by some combination of nonconscious and conscious norms (Markus, 2008). An individual cannot be assigned to a particular cultural group, therefore, without knowledge of his or her subjective experience. Although nationality and religious affiliation, for example, typically influence our worldview through cultural norms, there are many other characteristics by which we can identify ourselves as belonging to a normative group, such as age, gender, sexual orientation, occupation, and physical abilities. Because individuals have their own unique cultural identity, true collaboration within a shared therapeutic rationale can come only from listening and responding closely and empathically to each client's view of his or her place in the world.

The effective therapist is particularly sensitive to how expectations around culture can interfere with attending to the client's individual worldview (American Psychological Association, 2002). Because psychotherapists tend to believe that they are morally, ethically, and politically neutral (Ibrahim, 1996), we as a group are prone to assume that our theories and therapies are equally applicable to anyone—regardless of cultural worldview. We therefore tend to assume that others, whether from our same cultural group or not, share our worldview. This mistaken assumption has been termed *cultural encapsulation* (Wrenn, 1962) and can prevent us from understanding the world as our clients do. Much opportunity for therapeutic helpfulness has been lost—and even harms inflicted—by therapists assuming that their clients have the same cultural values as they do (Ponterotto, Casas, Alexander, & Suzuki, 2001; Sue & Sue, 2002).

Therapists can also be prone to assume that clients who are not of our cultural group do not share our worldview, turning then to whatever knowledge we possess (sometimes accurate, sometimes not) about the cultural group into which we have categorized them. Thus, we might expect that all individuals of a culture different from our own are all different in the same way from individuals of our cultural group. Sometimes we expect that persons who are members of a particular cultural group are inferior—the more common use of the concept of discrimination—and sometimes we idealize cultural stereotypes (e.g., the "noble savage"). In either case we miss the opportunity to collaborate with the client from within the client's personal worldview.

Remember also that what is viewed as a problem, solution, or goal from one worldview may not be seen as such from another. It follows that the nature of what is experienced as acceptable therapy—and thereby likely to be effective—will vary depending on the client's worldview. Sometimes a client will describe a problem or goal in an explicit way such that their worldview is relatively obvious, such as "I want to learn to control my anger" (empirical). More often it is implicit, such as, "If I could just figure out what is wrong with me, I wouldn't get so frustrated all the time" (rational). Therefore, an effective therapist who is working with one client will facilitate emotional expression and deep, personal disclosure, trying hard to relate to the client with unconditional positive regard while not judging, evaluating, or presuming to know what was best. The effective therapist knows that the active ingredient of this approach is the shared belief between the client and the therapist that people are best understood from what we would call a humanistic worldview. Yet, if another client holds a more empirical worldview, an effective therapist will take an active, directive stance and deliberately select tasks that promote logical thinking and adaptive behaviors intended to address specific problems and achieve pragmatic, measurable outcomes. Similarly, if a client holds a rationalist worldview, the effective therapist will adopt an introspective, skeptical stance and encourage a detailed description of events to foster honest self-perception so that patterns of personal experiences and old meanings can be discovered and understood and new more realistic decisions made in light of these personal insights. If the client has a collectivist worldview, the effective therapist will be an ally and advocate of the client's efforts at changing the nature of relationships with significant people within his or her social system so that the client experiences strong interpersonal ties, healthy role expectations, and nurturing relationships.

For therapists seeking a more overt source for learning from clients, the Outcome and Session Rating Scales (see Figures 11.2 and 11.3) are simple, valid, brief, and helpful tools (Duncan, Miller, & Sparks, 2004). They allow therapists to regularly monitor the quality of the alliance developed with clients and the clients' perception of the progress of therapy (Duncan, Sparks, & Miller, 2005). The information learned can be fed back into the therapy process and used to discuss with clients whether therapy should proceed in the same manner or adjustments should be made.

Conclusion

By adopting a theory that you believe in and adapting it to be congruent with who you are as a person, you will be able to clearly, sincerely, and convincingly articulate a rationale for therapy. If you then assimilate rationales, tasks, and goals from other theories and use them in the service of being responsive to your clients' worldview and experience of psychotherapy, you will be able to collaborate within a shared rationale. This ability to adapt your therapeutic approach to each client's worldview can be thought of as a sort of "disciplined improvisation" (Schacht, 1991, p. 309) and is the hallmark of effective therapy. This responsiveness is why seasoned therapists of differing theoretical orientations practice more like one another than like novice therapists of similar orientation (Dryden & Spurling, 1989; Goldfried, 2001; Orlinsky & Rønnestad, 2005). The effective therapist appreciates that each theory of psychotherapy speaks to an understanding of the human condition—a version of the truth—that is valuable and useful, without being definitive or absolute. Rather, each presents an opportunity to allay human suffering through collaborating with the client through their understanding of the problem and how it might be solved. Each ultimately requires a leap of faith in the merits of its foundational authority in order to adopt it (Mahoney, 2005). By adopting a theory of practice we believe in, we establish a conceptual base from which we can reach out to help others. By simultaneously holding our beliefs open to review and revision, we create a circumstance in which it is possible to continue to develop into even more effective therapists, be more helpful to more people more often, and have a long and satisfying career.

A Master Psychotherapist

Karen explored careers in law, teaching, and athletics (as an accomplished hockey player), but when she undertook personal

FIGURE 11.2

Looking back over the last week (or since your last visit), including today, help us understand how you have been doing in the following areas of your life, where marks to the left represent low levels and marks to the right indicate high levels.

Individually:
(Personal Well-Being)

I--I

Interpersonally:
(Family, Close Relationships)

I--I

Socially:
(Work, School, Friendships)

I--I

Overall:
(General Sense of Well-Being)

I--I

Institute for the Study of Therapeutic Change

www.talkingcure.com

© 2000, Scott D. Miller and Barry L. Duncan

Outcome Rating Scale (ORS). From the Institute for the Study of Therapeutic Change; available from http://www.talkingcure.com. Copyright 2000 by Scott D. Miller and Barry L. Duncan. Reprinted with permission.

therapy she knew with certainty that she wanted to become a psychotherapist. During graduate school she had the opportunity to work with a cognitive supervisor and found the approach very appealing. Her supervisor's characterization of therapy as "the

FIGURE 11.3

Please rate today's session by placing a hash mark on the line nearest to the description that best fits your experience.

Relationship:

I did not feel heard, understood, and respected

I--I

I felt heard, understood, and respected

Goals and Topics:

We did not work on or talk about what I wanted to work on or talk about

I--I

We worked on and talked about what I wanted to work on and talk about

Approach or Method:

The therapist's approach is not a good fit for me

I--I

The therapist's approach is a good fit for me

Overall:

There was something missing in the session today

I--I

Overall, today's session was right for me

Institute for the Study of Therapeutic Change

www.talkingcure.com

© 2002, Scott D. Miller, Barry L. Duncan, & Lynn Johnson

Session Rating Scale (SRS). From the Institute for the Study of Therapeutic Change; available from http://www.talkingcure.com. Copyright 2002 by Scott D. Miller, Barry L. Duncan, and Lynn Johnson. Reprinted with permission.

systematic application of common sense" really struck a chord with her. She also appreciated how he emphasized augmenting empirical knowledge with experiential learning, which instilled a life-long commitment to honing her psychotherapeutic skills through workshops and reflective practice.

Karen found the research findings on the importance of the client's experience of therapy for predicting outcomes particularly persuasive. She converted that knowledge into the routine of using S. D. Miller's (2004) Session and Outcome Rating Scales to solicit and quantify information she may have otherwise missed. One of the most powerful learning experiences she had was participating in one-way mirror sessions with therapists of differing therapeutic orientations. Observing and being observed by other therapists, and having them give her feedback, helped her to be keenly responsive to her clients' treatment needs.

Her athletic side had lain fallow while she immersed herself in her studies, until an internship supervisor invited her to consider applying the life lessons she learned in sports to her therapeutic practice. As she reflected on how she used imagery rehearsal and self-talk in her athletic career, she found herself feeling more confident as a therapist. She also began to include gentle physical activities, such as yoga and jogging with friends, in a stress-management regime that has continued throughout her career.

Just prior to entering graduate school, Karen married. She had her first child during school and her second child a year after graduating. She found the vicissitudes of marriage and motherhood sources of profound joy and tremendous strain. Through regular socializing with supportive friends—who are also therapists—she used these experiences and challenges as learning opportunities and incorporated the lessons learned into her work as a therapist.

Over her 20-year career, Karen explored a variety of theories of psychotherapy, including psychodynamic, gestalt, constructivist, and systemic. She attended workshops, undertook personal therapy periodically, read the psychotherapeutic literature regularly, and conferred with other congenial therapists. Although still fundamentally cognitive in her orientation to therapy, she often incorporates gestalt, constructivist, and systemic tasks and goals as appropriate for her clients. Today, Karen derives tremendous satisfaction from being an effective therapist and from mentoring other therapists. She looks forward to every day of practicing psychotherapy and to continuing to improve and hone her approach.

Learning Task

To further the process of consolidating your personal approach to psychotherapy, it can be helpful to prepare a case study from your practice that illustrates the application of your adopted theory (see Exhibit 11.1). Writing about what you have done is an opportunity to refine your understanding of what you do and to reflect on how your approach is more or less congruent with one theory or another. Upon completion of the task provided in Exhibit 11.1, you will probably notice that some of what you did was not entirely consistent with how you would like to practice.

EXHIBIT 11.1

Toward a Personal Approach to Practice

You will probably benefit most from this task if you write for a sympathetic audience. That is, if you do not attempt to convince anyone that your approach to practice is the best one. We all have our own preferred worldview, and others may or may not think that your approach is the right one. Therefore, trying to convince them will just distract you from what you need to do at this point. Instead, try to write in a manner that demonstrates that you believe in your approach.

It is also best if you do not try to convince anyone that you are a "good therapist." You will likely feel inhibited in your writing if you try to present a case that highlights what a wonderful therapist you are. Excessive concern about being good at psychotherapy tends to hinder becoming as effective as you can be. It may help to remind yourself that life is messy. And if you do not know it yet, let me be the first to tell you that therapy is usually just as messy. So, write your case study to describe how *you* make sense of what happened—the good, the bad, and the ugly.

As you are writing your case study, it may help to keep the following questions in mind:

1. Do I present my case study in a manner consistent with the worldview that underlies my adopted theory?
2. Do I present key concepts clearly and explain them as necessary?
3. Do I cite appropriate essential evidence relevant to my worldview?
4. Do I present my therapeutic rationale in a coherent, plausible manner?
5. Is the reasoning that I use to establish goals and choose change tasks consistent with my therapeutic rationale?
6. Do I establish how my adopted theory enables me to facilitate client goals?
7. Do I show sensitivity to what I am assuming or taking for granted?
8. Do I demonstrate appreciation for the value of other theoretical approaches?
9. Does my writing convince that I believe what I have written?

That's just fine—realizing that you have done so presents an opportunity to be more deliberate in your efforts to refine your approach. Trust the process, and you will become more confident and, ultimately, more effective.

Your Reflective Journal

Now is the time to consolidate your understanding of the approaches covered. Being able to decide for yourself what fits best for you is the most important task at this point in your career as a therapist. Therefore, take some time to review your reflective journal. What personal themes or trends do you notice? You might also want to review any chapters about which you still have some lingering questions or that you feel like rereading. Do you notice that you have an affinity for theories from a particular worldview, or are you drawn to theories that span two or more worldviews? To maximize your effectiveness as a therapist and satisfaction with your career, you should seriously consider settling on one theory, or at most two theories from the same foundational worldview. Returning to the learning task in the first chapter might be helpful for you at this point. Take time to record your personal process of adopting a theory for psychotherapeutic practice. You may not yet have settled on the right theory for you, and you may feel that you are near or far from that goal. Wherever you are, take as much time as you need to clarify your process.

This is also a good time to record your thoughts about how to stay refreshed and renewed throughout your career as a therapist. How could you use the information contained in this book, for example? Are there other opportunities for learning you want to pursue? Are there professional organizations you could join and conferences you could attend? What sort of therapeutic experiences might you participate in? Perhaps you want to undergo personal therapy or join a supervision group? Have you considered taking a well-experienced therapist to coffee or lunch, perhaps initiating a mentoring relationship? Who in your life sustains your aspirations? Who can help you to be successful and satisfied as a therapist? Who do you know who can delight in your successes and commiserate with your failures? How will you keep them close? What other resources could be helpful for you? Take some time now to record whatever ideas you have and plans you might want to make.

Summary

To be effective psychotherapists, we must first identify our preferred epistemological worldview and then become familiar with the various theories so that we can choose one that is compatible with our worldview. Once we have done this, we can then study a theory that we find particularly agreeable, becoming thoroughly familiar with its rationale and goals and mastering its associated change tasks. As we practice, we can maximize our effectiveness and our opportunities to develop if we strive to learn from our clients' experience of the therapy. Then, as we learn from our personal and professional experience, we can continuously revise and expand our personal theory by assimilating the rationale, goals, and change tasks from other theories. This ongoing process allows us to remain content and satisfied as therapists throughout our career and to be more helpful to more of the people who seek our services.

Further Resources

American Psychological Association (Producer). (2005). *Client-directed outcome-focused psychotherapy with Scott D. Miller, PhD* [Motion picture]. (Available from the American Psychological Association, 750 First Street, NE, Washington, DC 20002-4242)

Carlson, J., & Kjos, D. (Producers). (1999). *Client-directed interaction: Adjusting the therapy not the client with Scott D. Miller, PhD* [Motion picture]. (Available from Zeig, Tucker & Theisen, Inc., 3614 N 24th Street, Phoenix, AZ 85016-6509)

Dryden, W., & Spurling, L. (Eds.). (1989). *On becoming a psychotherapist*. London: Routledge.

Duncan, B. L., Miller, S. D., & Sparks, J. A. (2004). *The heroic client: A revolutionary way to improve effectiveness through client-directed, outcome-informed therapy*. San Francisco: Jossey-Bass.

Goldfried, M. R. (2001). *How therapists change: Personal and professional reflections*. Washington, DC: American Psychological Association.

Nevels, L. A., & Coché, J. M. (1993). *Powerful wisdom: Voices of distinguished women psychotherapists*. San Francisco: Jossey-Bass.

Orlinsky, D. E., & Rønnestad, M. H. (2005). *How psychotherapists develop: A study of therapeutic work and professional growth*. Washington, DC: American Psychological Association.

Skovholt, T. M., & Jennings, L. (2004). *Master therapists: Exploring expertise in therapy and counseling*. Boston: Allyn & Bacon.

Skovholt, T. M., & Rønnestad, M. H. (1995). *The evolving professional self: Stages and themes in therapist and counselor development*. New York: Wiley.

Stricker, G., & Gold, J. (Eds.). (2005). *A casebook of psychotherapy integration*. Washington, DC: American Psychological Association.

References

Ackerman, N. W. (1938). The unity of the family. *Archives of Pediatrics, 55,* 51–61.

Adler, A. (1931). *Guiding the child* (B. Gizberg, Trans.). New York: Greenberg.

Adler, A. (1963). *The practice and theory of individual psychology* (P. Radin, Trans.). Patterson, NJ: Littlefield, Adams.

Adler, A. (1964). *Problems of neurosis*. New York: Harper & Row.

Adler, A. (1992). *Understanding human nature* (C. Brett, Trans.). Oxford, England: Oneworld. (Original work published 1927)

Adler, N., & Matthews, K. (1994). Health psychology: Why do some people get sick and some stay healthy? *Annual Review of Psychology, 45,* 229–259.

Ahn, H., & Wampold, B. E. (2001). Where oh where are the specific ingredients? A meta-analysis of component studies in counseling and psychotherapy. *Journal of Counseling Psychology, 48,* 251–257.

Alexander, F. G., & French, T. M. (1946). *Psychoanalytic therapy: Principles and applications*. New York: Ronald Press.

Allen, F. (1995). Feminist theory and cognitive behaviorism. In W. O'Donohue & L. Krasner (Eds.), *Theories of behavior therapy: Exploring behavior change* (pp. 495–528). Washington, DC: American Psychological Association.

American Psychological Association. (1975). Report of the Task Force on Sex Bias and Sex Role Stereotyping in Psychotherapeutic Practice. *American Psychologist, 30,* 1169–1175.

American Psychological Association. (1978). Task force on sex bias and sex role stereotyping in psychotherapeutic practice: Guidelines for therapy with women. *American Psychologist, 33,* 1122–1123.

American Psychological Association. (2002). *Guidelines on multicultural education, training, research, practice, and organizational change for psychologists.* Washington, DC: Author.

Anderson, H. (1997). *Conversation, language, and possibilities: A postmodern approach.* New York: Basic Books.

Anderson, H. (2001). Postmodern collaborative and person-centred therapies: What would Carl Rogers say? *Journal of Family Therapy, 23,* 339–360.

Anderson, H., & Gehart, D. (Eds.). (2006). *Collaborative therapy: Relationships and conversations that make a difference.* New York: Routledge.

Anderson, H., & Goolishian, H. (1988). Human systems and linguistic systems: Evolving ideas about the implications for theory and practice. *Family Process, 27,* 371–393.

Angeles, P. A. (1992). *Dictionary of philosophy.* New York: HarperCollins.

Antony, M. M., & Swinson, R. P. (2000). *Phobic disorders and panic in adults: A guide to assessment and treatment.* Washington, DC: American Psychological Association.

Appel, M. A., Saab, P. G., & Holroyd, K. A. (1985). Cardiovascular disorders. In M. Hersen & A. S. Bellack (Eds.), *Handbook of clinical behavior therapy with adults* (pp. 381–416). New York: Plenum Press.

Atkinson, D. R., Thompson, C. E., & Grant, S. K. (1993). A three-dimensional model for counseling racial/ethnic minorities. *The Counseling Psychologist, 21,* 257–277.

Axline, V. M. (1964). *Dibs: In search of self.* New York: Ballantine Books.

Ayllon, T., & Azrin, N. H. (1968). *The token economy: A motivational system for therapy and rehabilitation.* New York: Appleton-Century-Crofts.

Baer, R. A. (2003). Mindfulness training as a clinical intervention: A conceptual and empirical review. *Clinical Psychology: Science and Practice, 10,* 125–143.

Baer, R. A. (2006). *Mindfulness-based treatment approaches: Clinician's guide to evidence base and applications.* San Diego, CA: Elsevier.

Baker, E. K. (2003). *Caring for ourselves: A therapist's guide to personal and professional well-being.* Washington, DC: American Psychological Association.

Bandura, A. (1969). *Principles of behavior modification.* New York: Holt, Rinehart & Winston.

Bandura, A. (1974). Behavior theory and the models of man. *American Psychologist, 29*, 859–869.

Bandura, A. (1977a). Self-efficacy: Toward a unifying theory of behavior change. *Psychological Review, 84*, 191–215.

Bandura, A. (1977b). *Social learning theory*. Englewood Cliffs, NJ: Prentice Hall.

Bandura, A., & Walters, R. H. (1963). *Social learning and personality development*. New York: Holt, Rinehart & Winston.

Barley, W. D., Buie, S. E., Peterson, E. W., Hollingsworth, A. S., Griva, M., Hickerson, S. C., et al. (1993). Development of an inpatient cognitive–behavioral treatment program for borderline personality disorder. *Journal of Personality Disorders, 7*, 232–240.

Barlow, D. H. (Ed.). (2002). *Anxiety and its disorders: The nature and treatment of anxiety and panic* (2nd ed.). New York: Wiley.

Barrett-Lennard, G. T. (1997). The recovery of empathy—Toward others and self. In A. C. Bohart & L. S. Greenberg (Eds.), *Empathy reconsidered: New directions in psychotherapy* (pp. 103–121). Washington, DC: American Psychological Association.

Barrett-Lennard, G. T. (1998). *Carl Rogers' helping system: Journey and substance*. London: Sage.

Baskin, T. W., Tierney, S. C., Minami, T., & Wampold, B. E. (2000). Establishing specificity in psychotherapy: A meta-analysis of structural equivalence of placebo controls. *Journal of Consulting and Clinical Psychology, 71*, 973–979.

Bateson, G. (1972). *Steps to an ecology of mind*. New York: Ballantine Books.

Bateson, G., Jackson, D. D., Haley, J., & Weakland, J. (1956). Toward a theory of schizophrenia. *Behavioral Science, 1*, 251–264.

Beck, A. T. (1967). *Depression: Clinical, experimental, and theoretical aspects*. New York: Hoeber.

Beck, A. T. (1976). *Cognitive therapy and the emotional disorders*. New York: International Universities Press.

Beck, A. T., & Emery, G. (1979). *Cognitive therapy of anxiety and phobic disorders*. Philadelphia: Center for Cognitive Therapy.

Beck, A. T., & Emery, G. (1985). *Anxiety disorders and phobias: A cognitive perspective*. New York: Basic Books.

Beck, A. T., & Hurvich, M. S. (1959). Psychological correlates of depression: 1. Frequency of "masochistic" dream content in a private practice sample. *Psychosomatic Medicine, 21*, 50–55.

Beck, A. T., Rush, A .J., Shaw, B. F., & Emery, G. (1979). *Cognitive therapy of depression*. New York: Guilford Press.

Beck, J. S. (1995). *Cognitive therapy: Basics and beyond*. New York: Guilford Press.

Beck, J. S. (2005). *Cognitive therapy for challenging problems: What to do when the basics don't work*. New York: Guilford Press.

Becker, R. E., Heimberg, R. G., & Bellack, A. S. (1987). *Social skills training treatment for depression*. New York: Pergamon Press.

Beisser, A. (1970). Paradoxical theory of change. In J. Fagan & I. Shepherd (Eds.), *Gestalt therapy now* (pp. 77–80). New York: Harper & Row.

Beitman, B. D., Goldfried, M. R., & Norcross, J. C. (1989). The movement toward integrating the psychotherapies: An overview. *American Journal of Psychiatry, 146,* 138–147.

Benjamin, L. T., Whitaker, J. L., Ramsey, R. M., & Zeve, D. R. (2007). John B. Watson's alleged sex research: An appraisal of the evidence. *American Psychologist, 62,* 131–139.

Bernfeld, S. (1944). Freud's earliest theories and the school of Helmholtz. *Psychoanalytic Quarterly, 13,* 341–362.

Bettelheim, B. (1983). *Freud and man's soul*. New York: Knopf.

Beutler, L., Malik, M., Alimohamed, S., Harwood, T. M., Talebi, H., Noble, S., & Wong, E. (2004). Therapist variables. In M. Lambert (Ed.), *Bergin and Garfield's handbook of psychotherapy and behavior change* (5th ed., pp. 227–306). New York: Wiley.

Bevan, W. (1991). Contemporary psychology: A tour inside the onion. *American Psychologist, 46,* 475–483.

Binswanger, L. (1958). The existential analysis school of thought. In R. May, E. Angel, & H. Ellenberger (Eds.), *Existence* (pp. 191–213). New York: Basic Books.

Binswanger, L. (1963). *Being-in-the-world* (J. Needleman, Trans.). New York: Basic Books.

Blocher, D. H. (1987). On the uses and misuses of the term *theory*. *Journal of Counseling and Development, 66,* 67–68.

Bohart, A. C., O'Hara, M., & Leitner, L. M. (1998). Empirically violated treatments: Disenfranchisement of humanistic and other psychotherapies. *Psychotherapy Research, 8,* 141–157.

Bowen, M. (1990). *Family therapy in clinical practice*. New York: Jason Aronson.

Bowlby, J. (1969). *Attachment.* New York: Basic Books.

Bowlby, J. (1977). The making and breaking of affectional bonds: 1. Aetiology and psychopathology in the light of attachment theory. *The British Journal of Psychiatry, 130,* 201–210.

Brabeck, M., & Brown, L. (1997). Feminist theory and psychological practice. In J. Worell & N. G. Johnson (Eds.), *Shaping the future of feminist psychology: Education, research, and practice* (pp. 15–35). Washington, DC: American Psychological Association.

Brantner, J. P., & Doherty, M. A. (1983). A review of time-out: A conceptual and methodological analysis. In S. Axelrod & J. Apsche (Eds.), *The effects of punishment on human behavior* (pp. 87–132). New York: Academic Press.

Brenner, C. (1982). *The mind in conflict.* New York: International Universities Press.

Breuer, J., & Freud, S. (1955). *Studies on hysteria.* In J. Strachey (Ed. & Trans.), *The standard edition of the complete psychological works of Sigmund Freud* (Vol. 2). London: Hogarth Press. (Original work published 1895).

Brody, C. M. (1984). *Women therapists working with women: New theory and process of feminist therapy.* New York: Springer Publishing Company.

Brown, K. W., & Ryan, R. M. (2003). The benefits of being present: Mindfulness and its role in psychological well-being. *Journal of Personality and Social Psychology, 84,* 822–848.

Brown, L. S. (1990). The meaning of a multicultural perspective for theory-building in feminist therapy. *Women & Therapy, 9,* 1–21.

Brown, L. S. (1994). *Subversive dialogues: Theory in feminist therapy.* New York: Basic Books.

Buber, M. (1947). *Between man and man* (R. G. Smith, Trans.). London: Kegan Paul. (Original work published 1929)

Buber, M. (1970). *I and thou* (W. Kaufman, Trans.). Edinburgh, Scotland: T&T Clark. (Original work published 1937)

Buckley, W. (1967). *Sociology and modern systems theory.* Englewood Cliffs, NJ: Prentice Hall.

Bugental, J. F. T. (1978). *Psychotherapy and process: The fundamental of an existential–humanistic approach.* New York: McGraw-Hill.

Bugental, J. F. T. (1987). *The art of the psychotherapist.* New York: Norton.

Bugental, J. F. T. (1990). *Intimate journeys: Stories from life-changing therapy.* San Francisco: Jossey-Bass.

Burchard, E. M. L. (1958). The evolution of psychoanalytic tasks and goals: A historical survey of Freud's writings on technique. *Psychiatry, 21*, 341–357.

Caballo, V. E. (Ed.). (1998). *International handbook of cognitive and behavioral treatments for psychological disorders.* Oxford, England: Pergamon Press.

Caplan, P. J. (1984). The myth of women's masochism. *American Psychologist, 39*, 130–139.

Carkhuff, R. (1969). *Helping and human relations* (Vols. 1 and 2). New York: Holt, Rinehart & Winston.

Carkhuff, R. (1981). *Toward actualizing and human potential.* Amherst, MA: HRD Press.

Carkhuff, R. (1983). *Interpersonal skills and human productivity.* Amherst, MA: HRD Press.

Carkhuff, R., & Berenson, B. (1967). *Beyond counseling and therapy.* New York: Holt, Rinehart & Winston.

Cartwright, D. E. (1955). Effectiveness of psychotherapy: A critique of the spontaneous remission argument. *Journal of Counseling Psychology, 2*, 290–296.

Cashdan, S. (1988). *Object relations therapy: Using the relationship.* New York: Norton.

Castonguay, L. G., Goldfried, M. R., Wiser, S., Raue, P. J., & Hayes, A. M. (1996). Predicting the effect of cognitive therapy for depression: A study of unique and common factors. *Journal of Consulting and Clinical Psychology, 64*, 497–504.

Castonguay, L. G., & Holtforth, M. G. (2005). Change in psychotherapy: A plea for no more "nonspecific" and false dichotomies. *Clinical Psychology: Science and Practice, 12*, 198–201.

Cautela, J. R. (1966). Treatment of compulsive behavior by covert sensitization. *Psychological Record, 16*, 33–41.

Cautela, J. R. (1967). Covert sensitization. *Psychological Reports, 20*, 459–468.

Cecchin, G. (1987). Hypothesizing, circularity, and neutrality revisited: An invitation to curiosity. *Family Process, 26*, 405–413.

Chambless, D. L., & Ollendick, T. H. (2001). Empirically supported psychological interventions: Controversies and evidence. *Annual Review of Psychology, 52*, 685–716.

Chesler, P. (1972). *Women and madness.* Garden City, NY: Doubleday.

Clarkin, J. F., & Levy, K. N. (2004). The influence of client variables on psychotherapy. In M. Lambert (Ed.), *Bergin and Garfield's handbook of psychotherapy and behavior change* (5th ed., pp. 194–226). New York: Wiley.

Cloitre, M., Koenen, K. C., Cohen, L. R., & Han, H. (2002). Skills training in affective and interpersonal regulation followed by exposure: A phase-based treatment for PTSD related to childhood abuse. *Journal of Consulting and Clinical Psychology, 70,* 1067–1074.

Cohen, J. (1988). *Statistical power analysis for the behavioral sciences* (2nd ed.). Hillsdale, NJ: Erlbaum.

Corsini, R. (1979). *Current psychotherapies.* Itasca, IL: F.E. Peacock.

Cottone, R. R. (1992). *Theories and paradigms of counseling and psychotherapy.* Boston: Allyn and Bacon.

Coyne, J. C. (1985). Toward a theory of frames and reframing: The social nature of frames. *Journal of Marital and Family Therapy, 11,* 337–344.

Craighead, W. E., Sheets, E. S., Bjornsson, A. S., & Arnarson, E. O. (2005). Specificity and nonspecificity in psychotherapy. *Clinical Psychology: Science and Practice, 12,* 189–193.

Crits-Christoph, P., Baranackie, K., Kurcias, J. S., Carroll, K., Luborsky, L., McLellan, T., et al. (1991). Meta-analysis of therapist effects in psychotherapy outcome studies. *Psychotherapy Research, 1,* 81–91.

Crits-Christoph, P., & Mintz, J. (1991). Implications of therapist effects for the design and analysis of comparative studies of psychotherapies. *Journal of Consulting and Clinical Psychology, 59,* 20–26.

Crook, K. H., & Truscott, D. (2007). *Ethics and law for teachers.* Toronto, Ontario, Canada: Thomson Nelson.

Cummings, N. A., & Lucchese, G. (1978). Adoption of a psychological orientation: The role of the inadvertent. *Psychotherapy: Theory, Research and Practice, 15,* 323–328.

Dattilio, F. M. (Ed.). (1998). *Case studies in couple and family therapy: Systemic and cognitive perspectives.* New York: Guilford Press.

Davanloo, H. (1980). *Short-term dynamic psychotherapy.* New York: Jason Aronson.

Dember, W. N. (1974). Motivation and the cognitive revolution. *American Psychologist, 29,* 161–168.

DeRubeis, R. J., Brotman, M. A., & Gibbons, C. J. (2005). A conceptual and methodological analysis of the nonspecifics argument. *Clinical Psychology: Science and Practice, 12,* 174–183.

de Shazer, S. (1985). *Keys to solution in brief therapy*. New York: Norton.

de Shazer, S. (1988). *Clues: Investigating solutions in brief therapy*. New York: Norton.

de Shazer, S., Berg, I. K., Lipchik, E., Nunnally, E., Molnar, A., Gingerich, W., & Weiner-Davis, M. (1986). Brief therapy: Focused solution development. *Family Process, 25*, 207–221.

DeVoe, D. (1990). Feminist and nonsexist counseling: Implications for the male counselor. *Journal of Counseling and Development, 69*, 33–36.

DiGiuseppe, R., & Tafrate, R. C. (2003). Anger treatments for adults: A meta-analytic review. *Clinical Psychology: Science and Practice, 10*, 70–84.

Dimidjian, S., Hollon, S. D., Dobson, K. S., Schmaling, K. B., Kohlenberg, R. J., Addis, M. E., et al. (2006). Randomized trial of behavioral activation, cognitive therapy, and antidepressant medication in the acute treatment of adults with major depression. *Journal of Consulting and Clinical Psychology, 74*, 658–670.

Dlugos, R. F., & Friedlander, M. L. (2001). Passionately committed psychotherapists: A qualitative study of their experiences. *Professional Psychology: Research and Practice, 32*, 298–304.

Dobson, K. S. (1989). A meta-analysis of the efficacy of cognitive therapy for depression. *Journal of Consulting and Clinical Psychology, 57*, 414–419.

Dobson, K. S. (Ed.). (2001). *Handbook of cognitive–behavioral therapies*. New York: Guilford Press.

Dobson, K. S., & Pusch, D. (1993). Toward a definition of the conceptual and empirical boundaries of cognitive therapy. *Australian Psychologist, 28*, 137–144.

Drapela, V. J. (1990). The value of theories for counseling practitioners. *International Journal for the Advancement of Counselling, 13*, 19–26.

Dryden, W., & Spurling, L. (Eds.). (1989). *On becoming a psychotherapist*. London: Routledge.

Duncan, B. L., & Miller, S. D. (2005). Treatment manuals do not improve outcomes. In J. C. Norcross, L. E. Beutler, & R. F. Levant (Eds.), *Evidence-based practices in mental health: Debate and dialogue on the fundamental questions* (pp. 140–149). Washington, DC: American Psychological Association.

Duncan, B. L., Miller, S. D., & Sparks, J. A. (2004). *The heroic client: A revolutionary way to improve effectiveness through client-directed, outcome-informed therapy*. San Francisco: Jossey-Bass.

Duncan, B. L., Miller, S. D., Wampold, B., & Hubble, M. A. (in press). *The heart and soul of change: Delivering what works* (2nd ed.). Washington, DC: American Psychological Association .

Duncan, B. L., Sparks, J. A., & Miller, S. D. (2005). Client, not theory, directed: Integrating approaches one client at a time. In G. Stricker & J. Gold (Eds.), *A casebook of psychotherapy integration* (pp. 225–240). Washington, DC: American Psychological Association.

Eddy, K. T., Dutra, L., Bradley, R., & Westen, D. (2004). A multidimensional meta-analysis of psychotherapy and pharmacotherapy for obsessive–compulsive disorder. *Clinical Psychology Review, 24,* 1011–1030.

Egan, G. (1979). *The skilled helper.* New York: Brooks/Cole.

Egan, G. (2006). *The skilled helper: A problem management and opportunity development approach to helping* (8th ed.). Belmont, CA: Thomson Brooks/Cole.

Eichenbaum, L., & Orbach, S. (1983). *Understanding women: A feminist psychoanalytic approach.* New York: Basic Books.

Elkin, I. (1994). The NIMH Treatment of Depression Collaborative Research Program: Where we began and where we are. In A. E. Bergin & S. L. Garfield (Eds.), *Handbook of psychotherapy and behavior change* (4th ed., pp. 114–139). New York: Wiley.

Elliot, R., Watson, J. C., Goldman, R. N., & Greenberg, L. S. (2004). *Learning emotion-focused therapy: The process-experiential approach to change.* Washington, DC: American Psychological Association.

Ellis, A. (1957a). Outcome of employing three techniques of psychotherapy. *Journal of Clinical Psychology, 13,* 344–350.

Ellis, A. (1957b). Rational psychotherapy and individual psychology. *Journal of Individual Psychology, 13,* 38–44.

Ellis, A. (1962). *Reason and emotion in psychotherapy.* Secaucus, NJ: Lyle Stuart.

Ellis, A., & Dryden, W. (1997). *The practice of rational emotive behavior therapy.* New York: Springer Publishing Company.

Ellis, A., & Whiteley, J. M. (Eds.). (1979). *Theoretical and empirical foundations of rational emotive therapy.* Monterey, CA: Brooks/Cole.

Emmelkamp, P. M. G., Kriji, M., Hulsbosch, A. M., de Vries, S., Schuemie, M. J., & van der Mast, C. A. P. G. (2002). Virtual reality treatment versus exposure in vivo: A comparative evaluation in acrophobia. *Behaviour Research and Therapy, 40,* 509–516.

Enns, C. Z. (1992). Toward integrating feminist psychotherapy and feminist philosophy. *Professional Psychology: Research and Practice, 23,* 453–466.

Enns, C. Z. (1993). Twenty years of feminist counseling and psychotherapy: From naming biases to implementing multifaceted practice. *The Counseling Psychologist, 21,* 3–87.

Epstein, S. (1994). Integration of the cognitive and psychodynamic unconscious. *American Psychologist, 49,* 709–724.

Erickson, M. H. (1954). Special techniques of brief hypnotherapy. *Journal of Clinical and Experimental Hypnosis, 2,* 109–129.

Erickson, M. H. (1965). The use of symptoms as an integral part of hypnotherapy. *American Journal of Clinical Hypnosis, 8,* 57–65.

Erikson, E. H. (1950). *Childhood and society.* New York: Norton.

Eysenck, H. J. (1952). The effects of psychotherapy: An evaluation. *Journal of Consulting Psychology, 16,* 319–324.

Eysenck, H. J. (1960). *Behaviour therapy and the neuroses.* Oxford, England: Pergamon Press.

Fairbairn, W. R. D. (1954). *An object-relations theory of personality: Psychoanalytic studies of personality.* New York: Basic Books.

Fairbairn, W. R. D. (1958). On the nature and aims of psycho-analytical treatment. *International Journal of Psychoanalysis, 39,* 374–385.

Feminist Therapy Institute. (2000). *Feminist therapy code of ethics* (Rev. ed.). Georgetown, ME: Author.

Ferenczi, S. (1980). Confusion of tongues between adults and the child: The language of tenderness and of passion. In M. Balint (Ed.), *Final contributions to the problems and methods of psycho-analysis* (Vol. 3, pp. 156–167). New York: Brunner/Mazel. (Original work published 1933)

Foa, E. B., Franklin, M. E., & Kozak, M. J. (1998). Psychosocial treatments for obsessive–compulsive disorder: Literature review. In R. P. Swinson, M. M. Antony, S. Rachman, & M. A. Richter (Eds.), *Obsessive–compulsive disorder: Theory, research, and treatment* (pp. 258–276). New York: Guilford Press.

Fowers, B. J., & Richardson, F. C. (1996). Why is multiculturalism good? *American Psychologist, 51,* 609–621.

Framo, J. L. (1996). A personal retrospective of the family therapy field: Then and now. *Journal of Marital and Family Therapy, 22,* 289–316.

Frank, J. D. (1961). *Persuasion and healing: A comparative study of psychotherapy.* Baltimore, MD: Johns Hopkins University Press.

Frank, J. D., & Frank, J. B. (1991). *Persuasion and healing: A comparative study of psychotherapy* (3rd ed.). Baltimore, MD: Johns Hopkins University Press.

Frank, R. (2001). *Body of awareness: A somatic and developmental approach to psychotherapy.* Hillsdale, NJ: Analytic Press.

Frankl, V. E. (1955). *The doctor and the soul: From psychotherapy to logotherapy* (C. Winston, Trans.). New York: Knopf.

Frankl, V. E. (1963). *Man's search for meaning: An introduction to logotherapy.* Boston: Beacon Press. (Original work published 1946)

Fraser, J. S., & Solovey, A. D. (2006). *Second-order change in psychotherapy: The golden thread that unifies effective treatments.* Washington, DC: American Psychological Association.

Freedheim, D. K. (1992). *History of psychotherapy: A century of change.* Washington, DC: American Psychological Association.

Freimuth, M. (1992). Is the best always preferred? *American Psychologist, 47,* 673–674.

Freud, A. (1936). *The ego and the mechanisms of defense* (C. Baine, Trans.). New York: International Universities Press.

Freud, S. (1953). The interpretation of dreams. In J. Strachey (Ed. & Trans.), *The standard edition of the complete psychological works of Sigmund Freud* (Vols. 4 and 5, pp. xi–338, 339–625). London: Hogarth Press. (Original work published 1900)

Freud, S. (1957). Mourning and melancholia. In J. Strachey (Ed. & Trans.), *The standard edition of the complete psychological works of Sigmund Freud* (Vol. 14, pp. 239–258). London: Hogarth Press. (Original work published 1917)

Freud, S. (1959a). Analysis of a phobia in a five-year-old boy. In J. Strachey (Ed. & Trans.), *The standard edition of the complete psychological works of Sigmund Freud* (Vol. 10, pp. 5–149). London: Hogarth Press. (Original work published 1909)

Freud, S. (1959b). The question of lay analysis. In J. Strachey (Ed. & Trans.), *The standard edition of the complete psychological works of Sigmund Freud* (Vol. 20, pp. 177–258). London: Hogarth Press. (Original work published 1926)

Freud, S. (1961). The ego and the id. In J. Strachey (Ed. & Trans.), *The standard edition of the complete psychological works of Sigmund Freud* (Vol. 19, pp. 1–66). London: Hogarth Press. (Original work published 1923)

Freud, S. (1964). New introductory lectures on psychoanalysis. In J. Strachey (Ed. & Trans.), *The standard edition of the complete psychological works of Sigmund Freud* (Vol. 22, pp. 1–182). London: Hogarth Press. (Original work published 1933)

Freud, S. (1999). *The interpretation of dreams* (J. Crick, Trans.). Oxford, England: Oxford University Press. (Original work published 1900)

Freud, S. (2003). *The joke and its relation to the unconscious* (J. Crick, Trans.). New York: Penguin Books. (Original work published 1905)

Friedan, B. (1963). *The feminine mystique.* New York: Dell.

Fromm-Reichmann, F. (1950). *Principles of intensive psychotherapy*. Chicago: University of Chicago Press.

Gay, P. (1988). *Freud: A life for our times*. New York: Norton.

Gendlin, E. T. (1970). A short summary and some long predictions. In J. Hart & T. Tomlinson (Eds.), *New directions in client-centered therapy* (pp. 544–562). Boston: Houghton Mifflin.

Gendlin, E. T. (1981). *Focusing*. New York: Bantam Books.

Gendlin, E. T. (1996). *Focusing-oriented psychotherapy: A manual of the experiential method*. New York: Guilford Press.

Germer, C. K., Siegel, R. D., & Fulton, P. R. (2005). *Mindfulness and psychotherapy*. New York: Guilford Press.

Gilbert, L. A. (1980). Feminist therapy. In A. Brodsky & R. T. Hare-Mustin (Eds.), *Women and psychotherapy* (pp. 245–265). New York: Guilford Press.

Gold, J., & Stricker, G. (2001). Relational psychoanalysis as a foundation of assimilative integration. *Journal of Psychotherapy Integration, 11*, 43–58.

Goldfried, M. R. (1980). Toward the delineation of therapeutic change principles. *American Psychologist, 35*, 991–999.

Goldfried, M. R. (2001). *How therapists change: Personal and professional reflections*. Washington, DC: American Psychological Association.

Goldfried, M. R., & Davison, G. C. (1994). *Clinical behavior therapy*. New York: Wiley.

Goldfried, M. R., & Wolfe, B. E. (1996). Psychotherapy practice and research: Repairing a strained alliance. *American Psychologist, 51*, 1007–1016.

Goldstein, K. (1939). *The organism: A holistic approach derived from pathological data in man*. New York: American Books.

Good, G. E., Thomson, D. A., & Brathwaite, A. D. (2005). Men and therapy: Critical concepts, theoretical frameworks, and research recommendations. *Journal of Clinical Psychology, 61*, 699–711.

Goodman, P. (1960). *Growing up absurd: Problems of youth in the organized society*. New York: Vintage.

Goodrich, T. J., Rampage, C., Ellman, B., & Halstead, K. (1988). *Feminist family therapy*. New York: Norton.

Goolishian, H., & Anderson, H. (1987). Language systems and therapy: An evolving idea. *Psychotherapy, 24*, 529–538.

Greenberg, J. R., & Mitchell, S. A. (1983). *Object relations in psychoanalytic theory*. Cambridge, MA: Harvard University Press.

Greenberg, L. S. (2002). *Emotion-focused therapy: Coaching clients to work through their feelings.* Washington, DC: American Psychological Association.

Greenberg, L. S., & Watson, J. C. (2006). *Emotion-focused therapy for depression.* Washington, DC: American Psychological Association.

Greene, B., & Sanchez-Hucles, J. (1997). Diversity: Advancing an inclusive feminist psychology. In J. Worell & N. G. Johnson (Eds.), *Shaping the future of feminist psychology: Education, research, and practice* (pp. 173–202). Washington, DC: American Psychological Association.

Greenspan, M. (1983). *A new approach to women and therapy.* New York: McGraw-Hill.

Greenwald, J. A. (1976). The ground rules in gestalt therapy. In C. Hatcher & P. Himelstein (Eds.), *The handbook of gestalt therapy* (pp. 267–280). New York: Jason Aronson.

Guerin, P. J. (1976). Family therapy: The first twenty-five years. In P. J. Guerin (Ed.), *Family therapy: Theory and practice* (pp. 2–22). New York: Gardner Press.

Guidano, V. F. (1987). *Complexity of the self: A developmental approach to psychopathology and therapy.* New York: Guilford Press.

Guidano, V. F. (1991). *The self in process: Toward a post-rationalist cognitive therapy.* New York: Guilford Press.

Guidano, V. F., & Lotti, G. (1983). *Cognitive processes and emotional disorders: A structural approach to psychotherapy.* New York: Guilford Press.

Gustafson, J. P. (1986). *The complex secret of brief psychotherapy.* New York: Norton.

Guy, J. D. (1987). *The personal life of the psychotherapist.* New York: Wiley.

Haley, J. (1984). *Ordeal therapy.* San Francisco: Jossey-Bass.

Haley, J., & Richeport-Haley, M. (2003). *The art of strategic therapy.* New York: Brunner-Routledge.

Halgin, R. P. (1985). Teaching integration of psychotherapy models to beginning therapists. *Psychotherapy, 22,* 555–563.

Hansen, N. E., & Freimuth, M. (1997). Piecing the puzzle together: A model for understanding the theory–practice relationship. *The Counseling Psychologist, 25,* 654–673.

Hare-Mustin, R. T. (1978). A feminist approach to family therapy. *Family Process, 17,* 181–194.

Harris, B. (1979). Whatever happened to little Albert? *American Psychologist, 34,* 151–160.

Hartmann, H. (1939). *Ego psychology and the problem of adaption* (D. Rapaport, Trans.). New York: International Universities Press.

Hecker, J. E., Losee, M. C., Fritzler, B. K., & Fink, C. M. (1996). Self-directed versus therapist-directed cognitive behavioral treatment for panic disorder. *Journal of Anxiety Disorders, 10*, 253–265.

Henry, W. E. (1966). Some observations on the lives of healers. *Human Development, 9*, 47–56.

Henry, W. P., Schacht, T. E., Strupp, H. H., Butler, S. F., & Binder, J. (1993). Effects of training in time-limited dynamic psychotherapy: Mediators of therapists' responses to training. *Journal of Consulting and Clinical Psychology, 61*, 441–447.

Henry, W. P., & Strupp, H. H. (1994). The therapeutic alliance as interpersonal process. In A. O. Horvath & L. S. Greenberg (Eds.), *The working alliance: Theory, research, and practice* (pp. 51–84). New York: Wiley.

Henry, W. P., Strupp, H. H., Butler, S. F., Schacht, T. E., & Binder, J. (1993). Effects of training in time-limited dynamic psychotherapy: Changes in therapists' behavior. *Journal of Consulting and Clinical Psychology, 61*, 434–440.

Hill, C. E. (2009). *Helping skills: Facilitating exploration, insight, and action* (3rd ed.). Washington, DC: American Psychological Association.

Hill, M., & Ballou, M. (1998). Making therapy feminist: A practice survey. *Women & Therapy, 21*, 1–16.

Homme, L. E. (1965). Perspectives on psychology: XXIV. Control of coverants, the operants of the mind. *Psychological Record, 15*, 501–511.

Horvath, A. O., & Greenberg, L. S. (Eds.). (1994). *The working alliance: Theory, research, and practice*. New York: Wiley.

Howard, G. S. (1985). The role of values in the science of psychology. *American Psychologist, 40*, 255–265.

Hubble, M. A., Duncan, B. L., & Miller, S. D. (1999). *The heart and soul of change: What works in therapy*. Washington, DC: American Psychological Association.

Ibrahim, F. A. (1996). A multicultural perspective on principle and virtue ethics. *The Counseling Psychologist, 24*, 78–85.

Imel, Z. E., Wampold, B. E., Miller, S. D., & Fleming, R. R. (2008). Distinctions without a difference: Direct comparisons of psychotherapies for alcohol use disorders. *Psychology of Addictive Behaviors, 22*, 533–543.

Ivey, A., Gluckstern, N., & Ivey, M. B. (1992). *Basic attending skills*. North Amherst, MA: Microtraining.

Ivey, A., & Ivey, M. B. (2007). *Intentional interviewing and counselling: Facilitating client development in a multicultural society*. Belmont, CA: Wadsworth.

Jacobson, E. (1929). *Progressive relaxation*. Chicago: University of Chicago Press.

Jacobson, N., & Margolin, G. (1979). *Marital therapy*. New York: Brunner/Mazel.

Jakubowski, P. A. (1977). Self-assertion training procedures for women. In E. I. Rawlings & D. K. Carter (Eds.), *Psychotherapy for women: Treatment toward equality* (pp. 168–190). Springfield, IL: Charles C Thomas.

Johnson, J. A., Germer, C. K., Efran, J. S., & Overton, W. F. (1988). Personality as a basis for theoretical predilections. *Journal of Personality and Social Psychology, 55*, 824–835.

Johnson, S. M. (1996). *The practice of emotionally focused marital therapy*. Philadelphia: Brunner/Mazel.

Jones, M. C. (1924a). Elimination of children's fears. *Journal of Experimental Psychology, 7*, 383–390.

Jones, M. C. (1924b). A laboratory study of fear: The case of Peter. *Journal of Genetic Psychology, 31*, 308–315.

Kabat-Zinn, J. (2005). *Coming to our senses: Healing ourselves and the world through mindfulness*. New York: Hyperion.

Kahn, M. (2002). *Basic Freud: Psychoanalytic thought for the 21st century*. New York: Basic Books.

Kalichman, S. C., Carey, M. P., & Johnson, B. T. (1996). Prevention of sexually transmitted HIV infection: A meta-analytic review of the behavioral outcome literature. *Annals of Behavioral Medicine, 18*, 6–15.

Kane, C. M. (1996). An experiential approach to family-of-origin work with marital and family therapy trainees. *Journal of Marital and Family Therapy, 22*, 481–487.

Kazdin, A. E. (1978). Behavior therapy: Evolution and expansion. *The Counseling Psychologist, 7*, 34–37.

Kazdin, A. E. (2005). Treatment outcomes, common factors, and continued neglect of mechanisms of change. *Clinical Psychology: Science and Practice, 12*, 184–188.

Keijsers, G. P. J., Schaap, C. P. D. R., & Hoogduin, C. A. L. (2000). The impact of interpersonal patient and therapist behavior on outcome in cognitive–behavior therapy: A review of empirical studies. *Behavior Modification, 24*, 264–297.

Keijsers, G. P. J., Schaap, C. P. D. R., Hoogduin, C. A. L., & Lammers, M. W. (1995). Patient–therapist interaction in the behavioral treatment of panic disorder with agoraphobia. *Behavior Modification, 19*, 491–517.

Kelly, G. A. (1955). *The psychology of personal constructs*. London: Routledge.

Kempler, W. (1981). *Experiential psychotherapy within families*. New York: Brunner/Mazel.

Kepner, J. (1987). *Body process: A gestalt approach to working with the body in psychotherapy*. New York: The Gestalt Journal Press.

Kernberg, O. (1980). *Internal world and external reality: Object relations theory applied*. New York: Jason Aronson.

Kimball, M. M. (2000). From "Anna O." to Bertha Pappenheim: Transforming private pain into public action. *History of Psychology, 3*, 20–43.

Kirschenbaum, H. (2007). *The life and work of Carl Rogers*. Ross-on-Wye, England: PCCS Books.

Kirschenbaum, H., & Jourdan, A. (2005). The current status of Carl Rogers and the person-centered approach. *Psychotherapy: Theory, Research, Practice, Training, 42*, 37–51.

Klein, M. (1948). *Contributions to psycho-analysis: 1921–1945*. London: Hogarth Press.

Koch, S. (1981). The nature and limits of psychological knowledge: Lessons of a century qua "science." *American Psychologist, 36*, 257–269.

Kohut, H. (1971). *The analysis of the self*. London: Hogarth Press.

Kohut, H. (1977). *The restoration of the self*. New York: International Universities Press.

Kohlenberg, R. J., & Tsai, M. (1991). *Functional analytic psychotherapy: Creating intense and curative therapeutic relationships*. New York: Plenum Press.

Koltko-Rivera, M. E. (2004). The psychology of worldviews. *Review of General Psychology, 8*, 3–58.

Kottler, J. A. (1986). *On being a therapist*. San Francisco: Jossey-Bass.

Kuhn, T. S. (1962). *The structure of scientific revolutions*. Chicago: University of Chicago Press.

Kurtz, R. (1990). *Body-centered psychotherapy: The Hakomi method*. Mendocino, CA: Life Rhythm.

Kurtz, R. (1995). The origins of the Hakomi. *Hakomi Forum, 11*, 3–13.

Laidlaw, T. A., & Malmo, C. (Eds.). (1990). *Healing voices*. San Francisco: Jossey-Bass.

Lambert, M. J. (1979). *The effects of psychotherapy*. St. Albans, VT: Edens.

Lambert, M. J. (1986). Implications of psychotherapy outcome research for eclectic psychotherapy. In J. C. Norcross (Ed.), *Handbook of eclectic psychotherapy* (pp. 436–462). New York: Brunner/Mazel.

Lambert, M. J., & Ogles, B. M. (2004). The efficacy and effectiveness of psychotherapy. In M. J. Lambert (Ed.), *Bergin and Garfield's handbook of psychotherapy and behavior change* (5th ed., pp. 139–193). New York: Wiley.

Lazarus, A. A. (1981). *The practice of multimodal therapy*. New York: McGraw-Hill.

Lazarus, A. A. (1993). Tailoring the therapeutic relationship, or being an authentic chameleon. *Psychotherapy, 30*, 404–407.

Lerner, G. (1993). *The creation of feminist consciousness*. New York: Oxford University Press.

Lerner, H. (1988). *Women in therapy*. New York: Jason Aronson.

Levant, R. F. (1996). The new psychology of men. *Professional Psychology: Research and Practice, 27*, 259–265.

Levin, L., & Shepherd, I. L. (1974). The role of the therapist in gestalt therapy. *The Counseling Psychologist, 4*, 27–30.

Levitsky, A., & Perls, F. (1970). The rules of the games of gestalt therapy. In J. Fagan & I. L. Shepherd (Eds.), *Gestalt therapy now* (pp. 140–149). Palo Alto, CA: Science and Behavior Books.

Lewandowski, L. M., Gebing, T. A., Anthony, J. L., & O'Brien, W. H. (1997). Meta-analysis of cognitive–behavioral treatment studies for bulimia. *Clinical Psychology Review, 17*, 703–718.

Lindsey, O. R. (1956). Operant conditioning methods applied to research in chronic schizophrenia. *Psychiatric Research Reports, 5*, 118–139.

Linehan, M. M. (1987). *Dialectical behavioral therapy: A cognitive behavioral approach to parasuicide. Journal of Personality Disorders, 1*, 328–333.

Linehan, M. M. (1993a). *Cognitive–behavioral treatment of borderline personality disorder*. New York: Guilford Press.

Linehan, M. M. (1993b). Dialectical behavior therapy for treatment of borderline personality disorder: Implications for the treatment of substance abuse. In L. Onken, J. Blaine, & J. Boren (Eds.), *Behavioral treatments for substance abuse and dependence* (Research Monograph No. 137, pp. 201–215). Rockville, MD: National Institute on Drug Abuse, National Institutes of Health.

Lovaas, O. I. (1977). *The autistic child: Language development through behavior modification*. New York: Irvington.

Luborsky, L. (1954). A note on Eysenck's article "The effects of psychotherapy: An evaluation." *British Journal of Psychology, 45*, 129–131.

Luborsky, L. (1984). *Principles of psychoanalytic psychotherapy: A manual for supportive–expressive treatment.* New York: Basic Books.

Lyddon, W. J. (1989a). Personal epistemology and preference for counseling. *Journal of Counseling Psychology, 36*, 423–429.

Lyddon, W. J. (1989b). Root metaphor theory: A philosophical framework for counseling and psychotherapy. *Journal of Counseling and Development, 67*, 442–448.

Lyddon, W. J., & Adamson, L. E. (1992). Worldview and counseling preference: An analogue study. *Journal of Counseling and Development, 71*, 41–47.

Maher, A. R. (2000). Philosophy of science and the foundations of psychotherapy. *American Psychologist, 55*, 1117–1125.

Mahler, M. S. (1968). *On human symbiosis and the vicissitudes of individualism: Infantile psychosis.* New York: International Universities Press.

Mahoney, M. J. (1988). Constructive metatheory: I. Basic features and historical foundations. *International Journal of Personal Construct Psychology, 1*, 1–35.

Mahoney, M. J. (2001). Behaviorism, cognitivism, and constructivism: Reflections on people and patterns in my intellectual development. In M. R. Goldfried (Ed.), *How therapists change: Personal and professional reflections* (pp. 183–200). Washington, DC: American Psychological Association.

Mahoney, M. J. (2003). *Constructive psychotherapy: A practical guide.* New York: Guilford Press.

Mahoney, M. J. (2005). Suffering, philosophy, and psychotherapy. *Journal of Psychotherapy Integration, 15*, 337–352.

Malan, D. (1979). *Individual psychotherapy and the science of psychodynamics.* Cambridge, England: Butterworths.

Markus, H. R. (2008). Pride, prejudice, and ambivalence: Toward a unified theory of race and ethnicity. *American Psychologist, 63*, 651–670.

Marsella, A. J., & Yamada, A. M. (2007). Culture and psychopathology: Foundations, issues, and directions. In S. Kitayama & D. Cohen (Eds.), *Handbook of cultural psychology* (pp. 797–816). New York: Guilford Press.

Martel, Y. (2001). *Life of Pi.* Toronto, Ontario, Canada: Knopf.

May, R. (1969). *Love and will.* New York: Norton.

May, R. (1981). *Freedom and destiny.* New York: Norton.

May, R. (1985). *My quest for beauty*. Dallas, TX: Saybrook.

May, R. (1991). *The cry for myth*. New York: Norton.

May, R., Angel, E., & Ellenberger, H. F. (1958). *Existence*. New York: Basic Books.

May, R., & Yalom, I. (2005). Existential psychotherapy. In R. J. Corsini & D. Wedding (Eds.), *Current psychotherapies* (pp. 269–298). Belmont, CA: Brooks/Cole.

McBride, M. C., & Martin, G. E. (1990). A framework for eclecticism: The importance of theory to mental health counseling. *Journal of Mental Health Counseling, 12*, 495–505.

McComas, J. J., Wacker, D. P., & Cooper, L. J. (1998). Increasing compliance with medical procedures: Application of the high-probability request procedure to a toddler. *Journal of Applied Behavior Analysis, 31*, 287–290.

McDaniel, S. H., Lusterman, D.-D., & Philpot, C. L. (Eds.). (2001). *Casebook for integrating family therapy: An ecosystemic approach*. Washington, DC: American Psychological Association.

McGlashan, T. H., & Miller, G. H. (1982). The goals of psychoanalysis and psychoanalytic psychotherapy. *Archives of General Psychiatry, 39*, 377–388.

McWilliams, N. (2004). *Psychoanalytic psychotherapy: A practitioner's guide*. New York: Guilford Press.

Meharg, S., & Woltersdorf, M. (1990). Therapeutic use for videotape self-modelling: A review. *Advances in Behaviour Research and Therapy, 12*, 85–99.

Messer, S. B. (1985). Choice of method is value laden too. *American Psychologist, 40*, 1414.

Messer, S. B. (1992). A critical examination of belief structures in integrative and eclectic psychotherapy. In J. C. Norcross & M. R. Goldfried (Eds.), *Handbook of psychotherapy integration* (pp. 130–165). New York: Basic Books.

Metzler, C. W., Biglan, A., Noel, J., Ary, D. V., & Ochs, L. (2000). A randomized controlled trial of a behavioral intervention to reduce high-risk sexual behavior among adolescents in STD clinics. *Behavior Therapy, 31*, 27–54.

Mikesell, R. H., Lusterman, D.-D., & McDaniel, S. H. (Eds.). (1995). *Integrating family therapy: Handbook of family psychology and systems theory*. Washington, DC: American Psychological Association.

Miller, J. B. (1986). *Toward a new psychology of women* (2nd ed.). Boston: Beacon.

Miller, R. B. (1992). Introduction to the philosophy of clinical psychology. In R. B. Miller (Ed.), *The restoration of dialogue: Readings in the philosophy of clinical psychology* (pp. 1–27). Washington, DC: American Psychological Association.

Miller, S. D. (2004). Losing faith: Arguing for a new way to think about therapy. *Psychotherapy in Australia, 10*, 44–51.

Miller, S. D., Duncan, B., & Hubble, M. (1997). *Escape from Babel: Toward a unifying language for psychotherapy practice.* New York: Norton.

Miller, S. D., Hubble, M., & Duncan, B. (2007, November/December). Supershrinks: What's the secret of their success? *Psychotherapy Networker,* 26–35, 56–57.

Miller, S. D., Wampold, B., & Varhely, K. (2008). Direct comparisons of treatment modalities for youth disorders: A meta-analysis. *Psychotherapy Research, 18*, 5–14.

Minuchin S., & Fishman, H. C. (1981). *Family therapy techniques.* Cambridge, MA: Harvard University Press.

Minuchin, S., Montalvo, B., Guerney, B., Rosman, B., & Schumer, F. (1967). *Families of the slums: An exploration of their structure and treatment.* New York: Basic Books.

Minuchin, S., Rosman, B. L., & Baker, L. (1978). *Psychosomatic families: Anorexia nervosa in context.* Cambridge, MA: Harvard University Press.

Mitchell, J. T., & Everly, G. S. (1996). *Critical incident stress debriefing: CISD: An operations manual for prevention of traumatic stress among emergency service and disaster workers* (2nd ed.). Ellicott City, MD: Chevron.

Morely, S., Eccleston, C., & Williams, A. (1999). Systematic review and meta-analysis of randomized controlled trials of cognitive-behaviour and behaviour therapy for chronic pain in adults, excluding headaches. *Pain, 80*, 1–13.

Moustakas, C. E. (1997). *Relationship play therapy.* Northvale, NJ: Jason Aronson.

Mowrer, O. H., & Mowrer, W. M. (1938). Enuresis: A method for its study and treatment. *American Journal of Orthopsychiatry, 8*, 436–459.

Neimeyer, R. A. (2000). George Kelly. In A. E. Kazdin (Ed.), *Encyclopedia of psychology* (Vol. 4, pp. 439–441). Washington, DC: American Psychological Association.

Neimeyer, R. A., & Stewart, A. E. (2000). Constructivist and narrative psychotherapies. In C. R. Snyder & R. E. Ingram (Eds.), *Handbook of psychological change* (pp. 337–357). New York: Wiley.

Nevels, L. A., & Coché, J. (1993). *Powerful wisdom: Voices of distinguished women psychotherapists.* San Francisco: Jossey-Bass.

Norcross, J. C., Prochaska, J. O., & Farber, J. A. (1993). Psychologists conducting psychotherapy: New findings and historical comparisons on the psychotherapy division membership. *Psychotherapy: Theory, Research and Practice, 30,* 692–697.

Nunnally, E., de Shazer, S., Lipchik, E., & Berg, I. (1986). A study of change: Therapeutic theory in process. In D. E. Efron (Ed.), *Journeys: Expansion of the strategic–systemic therapies* (pp. 77–96). New York: Brunner/Mazel.

O'Hanlon, B. (1986). Fragments for a therapeutic autobiography. In D. E. Efron (Ed.), *Journeys: Expansion of the strategic-systemic therapies* (pp. 30–39). New York: Brunner/ Mazel.

O'Hanlon, B., & Weiner-Davis, M. (1989). *In search of solutions: A new direction in psychotherapy*. New York: Norton.

O'Hara, M. (1995). Carl Rogers: Scientist and mystic. *Journal of Humanistic Psychology, 35,* 40–53.

O'Leary, K. D., & O'Leary, S. G. (1977). *Classroom management: The successful use of behavior modification* (2nd ed.). New York: Pergamon Press.

Orbach, S. (1986). *Hunger strike: The anoretic's struggle as a metaphor for our age.* New York: Norton.

Orlinsky, D. E., Geller, J. D., & Norcross, J. C. (2005). Epilogue: The patient psychotherapist, the psychotherapist's psychotherapist, and the therapist as a person. In J. D. Geller, J. C. Norcross, & D. E. Orlinsky (Eds.), *The psychotherapist's own psychotherapy: Patient and clinician perspectives* (pp. 405–415). New York: Oxford University Press.

Orlinsky, D. E., & Howard, K. (1980). Gender and psychotherapy outcome. In A. M. Brodsky & R. T. Hare-Mustin (Eds.), *Women and psychotherapy* (pp. 3–34). New York: Guilford Press.

Orlinsky, D. E., & Rønnestad, M. H. (2005). *How psychotherapists develop: A study of therapeutic work and professional growth*. Washington, DC: American Psychological Association.

Orlinsky, D. E., Rønnestad, M. H., & Willutzki, U. (2004). Fifty years of process-outcome research: Continuity and change. In M. J. Lambert (Ed.), *Bergin and Garfield's handbook of psychotherapy and behavior change* (5th ed., pp. 307–389). New York: Wiley.

Papp, P., Silverstein, O., & Carter, E. (1973). Family sculpting in preventive work with "well" families. *Family Process, 12,* 197–212.

Pavlov, I. P. (1927). *Conditioned reflexes: An investigation of the physiological activity of the cerebral cortex* (G. V. Anrep, Trans.). London: Oxford University Press.

Penn, P. (1982). Circular questioning. *Family Process, 21*, 267–280.

Perkins, R. (1991). Therapy for lesbians? The case against. *Feminism and Psychology, 1*, 325–338.

Perls, F. (1947). *Ego, hunger and aggression: A revision of Freud's theory and method.* Durban, South Africa: Knox.

Perls, F. (1969). *Gestalt therapy verbation.* Lafayette, CA: Real People Press.

Perls, F., Hefferline, R., & Goodman, P. (1951). *Gestalt therapy: Excitement and growth in the human personality.* New York: Julian Press.

Pine, F. (1990). *Drive, ego, object and self.* New York: Basic Books.

Plato. (1892). The Republic. In B. Jowett (Ed. & Trans.), *The dialogues of Plato translated into English with analyses and introductions* (3rd ed., Vol. 3, pp. 1–338). London: Oxford University Press.

Polster, E., & Polster, M. (1973). *Gestalt therapy integrated.* New York: Brunner/Mazel.

Pomerleau, O. F., & Brady, J. P. (1979). *Behavioral medicine: Theory and practice.* Baltimore: Williams & Wilkins.

Ponterotto, J. G., Casas, J. M., Alexander, C. M., & Suzuki, L. A. (Eds.). (2001). *Handbook of multicultural counseling* (2nd ed.). Thousand Oaks, CA: Sage.

Poznanski, J. J., & McLennan, J. (1995). Conceptualizing and measuring counselors' theoretical orientation. *Journal of Counseling Psychology, 42*, 411–422.

Poznanski, J. J., & McLennan, J. (1999). Measuring counsellor theoretical orientation. *Counselling Psychology Quarterly, 12*, 327–334.

Poznanski, J. J., & McLennan, J. (2003). Becoming a psychologist with a particular theoretical orientation to counselling practice. *Australian Psychologist, 38*, 223–226.

Prata, G. (1990). *A systemic harpoon into family games: Preventive interventions in therapy.* New York: Brunner/Mazel.

Prilleltensky, I. (1989). Psychology and the status quo. *American Psychologist, 44*, 795–802.

Prochaska, J. O. (1996). Revolution in health promotion: Smoking cessation as a case study. In R. J. Resnick & R. H. Rozensky (Eds.), *Health psychology through the life span: Practice and research opportunities* (pp. 361–376). Washington, DC: American Psychological Association.

Prochaska, J. O., & Norcross, J. C. (1983). Contemporary psychotherapists: A national survey of characteristics, practices, orientations, and attitudes. *Psychotherapy: Theory, Research and Practice, 20*, 161–173.

Propst, L. R., Ostrom, R., Watkins, P., Dean, T., & Mashburn, D. (1992). Comparative efficacy of religious and nonreligious cognitive–behavioral therapy for the treatment of clinical depression in religious individuals. *Journal of Consulting and Clinical Psychology, 60,* 94–103.

Ramsay, J. R. (2001). The clinical challenges of assimilative integration. *Journal of Psychotherapy Integration, 11,* 21–42.

Raskin, N. J. (1948). The development of non-directive psychotherapy. *Journal of Consulting Psychology, 12,* 92–110.

Redd, W. H., & Androwski, M. A. (1982). Behavioral intervention in cancer treatment: Controlling aversion reactions to chemotherapy. *Journal of Consulting and Clinical Psychology, 50,* 1018–1029.

Rescorla, R. A. (1988). Pavlovian conditioning: It's not what you think. *American Psychologist, 43,* 151–160.

Rice, L. N., & Greenberg, L. S. (1984). *Patterns of change: Intensive analysis of psychotherapy process.* New York: Guilford Press.

Rogers, C. R. (1942). *Counseling and psychotherapy: Newer concepts in practice.* Boston: Houghton Mifflin.

Rogers, C. R. (1951). *Client-centered therapy: Its current practice, implications, and theory.* Boston: Houghton Mifflin.

Rogers, C. R. (1954). *Psychotherapy and personality change.* Chicago: University of Chicago Press.

Rogers, C. R. (1955). Persons or science? A philosophical question. *American Psychologist, 10,* 267–278.

Rogers, C. R. (1957a). The necessary and sufficient conditions of therapeutic personality change. *Journal of Consulting Psychology, 21,* 95–103.

Rogers, C. R. (1957b). A therapist's view of the good life. *The Humanist, 17,* 291–300.

Rogers, C. R. (1961). *On becoming a person: A therapist's view of psychotherapy.* Boston: Houghton Mifflin.

Rogers, C. R. (1963). The concept of the fully functioning person. *Psychotherapy: Theory, Research and Practice, 1,* 17–26.

Rogers, C. R. (1967). Autobiography. In E. G. Boring & G. Lindzey (Eds.), *A history of psychology in autobiography* (Vol. 5, pp. 343–384). New York: Appleton-Century-Crofts.

Rogers, C. R. (1972). Some social issues that concern me. *Journal of Humanistic Psychology, 12*(2), 45–60.

Rogers, C. R. (1979). The foundations of the person-centered approach. *Education, 100,* 98–107.

Rogers, C. R. (1980). *A way of being.* Boston: Houghton Mifflin.

Rogers, C. R., Gendlin, E. T., Kiesler, D., & Truax, C. B. (1967). *The therapeutic relationship and its impact: A study of psychotherapy with schizophrenics.* Madison: University of Wisconsin Press.

Rogers, C. R., & Haigh, G. (1983). I walk softly through life. *Voices: The Art and Science of Psychotherapy, 18,* 6–14.

Rønnestad, M. H., & Skovholt, T. M. (2003). The journey of the counselor and therapist: Research findings and perspectives on professional development. *Journal of Career Development, 30,* 5–44.

Rosenzweig, S. (2002). Some implicit common factors in diverse methods of psychotherapy. *Journal of Psychotherapy Integration, 12,* 5–9. (Original article published 1936)

Rychlak, J. F. (2000). A psychotherapist's lessons from the philosophy of science. *American Psychologist, 55,* 1126–1132.

Ryle, A. (1989). *Cognitive analytic therapy—Active participation in change: New integration in brief psychotherapy.* New York: Wiley.

Ryle, A. (1994). Projective identification: A particular form of reciprocal role procedure. *British Journal of Medical Psychology, 67,* 107–114.

Ryle, A. (1995). *Cognitive analytic therapy: Developments in theory and practice.* New York: Wiley.

Ryle, A. (2005). Cognitive analytic therapy. In J. C. Norcross & M. R. Goldfried (Eds.), *Handbook of psychotherapy integration* (2nd ed., pp. 196–217). New York: Oxford University Press.

Safran, J. D., & Messer, S. B. (1997). Psychotherapy integration: A postmodern critique. *Clinical Psychology: Science and Practice, 4,* 140–152.

Safran, J. D., & Muran, J. C. (2003). *Negotiating the therapeutic alliance: A relational treatment guide.* New York: Guilford Press.

Salter, A. (1949). *Conditioned reflex therapy.* New York: Creative Age Press.

Samelson, F. (1981). Struggle for scientific authority: The reception of Watson's behaviorism, 1913–1920. *Journal of the History of the Behavioral Sciences, 17,* 399–425.

Sandell, R., Carlsson, J., Schubert, J., Broberg, J., Lazar, A., & Grant, J. (2004). Therapist attitudes and patient outcomes: I. Development and validation of the Therapeutic Attitudes Scales (TASC-2). *Psychotherapy Research, 14,* 469–484.

Satir, V. M. (1972). *Peoplemaking.* Palo Alto, CA: Science and Behavior Books.

Satir, V. M. (1988). *The new peoplemaking*. Mountain View, CA: Science and Behavior Books.

Sax, P. (2006). Developing preferred stories of identity as reflective practitioners. *Journal of Systemic Therapies, 25*, 59–72.

Schacht, T. E. (1991). Can psychotherapy education advance psychotherapy integration? *Journal of Psychotherapy Integration, 1*, 35–309.

Schacht, T. E., & Black, D. A. (1985). Epistemological commitments of behavioral and psychoanalytic therapists. *Professional Psychology: Research and Practice, 16*, 316–323.

Scharaf, M. (1983). *Fury on earth: A biography of Wilhelm Reich*. New York: St. Martin's Press.

Schwartz, J. (2003). Ways of knowing: Countertransference, neuroscience and the therapy relationship. In L. King & R. Randall (Eds.), *The future of psychoanalytic psychotherapy* (pp. 62–72). London: Whurr.

Selvini Palazzoli, M., Boscolo, L., Cecchin, G., & Prata, G. (1978). *Paradox and counterparadox* (E. V. Burt, Trans.). New York: Jason Aronson.

Shadish, W., & Baldwin, S. (2002). Meta-analysis of MFT interventions. In D. H. Sprenkle (Ed.), *Effectiveness research in marriage and family therapy* (pp. 339–370). Alexandria, VA: American Association for Marriage and Family Therapy.

Shapiro, M. B. (1961). The single case in fundamental clinical psychological research. *British Journal of Medical Psychology, 34*, 255–262.

Sherman, J. J. (1998). Effects of psychotherapeutic treatments for PTSD: A meta-analysis of controlled clinical trials. *Journal of Traumatic Stress, 11*, 413–435.

Sherman, L. W., & Denmark, F. (1978). *The psychology of women: Future directions of research*. New York: Psychological Dimensions.

Siegel, D. J., & Hartzel, M. (2003). *Parenting from the inside out: How a deeper self-understanding can help you raise children who thrive*. New York: Penguin.

Silverstein, L. B., & Goodrich, T. J. (2003). *Feminist family therapy: Empowerment in social context*. Washington, DC: American Psychological Association.

Skinner, B. F. (1953). *Science and human behavior*. New York: Free Press.

Skinner, B. F. (1954). A new method for the experimental analysis of behavior of psychotic patients. *The Journal of Nervous and Mental Disease, 120*, 403–406.

Skovholt, T. M., & Jennings, L. (2004). *Master therapists: Exploring expertise in therapy and counseling*. Boston: Allyn & Bacon.

Skovholt, T. M., & Rønnestad, M. H. (1992). *The evolving professional self: Stages and themes in therapist and counselor development.* Chichester, England: Wiley.

Sloan, D. M. (2004). Emotion-focused therapy: An interview with Leslie Greenberg. *Journal of Contemporary Psychotherapy, 34,* 105–116.

Smith, D. (1982). Trends in counseling and psychotherapy. *American Psychologist, 37,* 802–809.

Stein, D. M., & Lambert, M. L. (1995). Graduate training in psychotherapy: Are therapy outcomes enhanced? *Journal of Consulting and Clinical Psychology, 63,* 182–196.

Strupp, H., & Binder, J. (1984). *Psychotherapy in a new key: A guide to time-limited dynamic psychotherapy.* New York: Basic Books.

Sue, D. W., & Sue, D. (2002). *Counseling the culturally diverse: Theory and practice* (4th ed.). New York: Wiley.

Sukhodolsky, D. G., Kassinove, H., & Gorman, B. S. (2004). Cognitive–behavioral therapy for anger in children and adults: A meta-analysis. *Aggression and Violent Behavior, 9,* 247–269.

Sullivan, H. S. (1947). *Conceptions of modern psychiatry.* Washington, DC: William Allison White Psychiatric Foundation.

Sullivan, H. S. (1953). *Interpersonal theory of psychiatry.* New York: Norton.

Swinson, R. P., Fergus, K. D., Cox, B. J., & Wickwire, K. (1995). Efficacy of telephone-administered behavioral therapy for panic disorder with agoraphobia. *Behaviour Research and Therapy, 33,* 465–469.

Tarrier, N., Pilgrim, H., Sommerfield, C., Faragher, B., Reynolds, M., Graham, E., & Barrowclough, C. (1999). A randomized trial of cognitive therapy and imaginal exposure in the treatment of chronic posttraumatic stress disorder. *Journal of Consulting and Clinical Psychology, 67,* 13–18.

Tennov, D. (1973). Feminism, psychotherapy, and professionalism. *Journal of Contemporary Psychotherapy, 5,* 107–111.

Tillich, P. (1952). *The courage to be.* New Haven, CT: Yale University Press.

Tomm, K. (1984). One perspective on the Milan systemic approach: Part II. Description of session format, interviewing style and interventions. *Journal of Marital and Family Therapy, 10,* 253–271.

The top 10. (2007, March/April). *Psychotherapy Networker Magazine, 31*(2), 24–37.

Truax, C. B., & Carkhuff, R. R. (1967). *Toward effective counseling and psychotherapy: Training and practice.* Chicago: Aldine.

Truscott, D., & Crook, K. H. (2004). *Ethics for the practice of psychology in Canada*. Edmonton, Alberta, Canada: University of Alberta Press.

Tsai, M., Kohlenberg, R. J., Kanter, J., Kohlenberg, B., Follette, W., & Callaghan, G. (2008). *A guide to functional analytic psychotherapy: Awareness, courage, love and behaviorism*. New York: Springer.

Unger, R. K., Draper, R. D., & Pendergrass, M. L. (1986). Personal epistemology and personal experience. *Journal of Social Issues, 42*(2), 67–79.

Vachon, D. O., & Agresti, A. A. (1992). A training proposal to help mental health professionals clarify and manage implicit values in the counseling process. *Professional Psychology: Research and Practice, 23*, 509–514.

van Balkom, A. J., Bakker, A., Spinhoven, P., Blaauw, B. M., Smeenk, S., & Ruesink, B. (1997). A meta-analysis of the treatment of panic disorder with or without agoraphobia: A comparison of psychopharmacological, cognitive–behavioral, and combination treatments. *The Journal of Nervous and Mental Disease, 185*, 510–516.

van Deurzen-Smith, E. (1997). *Everyday mysteries: Existential dimensions in psychotherapy*. New York: Routledge.

van Emmerik, A. A., Kamphuis, J. H., Hulsbosch, A. M., & Emmelkamp, P. M. (2002, September 7). Single session debriefing after psychological trauma: A meta-analysis. *The Lancet, 360*, 766–770.

Vasco, A. B., Garcia-Marques, A., & Dryden, W. (1993). "Psychotherapist know thyself": Dissonance between metatheoretical and personal values in psychotherapists of different theoretical orientations. *Psychotherapy Research, 3*, 181–196.

Vervaeke, G. A. C., Vertommen, H., & Storms, G. (1997). Client and therapist values in relation to drop-out. *Clinical Psychology and Psychotherapy, 4*, 1–6.

von Bertalanffy, L. (1968) *General systems theory: Foundations, developments, applications*. New York: George Brazziler.

Wachtel, P. L. (1977). *Psychoanalysis and behavior therapy: Toward an integration*. New York: Basic Books.

Wachtel, P. L. (1997). *Psychoanalysis, behavior therapy, and the representational world*. Washington, DC: American Psychological Association.

Walker, L. E. A. (1989). Psychology and violence against women. *American Psychologist, 44*, 695–702.

Wallerstein, R. S. (1998). *Lay analysis: Life inside the controversy*. Hillsdale, NJ: Analytic Press.

Wampold, B. E. (2001a). Contextualizing psychotherapy as a healing practice: Culture, history, and methods. *Applied and Preventive Psychology, 10,* 69–86.

Wampold, B. E. (2001b). *The great psychotherapy debate: Models, methods, and findings.* Mahwah, NJ: Erlbaum.

Wampold, B. E. (2005). Establishing specificity in psychotherapy scientifically: Design and evidence issues. *Clinical Psychology: Science and Practice, 12,* 194–197.

Wampold, B. E. (2007). Psychotherapy: The humanistic (and effective) treatment. *American Psychologist, 62,* 855–873.

Wampold, B. E., & Brown, J. (2005). Estimating variability in outcomes attributable to therapists: A naturalistic study of outcomes in managed care. *Journal of Consulting and Clinical Psychology, 73,* 914–923.

Wampold, B. E., Mondin, G. W., Moody, M., Stich, F., Benson, K., & Ahn, H. (1997). A meta-analysis of outcome studies comparing bona fide psychotherapies: Empirically, "all must have prizes." *Psychological Bulletin, 122,* 203–215.

Watson, J. B. (1913). Psychology as the behaviorist views it. *Psychological Review, 20,* 158–177.

Watson, J. B. (1924). *Behaviorism.* New York: Norton.

Watson, J. B., & Rayner, R. (1920). Conditioned emotional reactions. *Journal of Experimental Psychology, 3,* 1–14.

Watzlawick, P., Weakland, J. H., & Fisch, R. (1974). *Change: Principles of problem formulation and problem resolution.* New York: Norton.

Weiner, I. B. (1975). *Principles of psychotherapy.* New York: Wiley.

Weiner, N. (1948). *Cybernetics.* New York: Wiley.

Westen, D. (1998). The scientific legacy of Sigmund Freud: Toward a psychodynamically informed psychological science. *Psychological Bulletin, 124,* 333–371.

Westen, D., & Gabbard, G. O. (2002). Developments in cognitive neuroscience: II. Implications for theories of transference. *Journal of the American Psychoanalytic Association, 50,* 99–134.

Whitaker, C. (1975). Psychotherapy of the absurd. *Family Process, 14,* 1–16.

White, M., & Epston, D. (1990). *Narrative means to therapeutic ends.* New York: Norton.

Whorf, B. (1956). *Language, thought, and reality.* Cambridge, MA: M.I.T. Press.

Wilkinson, S. (1994). *Women and Madness*: A reappraisal. *Feminism & Psychology, 4*, 261–267.

Williams, K. E., & Chambless, D. L. (1990). The relationship between therapist characteristics and outcome of in vivo exposure treatment for agoraphobia. *Behavior Therapy, 21*, 111–116.

Winnicott, D. W. (1956). On transference. *International Journal of Psychoanalysis, 37*, 386–388.

Winnicott, D. W. (1964). *The child, the family and the outside world*. Harmondsworth, England: Penguin.

Wogan, M., & Norcross, J. C. (1985). Dimensions of therapeutic skills and techniques: Empirical identification, therapist correlates, and predictive utility. *Psychotherapy, 22*, 63–74.

Woldt, A. L. (2005). Gestalt pedagogy: Creating the field for teaching and learning. In A. L. Woldt & S. M. Toman (Eds.), *Gestalt therapy: History, theory, and practice* (pp. xv–xxvii). Thousand Oaks, CA: Sage.

Wolitzky, D. L., & Eagle, M. N. (1997). Psychoanalytic theories of psychotherapy. In P. W. Wachtel & S. B. Messer (Eds.), *Theories of psychotherapy: Origins and evolution* (pp. 39–96). Washington, DC: American Psychological Association.

Wolowitz, H. M. (1972). Hysterical character and feminine identity. In J. Bardwick (Ed.), *Readings on the psychology of women* (pp. 307–314). New York: Harper & Row.

Wolpe, J. (1958). *Psychotherapy by reciprocal inhibition*. Stanford, CA: Stanford University Press.

Wong, S. E., Seroka, P. L., & Ogisi, J. (2000). Effects of a checklist on self-assessment of blood glucose level by a memory-impaired woman with diabetes mellitus. *Journal of Applied Behavior Analysis, 33*, 251–254.

Worell, J., & Johnson, D. (2001). Therapy with women: Feminist frameworks. In R. K. Unger (Ed.), *Handbook of the psychology of women and gender* (pp. 317–329). New York: Wiley.

Worell, J., & Remer, P. (2003). *Feminist perspectives in therapy: Empowering diverse women* (2nd ed.). New York: Wiley.

Wrenn, C. G. (1962). The culturally encapsulated counselor. *Harvard Educational Review, 32*, 444–449.

Yalom, I. D. (1980). *Existential psychotherapy*. New York: Basic Books.

Yalom, I. D. (1989). *Love's executioner and other tales of psychotherapy*. New York: Basic Books.

Yalom, I. D. (1991). *When Nietzsche wept*. New York: Basic Books.

Yalom, I. D. (2002). *The gift of therapy: An open letter to a new generation of therapists and their patients*. New York: HarperCollins.

Yalom, I. D. (2005). *The Schopenhauer cure: A novel*. New York: HarperCollins.

Yalom, I. D. (2008). *Staring at the sun: Overcoming the terror of death*. New York: Jossey-Bass.

Young, J. E., Klosko, J. S., & Weishaar, M. E. (2003). *Schema therapy: A practitioner's guide*. Guilford Press.

Index

About the Author

My desire to understand the human condition found a means through my undergraduate studies in psychology and philosophy. My desire to help others found a method while I was volunteering at a peer-counseling center at the same time. I still vividly remember saying to a fellow volunteer, "Wouldn't it be something if we applied psychology to helping people?" I have often wondered whether that question was motivated by ignorance or by a precocious grasp of the disconnect between the science and practice of psychology. Whatever the case, from that moment onward I knew I wanted to be a psychologist, and a psychotherapist in particular.

I became a registered psychologist in 1987 and earned my doctorate in clinical psychology from the University of Windsor, Windsor, Ontario, Canada, in 1989. I have practiced in psychiatric hospitals, community clinics, group homes, rehabilitation centers, and in private practice, and have served on the faculty at the University of Alberta, Edmonton, Alberta, Canada, since 1997.

When I began my training in psychotherapy, I thought that good therapy involved dispensing wisdom. Given that I was rather young, I assumed that I had time to fill as I waited to become older and thus wiser. So I decided to learn everything I could about ethics in order to stay out of trouble and in the profession while I gained the experience I needed. An ardent believer in "writing to learn," I wrote two books on ethics with my dear friend Ken Crook—*Ethics for the Practice of Psychology in Canada* (2004) and *Ethics and Law for Teachers* (2007)—as well as book chapters, articles, professional guidelines and standards, and conference presentations. I also continued to study, research, teach, and practice psychotherapy. To my great relief—having discovered firsthand that wisdom does not inevitably accrue with age—I learned that effective therapy is not about giving advice. I also learned that being ethical is not about receiving advice. Now I see my interests in ethics and psychotherapy as synergistic: An effective therapist is also an ethical one and vice versa.

I cannot imagine a better career than psychotherapy—it is always interesting, often satisfying, and ultimately deeply rewarding. I take pride in aspiring to be a good therapist and in striving to inspire others to do likewise.